Deciding
To Sell Your Business
The Key To
Wealth And Freedom

Ned Minor

Deciding

To Sell Your Business

The Key To
Wealth And Freedom

Ned Minor

First Edition
BUSINESS ENTERPRISE INSTITUTE, INC.

Copyright © 2003 Ned A. Minor
Printed in the United States of America
First Edition, 2003
Second Printing, 2004

Library of Congress Control Number: 2003101102
ISBN: 0-9655731-9-2 Hardcover
       0-9655731-8-4 Paperback

orders@decidingtosell.com
www.decidingtosell.com
www.exitplanning.com

Minor, Ned.
Deciding to sell your business: the key to wealth
and freedom / Ned Minor.–1st ed.
p.cm.
LCCN 2003101102
ISBN 0-9655731-9-2 (hardcover)

1. Sale of business enterprises–Decision making.
2. Corporate divestiture–Decison making.
3. Liquidation–Decision making. I. Title

HD1393.25.M56 2003   658.1'6
QB103-200472

Edited by Kathryn B. Carroll
Jacket Design by Susie Betts Hotz
Jacket Photos by John Meuller
Book Design & Production by
Jean Caggiano, Gryphon Design

Author's Invitation

No book can offer you specific answers to your unique situation and mine is no exception. If you have any questions or comments when reading this book, I encourage you to contact me.

You may email me at *nminor@decidingtosell.com* or call me directly at 303/320-1053.

Ned Minor

Dedication

I dedicate this book to: my beautiful wife, Nancy, who is my strength and inspiration, my wonderful daughter, Sarah, who makes me laugh, and my parents, whose early lessons continue to guide me.

I also dedicate this book to the many outstanding business owners I have had the privilege to represent who have become my good friends.

Acknowledgements

Without the assistance of my editor, Kathryn B. Carroll, I could not have written this book. Her ability to clarify my thoughts and to maintain a sense of humor through countless rewrites provided the support I needed.

To Anthony King, Lisa D'Ambrosia and James A. Thomas, Jr., three exceptional transaction attorneys, and to John Brown and Barbara J. Wells, business planning lawyers extraordinaire, my thanks for their invaluable input. Thanks also to my other partners, John A. Logan and Kim L. Ritter, for their support during the writing process.

Joseph M. Durnford, principal of JD Ford & Company, Investment Bankers, was especially helpful on issues of valuation and investment bankers.

I acknowledge all of the hardworking and dedicated business owners whose entrepreneurial drive and spirit make ours the greatest country in the world. May they reap the financial rewards they so richly deserve as they sell their companies.

Finally, I thank Sam Sargent, who urged me to finish this book just when I most needed encouragement.

Notes

Throughout this book, for simplicity's sake and for ease of reading, I chose to use the pronouns "he," "him" and "his" instead of the more cumbersome "she or he," "him or her," etc. By doing so, I mean no disrespect to women and trust that female readers will understand my intent.

And now, a word (or two) from my law partners and publisher:

This book is designed to provide information with regard to the subject matter covered. It is sold with the understanding that while the author is a practicing attorney, neither he, his law firm, nor the publisher is engaged by the reader to render legal, accounting or other professional service. If you require legal advice or other expert assistance, you should seek the services of a competent professional. The purpose of this book is to educate. Neither the author nor Business Enterprise Institute, Inc. shall have any liability or responsibility to any person or entity with respect to any loss or damage caused, or alleged to be caused, directly or indirectly by the information or sample forms contained in this book.

Contents

Introduction

When I started writing this book, the merger and acquisition market for privately-owned companies (like yours) was booming. From the mid-1990s through the third quarter of 2000, buyers were paying record prices in record numbers for privately-owned companies. The robust health of this market originally motivated me to write, in an effort to answer questions that all owners ask when contemplating the sale of their companies and to encourage owners to take advantage of this boom before it burst.

Well, the unprecedented boom has ended but the information in this book is more timely than ever. Owners who wish to maximize their sale prices in a less exuberant (but historically more realistic) market wrestle with the same emotional issues about selling their businesses as owners who sold during the boom. Today's owners, however, bear the additional burden of knowing that they missed the top of the cycle. The market they sell in is one of lower earnings, lower multiples and lower sale prices. Their goal, however, of achieving wealth and the freedom to enjoy it through the sale of their companies, remains unchanged.

Also unchanged is the fact that buyers will always pay reasonable prices for quality companies.

My goal is to help business owners through the decision-making process (*"to sell or not to sell?"*) regardless of the state of the merger and acquisition market at the time they are contemplating an exit.

After 25 years of working with successful business owners, I have found that there are two issues that preoccupy them, which left unresolved can stymie the most successful entrepreneur. First, they struggle with the decision to exit the companies they have created. The second is actually doing so.

Typically, owners grapple with these issues alone. Their usual sources of information – books, motivational tapes, consultants and even colleagues – can't help them with this often emotional, highly-personal and frustrating decision-making process. The traditional consultants (lawyers and CPAs) often fail to empathize with owners as they wrestle with the biggest decision of their business lives. Few owners feel comfortable discussing their feelings and concerns with their spouses. And rarely do owners discuss questions about exiting with employees – no matter how key or how trusted.

> "My purpose...is to supply business owners the information and guidance they need to move successfully through the process of deciding to sell their companies."

Business owners who want to leave their companies but don't know exactly when or how are often perplexed. They face the daily demands of running a business. They turn to accountants and lawyers for answers to their technical questions about selling. They are unsure, however, of where to go for input on their struggle with such personal and emotional issues as: "What will I do after I leave my company?" and "When should I leave my company?" These factors combine to prevent the typical owner from making any decision at all.

My purpose in writing this book is to supply business owners the information and guidance they need to move successfully through the process of deciding to sell their companies. Although each entrepreneur's situation differs, these questions (and their answers) apply to entrepreneurs universally.

In my one-on-one conferences with owners, the answers to these questions can be quite lengthy. It is difficult, absent that face-to-face dialogue, to cover every unique situation. It is my hope, however, that you will glean from this book the information you need to find your own answers and that your exit strategy will begin to take shape.

I have divided the process of deciding to sell your business into seven parts:

PERSONAL AND EMOTIONAL ISSUES

STRATEGIC DECISIONS

ALL ABOUT BUYERS

ASSEMBLING YOUR ADVISORY DREAM TEAM

VALUATION AND DEAL STRUCTURE

THE SALE PROCESS

CRITICAL LEGAL ISSUES

Each part is divided into those questions that owners routinely ask or should ask and answer when engaged in the decision-making process. In each of these parts, the business owner deals with objective data as well as subjective issues and feelings. Objective data may include multiples of cash flow, growth in revenues, and market conditions.

While important, the objective side of the equation is not the primary subject of this book. Of course, we will examine the entire sale process so that you, an owner, can gain a solid understanding of how the process works. This understanding of the process itself will clarify your decision-making process. Knowledge is a powerful ally when making the decision to sell.

My focus, however, is on the owner and how he manages the process. For example, we look at how the owner:

- *sorts through the often conflicting emotions in deciding to sell;*
- *creates his own definition of financial independence;*
- *manages a team of professional advisors (CPAs, investment bankers, financial planners/wealth managers, bankers, and transaction attorneys);*
- *behaves in negotiations;*
- *maintains his sanity during the sale process; and*
- *prepares for and lives a fulfilling life after the sale.*

My experience with business owners comes from two sources. First, I am one. With a partner, I started a law firm from scratch. We know how it feels to personally guarantee loans. Like yours, our workdays are long and not limited to Monday through Friday. We've experienced all of the growing pains that accompany the development of a successful company. And we've had to create our own plan for a successful exit.

Second, as a transaction attorney, many hundreds of owners have trusted me to hold their fears and doubts as well as aspirations and dreams in confidence. Having counseled owners for nearly three decades, I am intimately familiar with the issues that owners wrestle with when deciding to sell.

Over the years, few business owners have arrived at my office with all the answers necessary to move confidently through the sale process. They often carry impressions from friends who have sold or from rumors they have heard. They usually have some technical information about the process based on conversations with their accountants or attorneys but they lack experienced input on the subjective issues they confront. Consequently, I spend time explaining the sale process but we spend the bulk of our meeting time discussing the issues they do not, or cannot, discuss with anyone else. Issues that concern their feelings.

Owners meet with me when they are thinking about selling and are unsure of the best way to proceed. They typically enjoy longstanding relationships with competent attorneys but perceive the need to meet with "a specialist" regarding a possible sale. Our discussions during this pre-sale phase center on decision-making, identifying priorities, and setting objectives. I hope to share the essence of those discussions in this book. My goal is to provide you the tools necessary to make the best personal and family decisions about whether, when, and how to sell or transfer your company.

This book is not a technical manual on the sale process. Neither is it simplistic. I am confident that, as a successful owner, you have an understanding of accounting and financial concepts. I hope to equip you with enough legal and financial information about the sale process to allow you to converse effectively with and assess the performance of your transaction Team of Advisors as you pursue a transaction.

Throughout this book, I have made liberal use of the experiences of sellers I have represented. I hope you will learn from their experiences and be inspired by their victories. These owners have generously agreed to share their stories with you. They believe, as I do, that their insights into the anxieties and uncertainties they faced will help those currently contemplating a sale. By reading their accounts beginning on page 195, you will find that your concerns are normal, that you need not re-invent the wheel, that the "right" deal is out there, and that there is a reward for all of your hard work: wealth and personal freedom.

In their candid stories, you will learn that they experienced varying degrees of uncertainty during the sale. Each owner had doubts about whether a buyer would come through and was frustrated by the length of time it took to sell or the depth of the due diligence process. They wondered whether they would find new roles after that of "owner." But not one of these owners experienced "seller's remorse" after the sale nor have they second-guessed their decisions to sell. And not one would trade his newfound freedom for the demands of ownership and day-to-day business management.

Finally, remember one inviolate truth: Eventually, every owner leaves his business. The question is, will you leave feet first on a stretcher or will you sip champagne in celebration of your victory? The choice is yours. By answering the questions you have been asking yourself, I hope to help you crystallize your thinking and make that choice. If you are ready to prepare for the most exciting and financially rewarding part of your life, turn the page and let's get started.

Ned Minor

PART 1 | PERSONAL AND EMOTIONAL ISSUES

During 25 years of representing sellers, I have observed that in addition to wrestling with many of the same personal and emotional issues, they share several common traits. See how closely you match the profile of the typical seller.

The typical seller:

- *Is between 45 and 55 years old.*
- *Started the company with the help of a spouse who may still play a role.*
- *Has owned the company 15 to 20 years.*
- *Controls all or nearly all ownership interest.*
- *Has personal net worth tied primarily to the value of the company so will not achieve financial independence until the company is sold.*
- *Enjoys a good reputation.*
- *Usually undervalues his company.*
- *Takes one to two years to reach a decision to sell.*
- *Knows very little about the sale process.*
- *Lacks a team of transaction advisors.*
- *Wants a quality buyer with whom he is comfortable.*

- *Has received inquiries from buyers.*
- *Lacks a knowledgeable person to talk with about selling.*

If you see yourself in the traits above, I am confident that you will relate to and benefit from the following questions and answers.

Question 1

What will I do after I have sold my business?

Simple answer: "You will have so many demands on your time that you will wonder how you ever found time to run a company."

*A*lthough this may seem an unusual choice for a first question, this is the one I am most frequently asked when a business owner seriously starts thinking about selling.

Many business owners are quite naturally wary of the prospect of selling their businesses. For years, building and nurturing their companies have been the focal points of their day-to-day existence. For many business owners, everything, including friends, family, community, and personal desires have taken a back seat to their intense drives to survive and to succeed. Self-image is often defined by their role as "The Owner." Rarely do owners make a personal decision without relating its consequences to the business. Quite understandably, it is difficult for these owners to foresee a personal identity separate from that of owner.

If this sounds all too familiar, don't worry: All of these concerns will resolve themselves *if* the sale of your business generates your definition of wealth and personal freedom. You must, however, accept the fact that after you have completed the sale, you will still be the same person. Motivated by different goals perhaps, but nonetheless the same person.

The primary difference, however, will be that you will have exchanged your illiquid business for wealth and freedom. Instead of focusing on what it takes to survive as a business owner, you will be free to focus on fulfilling yourself as a person. Each day your activities will be self-initiated rather than motivated by the business demands thrust upon you.

One of my clients astutely anticipated the change that becoming a "former owner" would have on his life. He concluded that the one thing he could not give up, post sale, was an office. He knew that he needed a space, outside of his home, to use as a base so he rented an executive suite. Two months prior to closing, he had everything in place (furniture, computer, phone service) so that he could move smoothly through the transition process. To this day, when not traveling, he spends each morning in his office, reviewing financial publications, tweaking his portfolio, and analyzing potential new ventures. Initially, the office provided a bridge between his old life and his new life. Now, it is his safe haven. He is a classic example of the entrepreneur that does not retire – he refocuses.

> "Most rechannel their energies into new ventures that create additional wealth with less financial and personal risk."

It is not unusual for spouses of sellers to be apprehensive about how *their* lives will be affected by a business sale. In one case, the wife of a seller informed him that she agreed to marry him "for better or worse – but not for lunch everyday." This seller took the hint and structured an employment agreement that paid well, allowed flexible hours, and most importantly, kept him out of the house at lunch time. You, too, will have to find the right balance with your spouse.

Former business owners rarely spend the rest of their lives just playing. Most rechannel their energies into new ventures that create additional wealth with less financial and personal risk. If you have started and managed a successful business, and most importantly, have figured out the right time to sell your business, you are certainly capable of figuring out how to make the rest of your financially-independent life happy and fulfilling.

Don't wait until after the sale to start thinking about how you plan to refocus. Start this process now. If you are struggling with the decision to sell, start listing what you could be doing if your business did not consume your time. Many sellers have told me that once they had completed their lists, they could visualize wonderful lives after closing. The ability to imagine such a life facilitated their decisions to sell.

No one can tell you what it will take for you to be happy over a long period of time. I can, however, share my observations as to how many of my clients have dealt with their "PSSAS" (Post Sale Separation Anxiety Syndrome).

After you have sold your company, plan on doing **absolutely nothing**. This is not as easy as it sounds. If you are like most hard-charging entrepreneurs, *you will need to learn to relax*. While running your business, you are extremely focused, disciplined, and creative. You, of all people, know that it takes a tremendous amount of sustained energy to achieve success.

On the day you close on the sale of your business, you will have several conflicting emotions. You may feel simultaneously elated, relieved, melancholic, and nostalgic. The closing itself is anticlimactic. You may feel a sense of let-down and apprehension, i.e. "What do I do now?" It may simply take time to absorb the fact that you are off that disciplined, high speed treadmill that was your former business life.

Remember, however, that even while you were on that treadmill, you had a personal life. You traveled (albeit occasionally), golfed, skied, read, spent time with your kids, took photographs, or volunteered with your favorite charities. Something helped you to decompress from the stress of business. Once you've closed the sale, you will have the opportunity to enhance and to cultivate the activities that you enjoy.

It is imperative that you learn to relax, and having fun is one of the best ways to do so. Take a trip with your favorite person to that place you have always dreamed about. Immerse yourself in your favorite sport and achieve that level of excellence you could only hope for when you were working 80 hours each week. Buy the toys that will allow that "kid" inside you to reemerge. Surprise a loved one with a special gift. Do something for your favorite charity. The list of fun things to do is limited only by your imagination. Go ahead: Indulge. You've earned it. *Don't feel guilty about not being at the office.* This is your time to decompress. This is your time to start enjoying your newly acquired freedom.

Another concern common to business owners is that by selling their businesses they will lose their "platforms" in the community or in their trade associations. They worry that once they are separated from their businesses, their status as highly-respected civic leaders and leaders in their industries will be in jeopardy.

This should not be the case if you stay active and involved in organizations you've always belonged to. Join a few new organizations, as well. And remember, people will think more highly of you now than ever before. They will refer to you with a certain amount of awe, respect, and yes, envy. "Did you hear that John made a killing when he sold his company?" Think about it. You've known people who have successfully sold their businesses. What were your thoughts when you heard the news?

Colleagues and competitors are envious because you were shrewd enough to develop and execute an exit strategy. This attitude and respect is nourished by their speculation that you have sold the company for far more than you actually did. Savor this respect. Again, you've earned it.

Consider establishing your own private foundation. Nothing maintains high profile and visibility in the community more effectively than going into the business of giving money to worthwhile causes. You will have all of the influence and attention you ever wanted – and more.

Most of my clients simply cannot repress their entrepreneurial instincts. When you were running your own business, you had to live by the golden rule: *"The person with the gold makes the rules."* Now that you have sold your business and are financially independent, you are the person with the gold, so now, you make the rules. If word gets out that you are looking to invest in business opportunities, you will have a new full-time job sorting through and selecting those opportunities that meet your investment criteria. If your terms and conditions for

> "...never once has a client returned and complained, 'Gee, Ned, I wish I had never sold my business.'"

investment aren't met, you politely decline and start reviewing the next available opportunity. There is no such thing as the last good deal.

When you find the right investment opportunity and it is on your terms, then you choose how active or passive you want to be in the management. Rarely do former owners choose to involve themselves in day-to-day management. More likely, you will prefer a seat on the board of directors, thus enabling you to remain active in the business on a regular basis and on your terms. In addition, you will enjoy the satisfaction of telling your buddies that you are "dabbling in this and that company."

After the initial period of adjustment, you will discover so many fun, interesting, challenging, and fulfilling activities that you will wonder how you ever had enough time to run your business. If you remain unconvinced, I have one last assurance: In all of the transactions I have ever completed, never once has a client returned and complained, "Gee, Ned, I wish I had never sold my business."

If concerns about life after the sale are impeding your progress toward decisive action, I encourage you to skip to Part Eight. There, you will find the insight and inspiration only other owners who have wrestled with these issues can give. If they can find happiness and fulfillment, so can you.

If, on the other hand, you are confident of your ability to move through PSSAS successfully and adjust to your new role as "former business owner," we can focus on the process necessary to take you there. The rest of this book will do exactly that.

Question 2

When should I sell my business?

Simple answer: "Sell at the point when you achieve your definition of financial independence."

*T*wo sets of reasons dictate the "timing" for selling your business: one personal, the other financial. The personal reasons are unique to each individual and are too numerous to describe in detail here. You are already quite familiar with the thoughts that run through your head (at least ten times daily) with regard to selling your company. Since the personal reasons are complex, making the decision to sell can be extremely difficult. For that reason, I frequently counsel my clients to separate, at least initially, the personal from financial, and to focus exclusively on the financial opportunities a sale might yield. If, after analysis, the financial opportunity is the right one, then dealing with the personal issues becomes easier. Knowing that the sale will achieve your definition of wealth and financial independence, you can eliminate financial concerns from your list of worries and focus on the personal side. If, however, your company is not ready for sale and will not generate financial independence, then there is little reason to begin sorting through personal issues.

Let's examine the personal and financial decision-making process in greater detail.

The two most common personal reasons owners cite for wanting to sell are burn-out and a reduced tolerance for risk. Of course, owners are driven to burn-out or to a desire to take their chips off the table for more than one reason. Under the general heading of "burn-out," owners usually relate to one or more of the following symptoms:

- *I'm tired and I'm ready to start a "new chapter" in life;*
- *I'm feeling spousal pressure;*
- *I'm tired of managing people;*
- *The company doesn't provide the challenge that it once did;*
- *I do not want to work through another trough in the economic cycle;*
- *Industry consolidation has created a new 1,200 pound gorilla in my neighborhood that I do not want to fight;*
- *I'm worn out by recent company financial struggles; or*
- *The speed of technological change is outpacing my desire to keep up.*

Other owners find that their willingness to tolerate risk is on the wane. These owners tell me that:

- *Taking the company to the "next level" requires an assumption of debt and/or an infusion of equity that they simply are not willing to commit;*
- *They recognize that market multiples fluctuate and tomorrow's multiples may not be as good as today's; or*

• *They find themselves wondering if there are better returns in other investments.*

Of course, owners can (and usually do) experience more than one of these feelings.

How did you score? If you related positively to several of these symptoms, you may be closer than you think to a decision to sell.

From an economic standpoint, the best time to sell your business is when a sale will yield financial independence. As I define it, financial independence is having enough principal invested to generate an annual cash flow that supports the type of life you have always wanted to live – without ever having to draw upon the principal. For example, if your goal is to have an annual income stream of $300,000 before taxes, then you must sell your business for approximately $6 million.

> "...financial independence is having enough principal invested to generate an annual cash flow that supports the type of life you have always wanted to live – without ever having to draw upon the principal.'"

Generally speaking, if you sell your company for $6 million, you will net, after taxes (assuming federal and state capital gain rates of 20 percent) and transaction costs, approximately $4.4 million. This $4.4 million, invested at a rate of return of 6.8 percent, will yield an annual cash flow of $300,000. If you are more cautious and expect a lower rate of return, you will need to net more than the $4.4 million. Conversely, if you are a gambler and are confident that you can earn more than a 6.8 percent return, you can afford to net less than $4.4 million.

If you are convinced, after consulting your professional advisors, that no matter what management decisions you make, your company will **never** sell at a price that will generate financial independence, then you must ask yourself, "Am I in business just to pay myself a salary or to generate personal wealth?" If your goal is personal wealth, you should consider one of two courses of action. First, you can grow by acquisition, i.e., buying competitors or making strategic acquisitions. (See Question 11.) Second, you should consider selling your company at its maximum price and reinvesting the proceeds in the acquisition of another company that will ultimately generate financial independence. I have represented numerous entrepreneurs who have followed these paths. They have bought and sold several companies each one bigger than the one before until they sold the one that generated personal financial freedom.

To obtain the maximum sale price, you should sell when you can demonstrate that revenues and profits have increased consistently over a period of time. Don't be lured into thinking that the best time to sell is at the peak of this upward trend. Buyers won't pay top dollar in this situation, because they have no room to grow the business. They have no "upside" potential. Similarly, you want to avoid selling when revenues and profits have been consistently flat. You definitely do not want to sell if they have been steadily declining.

Several years ago, I referred one of my successful clients to a top investment banking firm to perform a valuation on his business. The investment banker felt confident that the business could be sold for approximately $25 million. With that piece of information, my client and I adjourned to a nearby coffee shop to discuss what he should do. He confessed that selling his company for $25 million would give him a lifestyle far better than anything he had ever imagined. He would certainly achieve financial freedom.

Being a typical entrepreneur, however, my client speculated that if he kept the business for another three to five years he could ultimately sell it for twice that amount. I reminded him that he had just said $25 million would give him financial freedom. I observed that if he chose to roll the dice, he did so not for financial reasons but rather for ego, greed, and the excitement of being in the hunt. I warned him that there was no guarantee that in three years he would be able to sell the company for a higher price or that he would even be able to sell it for the $25 million quoted by the investment banker.

Only 18 months after that meeting, my client's industry experienced significant negative change. My client was now more than ready to sell his business. When he had the same investment banker do a second valuation, he learned he would be lucky to sell the company for $10 million. Needless to say, $10 million is still a nice payday, but it did not meet my client's definition of financial freedom.

Having learned this tough lesson, he developed an exit strategy. Using the valuation, he focused on specific Value Drivers that would dramatically impact the value of his company. (Please see Question 20 for a more complete discussion of Value Drivers.) He set a three-year deadline to achieve an $18 million purchase price. Within two and one-half years, he reached his goal and sold his company for $18 million. This client was pleased with this exceptional recovery but understood what his original decision not to sell had cost him.

I hope this illustration will convince you to develop an exit strategy for your business today. Set the clock for the number of years you think it will take you to put the company in a position to sell and achieve financial independence. That may be three years, it may be five years. By establishing a timeframe, you can make decisions today which propel you toward the moment when you will maximize your return. If you get to that target date and for whatever reason you elect not to sell, then don't. But reset the clock for another date and stay on top of your exit plan.

Without a disciplined approach to staying on schedule, happenstance rather than planning may end up controlling when and for how much your business will be sold. Remember, all buyers are looking for two elements in acquiring your company: good cash flow and upside potential. If these elements can justify a purchase price that meets your definition of personal financial independence, then, from a financial standpoint, this is the time to sell. Knowing that a sale will achieve your financial objectives, you are in an excellent position to manage any unresolved personal issues about selling.

Question 3

Why should I sell my business?

Simple answer: "Sell to achieve wealth and freedom while you are still young enough to enjoy it."

Stop and think for a moment. What motivated you to get into this business in the first place? I suspect that there were many personal and financial incentives that inspired you to become an entrepreneur. Probably among the most important was the prospect of wealth accumulation, i.e. the potential to achieve financial freedom and the time to enjoy it. I firmly believe the day you start a business is the day to fix those personal and monetary goals in your brain and to establish an exit plan. Without goals and a good plan, it is unlikely that you will be able to exit when you want and for the money you want. Years slip by while your desire grows to sell and move on. Too late you realize that you don't know how to leave, or worse yet, you conclude that you are somehow incapable of leaving.

Over the years, I have observed that the average age of my clients who sell their businesses is 45. I believe that most owners expect to be much older when they give up control and leave their companies. At one time, this expectation may have reflected reality. The last generation of business owners was greatly influenced by its experience growing up during the Great Depression. They were driven equally by their fear of losing everything and of having nothing. They were builders and savers. They were not spenders. How times have changed.

The current generation of business owners consists of baby boomers now entering their late 40s and early 50s. Unlike any previous generation, they came of age during a time of sustained growth, and as a result, they have become the greatest consumers in history. They have worked hard but have consciously tried to balance work with outside interests. Unlike their predecessors, this generation of business owners has adopted the "I can't take it with me" attitude and has included "lifestyle" on its menu of choices. More and more, baby boomers are choosing to sell now, thus taking their chips off of the table and adopting the lifestyle afforded them by financial independence.

Many entrepreneurs answer the "Why Should I Sell Question" when they realize that the best time to sell is when they can receive a premium purchase price and are still young and healthy enough to enjoy the fruits of their labor. I can assure you that none of these entrepreneurs has sold out and gone quietly into the night. Just read the personal accounts in Part Eight, "Former Owners Reflect on Wealth and Freedom." These sellers can expect another 15 to 30 years of good health after the sale. They anticipate that during their post-sale lives they will take full advantage of the additional opportunities time and money will afford.

I have further observed that if a business owner reaches his 60s without having sold his company, he probably will never sell. For example, one of my clients told me that he planned to sell his company five years hence at age 62. He described all of the typical reasons he wanted to sell: more time with his wife, kids, church, and volunteer work in the community. Suspicious of the delay, I asked him what he could realistically expect to sell the company for today. He stated that he could net $10 million after taxes and closing costs. This, by his own admission, would make him financially independent. Astounded, I asked him why he wouldn't put his company on the market today. His hesitation resulted from his belief that he was too young to leave the company. He was confident that he would be able to do so five years from now. I warned him that if he procrastinated due to this arbitrary deadline based solely on his age, he'd find it even more difficult to sell then than to sell today. I shared with him my observation that once owners reach their 60s, they rarely sell. Once these owners realize that the anticipated number of years of good health left is minimal, many simply conclude that the changes wrought by a sale simply are not worth the trouble. They choose to continue working because they simply cannot envision not going to work.

> "Unless you understand the sale process and commit to an exit strategy, it becomes increasingly difficult for you to leave your business."

Unless you understand the sale process and commit to an exit strategy, it becomes increasingly difficult for you to leave your business. Think about it for a moment. If you are going to make a significant life change, doesn't it make sense to do so when you can project another 15 to 30 years of good health and prosperity? The longer you wait, the less time you will have to relish this change. Too many business owners I have met in their mid- to late 60s have resigned themselves to the notion of "dying in office." "Why should I quit now? It is too late for me to do anything else with my life. I'll just keep coming to work." When asked what they would have done differently if they could do it over again, the answer is always the same: "I should have sold out sooner when there was more life ahead of me to enjoy and still sufficient time to develop a new 'me.'"

When I shared these observations with the owner I described earlier, he realized that he had been concocting reasons not to sell when in reality that truly was what he wanted to do. Upon further reflection, he agreed that waiting to reach an arbitrary birth date would only make his decision to sell that much more difficult. He had mistakenly assumed that five years would magically change his attitude and give him the time he thought he needed to adjust to the reality of no longer being a business owner. Within a year of our discussion, he was one of the first to sell to a publicly-traded acquirer who was consolidating his industry. He has subsequently achieved the best of both worlds. He was acquired and continues to work part time for his former company. He is enjoying building his former company with someone else's money: The pressure is off. He has accomplished what he set out to do: spend more time with family, church, and civic activities.

In another case, I met with a 70-year-old owner who expressed an interest in selling his company. I questioned him extensively about his decision. He confided that he had tried to sell several years earlier but had been unable to pull the trigger. His motivation to meet with me was that his son (active in the business) and wife were encouraging him to sell. When I told him my theory that 60-year-olds (never mind 70-year-olds!) just aren't sellers, he insisted that he was the exception.

Within six months, we brought a qualified and committed buyer to the table. The offer was all cash and several million dollars greater than this owner's stated target. I wish I could say that I was surprised when he balked and walked away from the deal. When I asked him why he didn't sell, he simply stated that he was "scared to death" of what he would face each morning if he couldn't go to work. As his attorney I accepted his explanation, but I was saddened, as well. Here was a classic example of an owner who stays at the helm, not for the thrill of being the captain, but because of a fear of not being the captain.

Don't allow Father Time to sneak up on you. Review your exit strategy annually. Frequent periodic reviews allow you to gauge the progress you are making toward your personal and financial objectives. Fail to do so and one morning you may realize that it is too late to sell.

Question 4

Should I sell my business to a key employee or a group of key employees?

Simple answer: "Sell to employees only if their purchase price matches or exceeds one that a third party would pay."

If you have conscientiously assembled and groomed a solid management team, this individual or group of individuals is a logical, readymade buyer. The advantages of a sale to employees are obvious.

First, you know the capability of the potential owner(s). Second, you can anticipate how the business will be run after you leave. Third, the buyer knows and understands the inner workings of the business. And fourth, you will likely have greater flexibility in defining your role, if any, as a consultant to the buyer after the sale is completed.

Of course, there are disadvantages to pursuing a sale to employees. The most significant, of course, is money. Employees' purchase offers rarely match the sums paid by outside third parties. Do your existing employees have or can they come up with sufficient cash to pay you 100 percent (or a substantial portion) of the purchase price at closing? If they cannot and an outside third party can, it may be unwise to consider this option. Recall that one of the main objectives when selling your business is to leave worries behind you. If you sell to employees and must carry back a substantial portion of the purchase price in the form of a promissory note, then your real worries have only just begun. You have now traded your role as "Owner in Control" to that of "Banker" with very little say about the day-to-day operations that determine success or failure. Will you be able to enjoy your new life as you worry about receiving your monthly note payments?

A second risk of financing an acquisition by employees is that although your management team may be composed of the best employees you have ever had, you are well aware that "best employee" is not synonymous with "most successful entrepreneur." Employees are employees for a reason. They are comfortable letting you, the entrepreneur, assume all of the risk. Once the risk is placed on their shoulders, they may not perform. When evaluating your employees' entrepreneurial instincts, avoid letting personal loyalties or wishful thinking cloud your judgment. Knowing that the security of your retirement is at stake, ask yourself one question: "Does the potential employee/buyer have what it takes to succeed?"

As a client of mine discovered, the risk of a sale to employees continues well beyond closing. "Mr. Seller" sold his successful company to a group of trusted employees in what he considered to be, for them, a "sweetheart" deal. For a variety of reasons, Mr. Seller agreed to carry back 80 percent of the purchase price.

Nine months after the closing, the company's revenues fell off dramatically due to both mismanagement and an economic downturn. Not surprisingly, the buyers chose to ignore their contribution to the company's demise, perhaps, in large part, because they were short on cash (owing Mr. Seller $50,000 per month note payments). Blaming Mr. Seller for their misfortune, they refused to make any further payments.

They argued that Mr. Seller had misrepresented various warranties and representations about the condition of the company. (See Question 47 for a discussion of warranties and representations.) Mr. Seller knew that these allegations were false, especially since the buyers had been instrumental in running the company on a day-to-day basis.

Nonetheless, Mr. Seller faced a difficult dilemma. He wanted his note paid and had no desire to resume control of the company. Any litigation would be an additional cash-drain on his beleaguered former company and would distract management, thus fatally jeopardizing the company's survival and its ability to pay the note.

Mr. Seller decided to re-negotiate the terms of the note, hoping that, in time, the company could recover. During the ensuing turnaround years, Mr. Seller and the buyers engaged in painful and expensive negotiations. In addition to Mr. Seller's financial losses, he lost faith in the employees who he believed had betrayed his trust. This was not the retirement he had envisioned.

If your employees have the cash to buy your company, by all means let them. If they don't, allow them to borrow from someone other than you. Do not act as senior lender, or worse yet, as a junior subordinated lender, on a deal. Allow others to enjoy the risk and reward of lending money. Your investment banker can help you to identify groups (such as a bank or private equity buy-out funds) who loan to and invest in management buyouts.

If, for whatever reason, you must carry back some portion of the purchase price, make sure that as a subordinated creditor to the senior lender, you have negotiated as much security for your note as possible. Clearly, if there are potential buyers other than your employees, carefully weigh which type of buyer best serves your long-term retirement and family interests. When deciding to sell to

> "If your employees have the cash to buy your company, by all means let them."

employees, make your choice for the right reasons.

I expect that at this point, I have discouraged you from even thinking about selling to employees. My intention is not to dissuade you but to demonstrate the pitfalls of a poorly-planned sale to employees. Sales to employees are indeed possible and even profitable **IF** you can meet two conditions. First, you must have at least five to seven years between your decision to attempt a sale to employees and the moment you plan to leave your company. Second, you must have a skilled set of advisors who are experienced in orchestrating the planning necessary to make this type of sale successful.

In Questions 21, 22, and 23, we discuss how to groom a group of key employees capable and motivated to buy your company. We cover how to motivate this group and how to put the cash in their pockets to pay for your ownership interest. Before you delete this category of buyer from your list of "possibles," I urge you to read further.

Question 5

Should I transfer my business to a family member?

Simple answer: "When it comes to family, the answer is never simple."

Various business surveys have reported that as many as eighty percent of family business owners anticipate transferring the company to a family member to carry on the business. Ultimately, the majority of those polled sold their businesses to a third party. Why? Because Junior could not afford to buy Dad out.

Many business owners dream of transferring their lives' work to their children. Clearly, this dream has worked successfully on many occasions, but dealing with family members in a business relationship is one of the thorniest challenges I have watched my clients undertake. First, family members encounter all of the inherent tensions that exist between co-owners. Stir in a lifetime of intrafamily dynamics and top it all off with the day-to-day pressures of running a business and you have a recipe for disaster.

> "...dealing with family members in a business relationship is one of the thorniest challenges I have watched my clients undertake."

If you are already in a family-owned business, you are well aware of the volatility of these ingredients. If you are not in a family-owned business, you have probably witnessed the trials and tribulations of friends who are.

The same logic used in selling your company to key employees (Question 4) should be employed here. If Junior can afford to buy you out for top dollar without using your money and you are convinced that after the closing, you can detach yourself from the fear of Junior ruining your company, then sell to Junior. If, on the other hand (and you truly need to be honest with yourself), you know that you are going to worry constantly about whether Junior will be successful or not, then do yourself, Junior, and the rest of the family a favor: Sell to a non-related third party.

The relationship between parent and child/children in business typically falls into the following categories.

> **Father and Child.** Father is strong and competent. Child does not have the skills to run company and allows Father to dominate. Father assigns Child responsibilities, but because Child really does lack skills, Father continually interferes (even when not necessary) with the role Child is to perform. Therefore, Child never succeeds and never matures. Neither Father nor Child is happy.
> *Conclusion: Father should not sell to Child.*

> **Father and Child.** Father is strong and competent. Child possesses the skills necessary to run company but Father's ego causes him to constantly second-guess Child. Why? Because Father can't give up control. As a result, there is a great deal of tension. There will be lulls when things seem to be going well, followed by strong confrontations between the two. These are typically brought on because Father interprets Child's success as a challenge to his control and Father needs to show Child who is boss.

Conclusion: A sale to Child can only work if Father gives up control and accepts the fact that although Child will experience some failures, he will learn from them and will ultimately be successful.

Father and Multiple Children. One child is more competent than the others. One or all children compete for Father's endorsement as successor. Father constantly pits one child against the other.

Conclusion: Good luck!! If there was ever a scenario in which Father should be cashed out by a third party at closing, this is it.

If any of the scenarios above sound familiar, tread cautiously if you are considering a sale to Child.

Despite these common scenarios, family transfers can be successful. The odds of success dramatically improve when both parent and child are mature and can communicate well with each other. Too often, however, Dad assumes that Child wants to control and operate the business when in reality Child does not. Child joined the company fresh out of college or shortly thereafter, because the business offered security, compensation, and good benefits. Years pass quickly, and although Child has enjoyed a nice life, the company's blood may not run through his veins. He goes through the motions because he does not want to disappoint Dad, but he would prefer to be elsewhere, "doing his own thing."

It is imperative, if you are in this situation, that you analyze Child's true desires as they relate to assuming the role as your successor. If Child does not want to own your business, you can sell to a third party and invest part of the sale proceeds in a venture that Child yearns to undertake. Give him the opportunity to steer his own ship.

It is never too early to start communicating with your child/employee. Tell the child that someday you may want him to

succeed you. Be honest about the realities, risks, and rewards of ownership. Make sure he understands that your financial freedom depends
on a proper buyout and on his performance. Don't assume to know
what he is thinking or what is best for him. Ask him. Ask him what he
wants and listen carefully to his answers. Don't try to subtly influence
his answers or filter out what you may not want to hear.

These are discussions that are best continued over time. Parent and
child need ample opportunity to communicate evolving goals, wants,
and needs relating to the business. Seriously consider retaining a facili-
tator, perhaps an industrial psychologist to help expedite these ongoing
discussions.

Without this type of honest and caring communication, it is likely
that your attempt to transfer your business to the next generation will
fail and your financial independence will be exposed to unnecessary
risk.

Question 6

Should I sell my business to a third party?

*B*ased upon my nearly 30 years of experience representing
owners who have successfully sold their companies to third
parties, I believe that, in most cases, the answer to this question is "yes."
Let's examine why.

ADVANTAGES
There are many advantages to selling your business to an inde-

pendent third party. Many of these advantages mirror the disadvantages of selling to a key employee or to a family member. First and foremost, you have a greater probability of receiving the bulk of the purchase price in cash or publicly-traded stock. Second, your chances of hitting a financial home run are much greater.

Objectivity. In selling to a key employee or family member, you will need to resist the temptation to make the deal too generous or too easy. In dealing with a third party, you will act more objectively and your transaction advisors are free to do their best to negotiate the most favorable deal for you.

More specifically, your goal will be to negotiate the highest possible purchase price and to receive as much of the purchase price in cash as possible. In addition, terminating the negotiating process with a third party is much easier than doing so with a key employee or family member. If you must terminate the negotiations, you never have to deal with that third party again as it relates to buying your business. Obviously, if you are negotiating with a key employee or family member, your relationship will continue beyond any termination of negotiations. Negotiating with "insiders" as objectively and perhaps as aggressively as you would with a third party can put that future relationship at risk.

Financial Flexibility. Selling your business to a third party will give you the most financial and personal flexibility. A third party will pay the purchase price for your business in one of the following ways: (1) cash; (2) cash plus a promissory note; (3) stock; or (4) a combination of stock and cash or promissory note. If you sell to an employee or family member, you will be limited to only the first two options. If the third party buyer is a publicly traded company, any of the four payment methods may be used.

If you are willing to accept stock from a publicly-traded company, you must first, with the help of your advisors, analyze the current value and future potential of that stock. How has this stock traded histori-cally? Has it had a steady growth pattern? Has it remained relatively flat or shown a tendency to be volatile? How strong is the management team? You must be comfortable with the degree of risk that you will bear if you accept stock as payment of the purchase price.

Further, you must determine what restrictions, if any, will be placed on your ability to sell the stock. Will it be freely transferable immedi-ately after the closing, or will you have to hold on to the stock for a specified period? Is the stock that you will receive currently registered or will the buyer have to initiate and complete the registration of your stock? If the stock is not currently registered, then you must again assess the degree of risk that you are willing to bear.

I have closed transactions in which the buyer, a publicly-traded company, has had a history of successful registrations and offerings, and warranted to the seller that it would use its best efforts to complete its next registration within a certain timeframe. Based upon thorough analysis, my clients were willing to assume the risk inherent to unregis-tered stock. In essence, they concluded that the risk was minimal since their stock would ultimately be registered and therefore, tradable. Their conclusions proved to be correct.

Personal Flexibility. A third party sale can afford a seller greater personal flexibility because the buyer (unlike your employee/buyer) will likely want you to stay with the company, either in your current capacity or to perform those duties hammered out between you and the buyer. Almost every buyer wants the seller to remain with the company for a minimal period to effect an orderly transition. "Minimal" ranges from 30 days to six months.

If you sell to an established company, whether public or private, and you wish to continue in your same or a similar capacity, most buyers are happy to accommodate you. Your strong management team is a selling point for your buyer. If you, as the head of that management team, are willing to stay on, many buyers will pay a higher purchase price. If you do stay, expect a lower base compensation than you currently receive, but don't worry. Payment of the purchase price at closing means you will have achieved financial independence and you can afford to take less. Having said that, if you sell to a publicly-traded company, its benefit package, including stock options, can be quite generous.

> "Many sellers elect to stay on after the sale because they want to participate in taking the company to the next level."

Many sellers elect to stay on after the sale because they want to participate in taking the company to the next level. If the company achieves certain objectives, the seller may receive additional compensation, either through cash, cash bonuses, stock bonuses, or stock options.

I once helped sell a company whose two owners (Partner A and Partner B) were quite young. This company was in an especially "hot" industry and therefore sold at a premium. When I first met these two individuals, Partner A explicitly stated that after the closing he would retire to a sun-drenched Florida beach. Partner B, because he truly enjoyed this dynamic industry, wanted to stay with the company so that he could become one of the industry's key players. Both partners succeeded. Partner A, at the time of this writing, is still collecting shells in Florida. Partner B continued to run his company until he decided to pursue other outside interests. (See Bob Quinette's story beginning on page 209.)

In another situation, one of my clients convinced his buyer, a leader in their industry, that there were numerous strategic reasons why this buyer should acquire the seller's company. As part of the transaction, my client, a highly-regarded industry player, agreed that he would remain after closing for a period of time so that he, on behalf of the buyer, could consolidate the industry. Using the buyer's stock and cash as currency, the seller completed numerous acquisitions in the same industry. This buyer is now the second largest player in its industry in the United States. In addition, each time the seller acquired another company, he received cash bonuses and additional stock in the parent company. As you can see, a sale to a third party can provide a seller a great deal of flexibility and valuable potential opportunities.

> "I see no disadvantages whatsoever in selling to a financially qualified third party."

Probability of closing. Let's not overlook another key advantage to selling to a third party; namely, the improved probability of closing the deal. Employees and relatives often lack the sophistication and independence necessary to facilitate a smooth transaction. Their lack of experience in the merger and acquisition arena can lead to a series of false starts and sudden stops. Separating themselves from their traditional roles of "employee" or "son" in order to negotiate on an equal level with "Boss/Dad" can be a daunting challenge. These buyers see themselves at risk. All of a sudden, because of the natural give and take of the negotiation process, they are taking positions (e.g. arguing for a lower valuation) that directly oppose that of their boss. The underlying fear of "What will happen to my job if this transaction fails?" can poison the negotiations. If properly represented by able counsel, this (and other) hurdles can be overcome. If not handled properly, these land mines will explode and jeopardize the deal's chances of closing.

Risk. This discussion of advantages would be incomplete without comment about the risk involved in accepting stock (in place of cash) for the purchase price. Indeed, third parties offer owners the flexibility of accepting payment in some combination of cash and stock. But does this advantage really benefit owners? Over the years, the vast majority of my clients have declined offers of stock. Why? Because no amount of research indicating future growth potential could outweigh the security owners felt when pocketing cold hard cash.

DISADVANTAGES

I see no disadvantages whatsoever in selling to a financially quali-fied third party. Owners who reject a sale to a third party because they believe that the third party will run the company differently than it has been run, or will conduct business under a different philosophy, need to re-evaluate their objectives for selling their companies. If fears regarding continuity issues prevent you from making the best possible financial decision for yourself and your family, you are not ready to sell. You must accept the fact that once you have closed the deal and received your sale proceeds, you surrender the right to worry about management techniques and business philosophy. That is now someone else's job. Let them do their job while you move on.

Question 7

Will my employees lose their jobs?

Simple answer: "No."

Assuming that you sell your company as a going concern, your employees' jobs should be secure.

Every buyer considers the existing employees to be a highly valu-able asset. In fact, having a strong, motivated group of employees drives the value of a company upward. Historically, buyers recognize the importance of a committed employee base and are willing to pay a premium price for it. This is true if the labor market is tight or abun-dant. In a tight market, a key factor motivating a buyer can be its desire to acquire more employees for its existing operations.

In the mergers and acquisitions of industry giants, hundreds and often thousands of employees lose their jobs as inefficiencies and dupli-cations are eliminated. We rarely see layoffs in middle market acquisi-tions. Acquisitions of this size do not involve such large economies of scale. Rarely are departments eliminated or sales forces slashed. That said, there is a risk that some positions will become redundant. For example, chief financial officers and controllers are often released because the buyer already has these positions filled and their own people are capable of taking on the additional responsibility.

It is not uncommon for sellers who suspect that certain key employees will be laid off to negotiate employment agreements (that specify a period of continued employment) or severance payments for those individuals. If you have loyal key employees and you are con-cerned about their future with the buyer, make it known at the outset. Obviously, there is only so much you can do. I assume you are unwilling to drive your buyer from the table over the issue of your employees' future. If you are convinced, however, that your employees' jobs are at risk, you can financially reward these employees from your own sale proceeds.

Question 8

Should I feel guilty about my employees after the sale takes place?

Simple answer: "No."

As a seller, you have absolutely no cause to feel responsible for or guilty about your employees once you have sold your company. For years, you have provided them with jobs, careers, opportunities, salaries, and benefits. The closing on the sale of your company is *your* payday. Don't let it be tainted by undeserved guilt.

Your forward-looking employees will understand that closing is their payday as well. This is true because many privately held businesses are often sold to larger companies – often publicly traded ones. These companies often provide employees better long-term career opportunities, better compensation, and better benefit packages than you ever could. In fact, many of these companies may offer your employees a chance to purchase stock – an opportunity that they would probably never have seen during your ownership.

Employees rarely quit their jobs after receiving news that a company has been sold. First and foremost, most employees are driven by their desire for job security. Additionally, they know and understand their existing job, duties, and responsibilities. They presumably like working for your company (whether or not you own it) and they have formed friendships with co-workers. The only unknown factor they face post-closing is the "new" owner. "Is he a good guy?" "Do I still have a future with this company?" etc. Rarely do employees choose to leave and move to another company where everything – including the owner – is unknown. Most employees are willing to remain in place long enough for the new owner to prove himself.

If you suspect that one of your key employees will lose his job because the buyer already has someone in his position, the closing will put you in the financial position to reward that employee for years of loyal service. In Question 42, we discuss how you go about making the announcement of a sale to your employees.

Question 9

How do I keep the sale process confidential?

Simple answer: "Don't tell anyone."

*A*ll sellers are and should be paranoid about keeping a potential sale confidential. For obvious reasons, employees, customers, competitors, and vendors should only learn about the sale **after** the closing and in a manner that you, the seller, control. A knowledgeable team of transaction advisors knows how to orchestrate the sale process without breaching confidentiality. Contrary to popular belief, most deals close without leaks. Almost without exception, when a leak does occur, it can quickly be traced back to the seller himself. Despite their paranoia, owners cannot resist the urge to tell someone in their confidence about the impending sale. Once one "confidant" learns of an impending sale, rest assured that shortly, the rest of the world will know, as well.

> "...when a leak does occur, it can quickly be traced back to the seller himself."

At one time, I represented the owner of a very successful family business who was especially sensitive that anyone discover his sale plans – including other family members – until the deal was near closing. My client lectured me endlessly about how the deal must be kept absolutely confidential. Shortly after one of these lectures, my client and I were on the golf course with another twosome. We hadn't reached the second green before my client told these gentlemen, two complete strangers, that he was selling his company!

At some time during every transaction, an employee, customer, or outside third party will ask an owner, point-blank, "Are you selling your company?" I prepare owners for this inevitability during our very first meeting. "When this happens," I advise, "cross your fingers behind your back, look the questioner directly in the eyes and fib." For those who simply can't bring themselves to utter a clear and resounding, "No," I suggest that they finesse the confrontation as follows: "Everything is for sale. If someone offers me $100 million cash to buy this company, I'll sell in a heartbeat. Unfortunately, no one has made such an offer." This response is a great way to deflect attention from the inevitable question. After closing, if you so desire, you can explain that you were bound to a confidentiality clause and thus you were forced to finesse when asked the question. The questioner will understand your actions.

At some point before the closing, you may have to tell a key employee (or several) that the company is for sale. Limit this disclosure to as few employees as possible. Key members of management often participate in the sale process by gathering critical information, participating in presentations to buyers, and ultimately being interviewed by the buyer.

If, during the sale process, you must rely heavily upon a key employee(s), consider offering a "loyalty bonus" to that employee. Your offer provides an incentive to work diligently to close the deal without disclosing to anyone that the company is on the market. This bonus will only be paid if the transaction remains confidential and closes. I have seen sellers pay a vital employee as much as twice his annual salary in return for his help. As to the size of this bonus, I leave that to you. You know your employees. Figure out what it will take to inspire your dedicated employee(s) to focus on and support you in the sale of your company.

Of course, your advisors must take the necessary precautions to preserve your confidentiality. My firm asks every owner to evaluate the security of his internal channels of communication. If, for example, we mark envelopes "PERSONAL AND CONFIDENTIAL," can the owner be absolutely sure that they will reach his desk unopened? Some owners prefer that bills for services rendered be sent to their homes. When so requested, my firm sends a detailed invoice to the owner's home and a bare-bones invoice (one showing only "For Services Rendered" and a dollar amount) to the business address. In this way, the owner sees a detailed accounting of our services while his accounts payable person sees nothing that will reveal the owner's plan to sell.

Similarly, my firm does not send documents via facsimile without first calling the owner to make absolutely sure that the person standing at the machine on the receiving end knows about the deal. In addition, owners should determine whether their email communications are secure. In one case, a client asked members of my firm to use fictitious names when phoning his company. That is an extreme example but it does illustrate the lengths to which some owners will go to protect their plans.

At some point in the process (usually near the end of their due diligence), buyers and their advisors will insist on inspecting your facility. Sellers unaccustomed to hosting a steady stream of "professional-looking" visitors are especially apprehensive about such tours. This concern can be alleviated in several ways. Buyers and their teams can dress down, leaving their pinstripes at home. They can arrive after hours, or, if during operating hours, they can be introduced as bankers, auditors, prospective customers, or friends who want to see the company. Any combination of these ruses usually keeps the lid on your plans to sell.

If news of the sale does leak and you find the buyer at the source, your investment banker and attorney will alert the buyer that you will not tolerate any more breaches of the confidentiality agreement. Your advisors should also ask for and receive proof that the buyer has taken the necessary precautions to prevent further leaks. Remember, if *you* can keep a secret, confidentiality, in most cases, will be maintained.

PART 2 | STRATEGIC DECISIONS

Once owners have resolved the emotional issues that can delay a decision to sell, they begin to ask another set of questions that I consider to be "strategic."

Strategic decisions concern how to pursue a sale: whether, in order to achieve a viable size, they should merge with industry peers or grow through acquisition. Owners at this point in the decision-making process wonder if they can orchestrate a sale themselves. They have received unsolicited offers (and don't feel prepared to respond) and wonder how they will inform those around them that they are considering a sale.

If you find yourself at this point in the process, the answers in this Part Two will help you to move forward.

Question 10

Should I take my company public?

Simple answer: "If your goal is to exit, no."

Taking a company public is typically not an exit strategy – at least in the short term. As a general rule, converting your company from a privately-held entity to a publicly traded company is a strategy used to raise capital. It is often a financing tool used to grow a company to the next level. If your objective is to sell your company, leave and start a new chapter in life, then the answer to "Should I take my company public?" is no.

In the short term, a public offering may allow you to take some of your chips off the table, but the success of the offering relies heavily on the management team that you will lead. As CEO of a publicly traded company, you will spend much of your time on the road educating analysts in the finer points of why they should jump at the opportunity to own and promote your company's stock. As a CEO and substantial shareholder, you will have none of the financial privacy or authority to make decisions that you enjoyed as the owner of a private company. You will be an employee of the publicly-held entity and will report directly to your board of directors. You will live in a fish bowl where all of your decisions are open to the brokerage community's and to the market's second guesses.

In addition, your investor agreements and the underwriters who took you public will restrict your ability to leave the company and cash out your stock. It is not uncommon to be prohibited from selling your stock from 12 months to three years or more and then be allowed to sell only in fractions that comply with SEC regulations.

If your objective is to grow your company and to stay actively involved for a reasonable amount of time, consider using a public offering as a means to achieve those goals. If, on the other hand, your objective is to sell and walk away, going public is not the right path for you. (See Bill Clymor's story on page 203.)

Question 11

If my business is not worth enough today, should I grow through acquisition?

*I*f the value of your company is insufficient to generate your definition of wealth and freedom, you must increase it. You can let your company grow organically, or you can graft on new growth through the process of acquiring other companies. Those owners who have depended on organic growth to increase revenue and profitability know how much human and financial capital such growth requires. These owners also know that organic growth takes time. Knowing the ingredient list for organic growth, you must determine whether you can achieve the greater value you desire more quickly and with less risk via acquisition.

In some ways, these two growth strategies are comparable to the tortoise and hare of fable fame. Organic growth can be slow, steady, and may involve fewer resources and less risk. Like the hare, growth through acquisition allows you to grow as quickly as your appetite demands. If you properly analyze the potential acquisition opportunities (gained through due diligence), structure your financing intelligently, and negotiate a fair purchase price with reasonable terms and conditions, the growth-through-acquisition hare can finish well ahead of the tortoise.

Let's look at eight common reasons for choosing an acquisition growth strategy:

1. *Enhance diversification of products and services;*
2. *Reduce competition;*
3. *Increase market share;*
4. *Achieve economies of scale;*
5. *Expand geographically;*
6. *Achieve strategic alliances;*
7. *Achieve greater leverage with vendors;*
8. *Add new product or service lines.*

If you do decide to grow through acquisition, resist the temptation to acquire a "turnaround company." Turnarounds are companies in serious trouble which can be acquired cheaply. Professionals in the business of buying distressed companies are typically the only parties who can successfully turn around these companies. These buyers employ a team of financial and management experts and have sufficient time and capital to rebuild the company. These experts adhere to their own strict financial criteria in purchasing a turnaround and are not prone to "falling in love" with the acquisition target.

One compelling reason to avoid a turnaround is the inability to fully diagnose the depth and severity of the turnaround's problems. For example, until you have operated the company for some time after closing, you may not discover just how sick the patient is. The seller may have treated customers, employees, and vendors far worse than you would ever have imagined and he may have failed to fully disclose certain liabilities. In addition, the intensity of this effort could distract you and your management team from profitably operating your primary business. For these reasons, turnaround purchases can end up costing the inexperienced buyer far more money in the long run than anticipated while never achieving the turnaround success originally contemplated.

If you grow by acquisition, I recommend finding a good company with a strong history of performance and with many of the "Value Drivers" discussed in Question 20. In that case, you will assume the role of buyer and should carefully consider the Questions in Part Three, "All About Buyers." In buying a good company, you will pay a price that reflects quality, but the road to success will be more certain. One rarely regrets paying for quality. I recommend that you avoid the brain damage and potential unforeseen costs inherent to turning around a turnaround.

Question 12

Should I consider merging with industry peers prior to a sale?

I routinely encounter this question from business owners. The typical scenario involves multiple industry players who know each other through their trade association, are friends, and don't compete against each other. Their theory is simple. First, merge the companies, achieve greater economies of scale, reduce duplicate expenses, achieve expanded geographic coverage, and add more product lines and services. Second, sell the new and larger entity to a third party or go public. Does this sound familiar?

This plan may be logical but it rarely reaches fruition. Why? Because executing this plan is similar to herding cats. Rarely does one person assume leadership of the process. Multiple owners armed with various agendas and differing opinions rarely arrive at valuations that they can agree upon. It is even more difficult to agree on who receives what percentage of ownership or whose employees will be terminated. Finding agreement on who will control the new enterprise is also a significant hurdle. Owners who have known each other for years as *peers* find it difficult to elevate one to a position of control. Finally, day-to-day business demands distract each owner from concentrating on the mega-deal. The result? The would-be partners continue to meet and meet until the lack of tangible progress numbs all initiative and enthusiasm. They never reach a formal decision to stop exploring the concept; they just eventually stop talking about it.

All that said, I have seen a variation of this concept work – once. During a number of meetings, one particular client proposed to me the "cat herding" scenario. As I continued to point out the significant obstacles described above, he failed to convince me and ultimately himself that in *his* case the concept would succeed. During our last discussion on the topic, I suggested that, as an alternative, he designate his company a platform company and seek a buyer who would "roll up" this particular industry.

He subsequently adopted this strategy, abandoned the merger idea, and sold his company to a publicly-traded company. He assured his buyer that he would bring many of his fellow cats to the table and that he would assist in their acquisition. This is exactly what he did. His fellow cats were most appreciative that he had conceived and executed an exit strategy that enabled many of them to leave their businesses and achieve their definitions of wealth and freedom.

Question 13

How do I respond to unsolicited inquiries about buying my business?

Simple answer: "Very carefully."

When you receive an unsolicited inquiry, it will be tendered in one of two ways: You will receive a letter or you will receive a phone call. To a letter, no immediate response and often no response at all is necessary. Most come from business brokers trying to solicit a listing. They usually read something like this:

> *Dear Captain of Industry,*
>
> *I represent a buyer who has identified your company as a target acquisition. This buyer has chosen your company because of its profitability, its sound business practices and excellent reputation in the region. This buyer believes that acquiring your company will elevate both companies to new levels of profitability and earnings.*
>
> *I urge you to contact me immediately to pursue discussions that could open the door to your financial security.*
>
> *I.M. Fishin*

Rarely does such a buyer exist. The writer simply wants more information about your company so that he can meet you and convince you to sell it. These letters generally do not warrant a response. If, however, you suspect that the letter is legitimate, you should ask one of your advisors to respond with a letter such as the one I use for my clients.

Dear Mr. Fishin:

I represent Mr. C.O. Industry. He has received your letter describing a buyer interested in acquiring his company. Let me state, most emphatically, that Mr. Industry is not seeking to sell his company at this time.

Like all forward-looking entrepreneurs, Mr. Industry recognizes that someday he will transfer his company, for the right price, to the right suitor. Your timing is, therefore, premature. As his advisor, however, it is my duty to probe your offer more completely. If your client is interested in pursuing this matter further, I will need to review the following items:

1. Company literature (brochures, marketing materials, etc.)

2. Company or individual financial statements (preferably audited) and

3. Company or individual tax returns for the last three, and preferably the last five years.

All future communication should be directed to me.

This letter effectively separates the genuine expressions of interest from the false come-ons.

In the case of a phone call, you have two goals. First, and foremost, reveal nothing about your exit plans. Second, gather as much information as you can so your attorney can return the call.

Let's look at the first goal – revealing nothing. Your script should read something like this: *"I am not in the market to sell my company. Of course, if the opportunity is right, anything can be for sale. I am flattered by your call. If I decide to take any action, I'll have one of my advisors contact you."* At that point you should gather contact information, the name of the company he represents, and any other information you think will help you and your advisors decide if any response is necessary.

After you pass this information to your transaction attorney, he can follow up with a letter requesting the three items listed earlier.

It is crucial that owners show no interest whatsoever in these callers. Keep in mind that you have no idea who is on the other end of the phone. A competitor? A potential customer? A creditor? A journalist? To engage in lengthy discussions – even hypothetical ones – divulges information and essentially opens negotiations. Your best course is to remove yourself from the loop and hand over the information to your advisors. If, in fact, you are ready to sell, seek your advisors' counsel to help you decide if this is a buyer you wish to pursue or if another sale strategy would better serve your exit objectives.

Question 14

Can I sell the business myself?

Simple answer: "No."

For a variety of reasons, some business owners are tempted to fly solo on the sale of their businesses. I have rarely seen one of those solo flights reach its intended destination. If I am unsuccessful in convincing an owner to retain an experienced transaction team to navigate the turbulence of a transaction, I sadly await the inevitable crash and burn.

Think about it. You have successfully built your company due to your keen understanding of your business, your customers, and your market. You may not, however, have the expertise necessary to orchestrate a successful sale. Keep in mind that nothing less than your financial security is at stake. This is a good time to let transaction experts guide you through the most important transaction of your business life.

Here I will try to dissuade you from attempting to orchestrate the sale of your company and convince you to use the valuable services of a Team of Advisors. Let me do so by describing just one member of the Advisory Team, the investment banker. Other Team members include your transaction attorney, CPA, and financial planner and possibly a business broker. For more information on their roles, please see Part Four.

As a key member of this Team, your investment banker adds value to the sale process in ways that few owners are capable of duplicating.

- *The investment banker will identify potential buyers that you have probably not considered.*
- *He will pre-qualify buyers so that you don't waste time with "looky-loos" or tire-kickers.*
- *He can determine what the buyer's motives are in the acquisition.*
- *Once those motives are determined, he constantly educates the buyer about how your business satisfies and even exceeds his criteria.*

> "...your investment banker adds value to the sale process in ways that few owners are capable of duplicating."

- *He creates a controlled auction. (See Question 41.)*
- *He has the financial expertise to take on the buyer's accountants in the war of numbers. He speaks the same language as the buyer's financial advisors and can protect and defend your valuation.*
- *He acts as a buffer between you and the buyer, protecting you from on-the-spot decision-making. Answering the seller's demands with "I'll discuss that with my client and get back to you" gives both you and your Advisory Team the*

time needed to make thoughtful, informed decisions. This buffer enables you to keep your ego and emotions from jeopardizing the transaction.

- *He allows you to retain your role as the "good guy" in the process.*
- *He negotiates the nitty-gritty while you maintain the "let's get the deal done" relationship with the buyer. This is crucial if you will continue to work for the new owner post-closing.*
- *The investment banker brings instant credibility to the process. Sophisticated buyers lick their chops when they stumble upon an under-represented seller.*
- *An investment banker increases the probability that your deal will close and the company will sell. On your own, you might attract a reasonable offer but knowing how to orchestrate the process that converts an offer to cash is critical.*
- *Perhaps most importantly, when the investment banker is guiding the process, you keep your focus where it belongs – on running your business. This is not the time to become distracted and create a financial hiccup in your profits or sales.*

That said, I have participated in transactions in which the seller assumed a major role in the negotiations. This role, however, was played in a tightly controlled environment. Before the seller communicates with the buyer:

- *We conduct a "dress rehearsal" during which we advisors ask the seller questions that the buyer will likely ask;*
- *We prioritize the exact points to be won and those we are willing to give up;*
- *We anticipate the buyer's presentation and arguments;*
- *We identify key words and phrases (bullet points) for the seller to emphasize in order to make his case;*

- *We identify issues that the seller will not discuss and make sure that whenever the seller feels uncomfortable, he will say, "I'll have to talk to my advisors before I can make a decision."*

It is this detailed preparation that enables sellers to play an important role in the negotiations. In most cases, any approach less disciplined than this causes the seller to place his deal in jeopardy. Remember, any fee that you think you may save by arranging your own sale becomes immaterial if you fail to close the transaction.

If you do try to sell the company yourself and fail, there is a strong probability that you will have tainted the market. This will become apparent when, at a future date, you re-enter the market to sell. Those potential buyers that you approached earlier will know that you failed to sell. Based on this knowledge, they typically will make negative assumptions: There must be something wrong with you, your company, or both. You will have to spend time overcoming their doubts rather than highlighting the opportunities your company offers. Potential buyers whom you did not approach in your first foray into the market may make the same assumptions, because through the grapevine they will know of your earlier attempt and failure.

The sale process contains a number of obstacles. Do not let yourself become the biggest obstacle of all.

Question 15

When do I tell my employees, customers, bankers and vendors that I am selling?

EMPLOYEES

Keeping your cards close to the vest before and during the sale process is critically important. As discussed earlier, your first task will be to determine which key employees need to know about the sale. Only inform those whose help you, or your advisors, will require during the process. The other employees have no need to know anything until the deal is closed. The reason for this selectivity is simple. If your employees learn of the deal prematurely, they will justifiably become fixated on one issue: "What is going to happen to me?" A distraction of this magnitude can create a devastating downturn in a company's performance. It is imperative that everyone focus on company performance before and during the sale process.

Keep in mind that many buyers will want to size up your key employees before the deal closes. A buyer will want to determine the caliber of your key employees and whether they are likely to stay once the transaction is complete. Ideally, you postpone that meeting as long as possible. At a minimum, you should prevent the buyer from talking to your key employees until all other conditions precedent or contingencies are satisfied and you are 99 percent sure that you will close. (See Question 48 regarding conditions precedent.)

Of course, the day will come when the buyer meets your key

employees. I suggest that you sit down with your employees prior to that meeting and explain that you are in negotiations to sell the company. Offer to answer any questions your employees have so that they can go into that meeting with some information and hopefully with some thought about their future. Properly prepared, your employees will likely handle their first meeting with the buyer quite well. Usually, they understand that when they speak highly of you to the buyer, they speak well of themselves.

CUSTOMERS

As a rule, your customers can remain blissfully unaware of the transaction until the deal is closed. Apply the same standards of confidentiality to your customers that you do to your employees. You certainly do not want customers to worry unnecessarily about your continued ability to meet their needs. If, however, you have a limited number of customers who make up a significant portion of your business, your buyer will likely want to meet them. He wants some assurance that these major customers will continue to do business with him once he assumes the reins. Again, as understandable as this desire is, postpone this meeting as long as possible. You don't want to threaten a relationship that you have worked so hard to cultivate. Typically, you will allow direct communication between your buyer and customers only after all other contingencies have been satisfied. When the meeting occurs, plan to attend so that you have a measure of control over how and what questions are answered.

I have represented many owners who were convinced that face-to-face meetings between buyer and customer were either unnecessary or too risky. Therefore, they asked their buyers to approach customers more discreetly. For example, a buyer can contact customers under the guise of a customer service survey. Alternatively, a buyer can tell a customer that he is considering using the seller's services and would like a candid opinion. In this manner, buyers collect the information they need without putting your relationship with your customers at risk or disclosing that a sale is in the works.

BANKERS

A seller's banker is usually the last person to learn that his customer is selling his company. This occurs for two reasons. First, most sellers don't consider their bankers to be trusted confidants, knowledgeable about the decisions involved in the sale process. Second, many sellers anticipate that bankers will respond negatively to news about a sale and change the existing credit facility. In my experience, both of these assumptions are incorrect.

> "No other lender will know your company, your management team, and your industry as well as your existing lender."

If you know your banker well and have, over the years, been candid about your desire to sell, then alerting him that that day draws near is probably a good idea. Whether you know him well or not, if you have a bank loan that you will pay off at closing, you must notify your bank of this payoff at least as early as the terms of your loan require.

I suggest that bringing your banker into your confidence well before any transition is a good idea because your existing bank may be the logical place for your buyer to look for financing. No other lender will know your company, your management team, and your industry as well as your existing lender. When credit is difficult to obtain, your bank may be the only lender willing to finance the purchase. In addition, your banker will be eager to help you to invest the sale proceeds. He will also be a likely source of financing for any of your future entrepreneurial ventures.

If you do not know your banker well, and your gut tells you to keep your cards close to your vest, use your Advisory Team as a sounding board and discuss your doubts with them. If your Team agrees with you, trust your instincts. (See Question 24 for a more complete discussion for the role your banker can play as a member of your Advisory Team.)

VENDORS

Your vendors have no reason to know about a pending transaction until it has closed. Most likely, they will continue to do business with the new owner as long as their bills are paid.

PART 3 | ALL ABOUT BUYERS

This book is about deciding to sell your company at a price that will yield your definition of personal wealth and freedom. For all of the reasons already discussed, selling to a third party for cash is often the best way to achieve that objective. Therefore, this Part contains a description of the types of third party buyers.

But let's assume for a moment that market, economic, or industry conditions make a sale to a third party on your terms impossible. Or perhaps your company has strong cash flow, a superior management team, and a bright future but it is too small to attract the interest of financial or strategic buyers. Is there a way to exit your company without sacrificing your objectives?

Owners are often surprised to learn that given both adequate time and thoughtful planning, a sale to insiders – key employees – not only meets their financial objectives but that such a sale can be designed to minimize the risk to the owner of receiving anything less than full payment. For that reason this Part contains a discussion of how an owner can achieve a successful sale to insiders.

To orchestrate this kind of sale, an owner must first design a key employee incentive plan that handcuffs key employees to the company. Doing so not only makes a company more valuable to a third party buyer but it also makes a sale to key employees (using an ESOP or conventional buy-out) possible. Because they serve this dual purpose, key employee incentive plans are well worth considering no matter who your potential buyer is.

Second, an owner must work with his Advisory Team to design a plan that will bonus to the key employees (over time) the cash they need to buy him out. (See Question 22 for details on Non-Qualified Deferred Compensation Plans.)

Finally, some owners whose companies meet several specific criteria can exit via a sale to their employees through an Employee Stock Ownership Plan. While complex, a properly designed sale to an ESOP is often no more difficult than a sale to a third party. For owners who cannot locate a third party or who wish to provide employees the benefit of indirect ownership, the ESOP can be an ideal exit opportunity. (See Question 23 for a description of ESOPs.)

For the information in this Part regarding techniques used to sell to key employees, I owe a great debt to my law partner, John H. Brown. He is the author of **The Completely Revised How To Run Your Business So You Can Leave It In Style**, a book which covers the transfer to insiders in greater detail. (To order a copy, visit **www.exitplanning.com** or any bookstore.)

Question 16

Should I sell my business to a strategic buyer?

A "strategic buyer" comes from the pool of companies that conducts business, directly or indirectly, in your industry. For example, a business that sells goods or services to your industry, distributes your industry's products, or provides financing to your industry is considered to be a strategic buyer. Of course, this group of strategic buyers also includes your direct competitors.

Strategic buyers are logical prospective buyers. They are motivated to acquire your company for one or more of the following strategic reasons:

- *To increase revenues;*
- *To become more diversified;*
- *To reduce competition;*
- *To increase market share;*
- *To attain economies of scale and market share;*
- *To expand geographically;*
- *To establish strategic alliances;*
- *To achieve greater leverage with vendors;*
- *To add new lines of goods or services; and*
- *To provide enhanced growth opportunities to employees.*

More often than not, a strategic buyer will pay a higher purchase price than a financial or entrepreneurial buyer. (See Questions 17 and 18.) Strategic buyers compare the cost of purchasing your business to the cost of starting a business in your area and competing head-to-head against you. The strategic buyer knows your industry well and may be willing to pay a premium because he fully understands the opportunities, dangers, pitfalls, market conditions, and trends in the industry. The strategic buyer often agrees to pay a premium to acquire a company with a positive historical track record because he can use that to predict future performance more accurately.

If you have more than one buyer competing to buy your company, the ultimate buyer may pay a premium just to prevent competitors from acquiring you. This is an example of how the controlled auction process (discussed in Question 41) is a very effective technique for selling your company. Similarly, if your company is extra-special in its own right and provides a perfect fit, the strategic buyer should reward you handsomely. If he doesn't, wait for one who will.

In determining what your business is worth, strategic buyers will project future cash flow, taking into consideration its estimates of both the increased revenue and anticipated reduced costs. Thus, the future cash flow to the strategic buyer may be significantly more than what your business can generate on a stand-alone basis. From the strategic buyer's perspective, as the projection of future cash flow improves, the value of your business increases. Your advisors must demonstrate to the buyer how it can enjoy the "upside potential" that the combined entity will realize.

The potential for financial and operational synergies is a strong motivator for strategic buyers to pay more for your business than will financial buyers, entrepreneurial buyers, or related parties. Strategic buyers can cut costs, eliminating areas of duplication. For example, once the post-closing transition phase is complete, your in-house controller will most likely be looking for a new job. Most strategic buyers already have strong accounting/financial departments in their home offices. The strategic buyer may consolidate multiple locations, thus saving significant rental expense. Some strategic buyers may cease to do business with smaller, lower margin customers in order to cut costs.

Special considerations when dealing with competitors

Not surprisingly, there are many sellers who won't consider a competitor as a potential buyer because they fear that if the transaction fails to close, the competitor will know everything there is to know about the selling company and thus will have obtained an unfair advantage. Carefully consider this concern before approaching a competitor or before responding to a competitor's inquiry about whether your company is for sale.

A confidentiality agreement (discussed in Question 44) is intended to give you the legal protection you need to prevent the competitor from using information to compete against you. Although assurances look good on paper, if the sale does not occur, it is obviously difficult for you to police whether or not the competitor uses the information you provided him. Nonetheless, if properly drafted, the confidentiality agreement should act as a strong deterrent against misbehavior.

I have represented sellers who were simply unwilling to depend on confidentiality agreements. Therefore, because they did not trust certain competitors, they simply excluded them from consideration. Most sellers have some information on which to base their assessments of a competitor's integrity. If you lack knowledge about a particular competitor, you or your advisors can make some discreet inquiries about that competitor's reputation. If you are unsatisfied with the results of these inquiries, you, too, can exclude that competitor from consideration.

Fortunately, I have not seen a prospective buyer fail to close and then proceed to violate a confidentiality agreement and use information for competitive purposes.

Competitors can be ideal buyers. One of my clients sold his company to one of his largest industry competitors. This competitor moved to town with the expressed purpose of capturing the market. It

"The challenge for you, and for your transaction Advisory Team in negotiating the sale, is to make the strategic buyer pay a premium for the opportunity to prove just how smart he really is."

wrongly calculated that it would be cheaper to start a branch office from scratch than to purchase my client's established company.

This competitor underestimated the strength of the local competition and did not adapt its style to the customers in the local market. After two years of battle, the competitor gave up and bought my client for a multiple of ten times earnings. This multiple was one of the highest ever to be paid by one private company for another in this industry.

One last word about buyers.

One fundamental principle applies to all buyers – strategic perhaps most of all. No matter how successful you are, your buyer believes he is smarter and can make more money running your business. The challenge for you, and for your transaction Advisory Team in negotiating the sale, is to make the strategic buyer pay a premium for the opportunity to prove just how smart he really is.

Question 17

What is an entrepreneurial buyer?

*A*n entrepreneurial buyer is typically an *individual* who decides to acquire and subsequently run a business. Some entrepreneurial buyers have left careers in larger, often publicly-traded, companies to pursue lifelong dreams of owning their own companies. Others have owned companies previously but now desire to invest while taking a more passive role in management. In short, entrepreneurial buyers are often people just like you.

Over the years, I have represented many entrepreneurial buyers. In an interview, a series of carefully-worded questions quickly determines if the person sitting in my guest chair is a serious buyer or if he simply enjoys shopping. You should know that many would-be entrepreneurial buyers are perennial tire-kickers. They truly believe that they want to buy a company but they never do pull the trigger. They can look at 50 quality buying opportunities and find 50 different reasons not to pursue each. Don't be drawn into an activity trap with a buyer like this. If you sense that a prospective buyer is just looking, have one of your advisors eliminate this buyer from further involvement in the process.

Typically, entrepreneurial buyers look to acquire smaller companies with sale prices between $1 million and $10 million. Unfortunately (for sellers), they often lack sufficient equity to consummate a deal and will frequently ask sellers to carry back a significant part of the purchase price.

When I ask entrepreneurial buyers how much they can afford to pay for a company, many don't have an answer. If I pursue that line of questioning, asking how much equity can be gathered from personal assets, friends, and family, the answer typically ranges from $250,000 to $1 million.

Due to these financial limitations, you and your advisors should know approximately how much a bank will be willing to loan to a buyer before you put your company on the market. (Another reason to bring your existing banker into the process!) Your investment banker and attorney should also consider how your desired purchase price can be structured with a lender.

Be prepared to assist an entrepreneurial buyer in the financing process. If capital markets are tight and lenders' requirements difficult to satisfy, your attorney and investment banker should take the initiative with their lending sources, and to the extent possible, pre-arrange the financing. When notifying their banking sources that your company is for sale, your advisors will ask these sources to structure a potential financing package. Once the appropriate buyer is identified, your advisors can introduce him to the banker who is prepared and has been waiting for the buyer's call.

If you are negotiating with an entrepreneurial buyer, it is critical that you (or better yet, your advisors) determine his commitment and financial ability to make the purchase as soon as possible. As stated earlier, you can't afford to be distracted from operating your business by dealing with "tire kickers." On the other hand, a sophisticated and financially capable entrepreneurial buyer can often close a deal more quickly than a larger strategic or financial buyer because he has a committee of one making the ultimate decision to buy.

Question 18

What is a financial buyer?

*F*inancial buyers typically operate as private investment funds controlling millions of dollars. They identify an industry with significant growth potential and make direct investments in mature and stable middle market businesses. They look for companies that provide the opportunity to create value. Once such companies are acquired, financial buyers will install their own management teams or rely upon the management team already in place. In either case, financial buyers believe that to be most effective, management must have a significant financial commitment to the company as well as an opportunity for additional equity participation based on performance.

Frequently, the financial buyer will offer a lower multiple than a strategic buyer. This is true for several reasons. The financial buyer's objective is to realize a fairly high internal rate of return on its invested capital over an average five-year period. In my experience, this return ranges from 35 to 40 percent. To achieve this rate of return, the financial buyer must not overpay or over-leverage at the outset. Similarly, financial buyers are less likely than strategic buyers to "fall in love with the deal." Driven more by bottom line numbers, financial buyers look for reasons why not to do the deal. On the other hand, strategic buyers are often influenced by the perceived *long-term* benefits (see Question 16) and are therefore more apt to justify a higher multiple. Finally, the financial buyer anticipates that most of its portfolio companies will ultimately be sold to strategic/corporate buyers or taken public. Their strategy is to buy at the low end of "reasonable" and sell high.

Please don't infer from my description that financial buyers are "bottom feeders" or that strategic buyers always pay more. They aren't and they don't. I recently represented a highly successful family-owned business during a controlled auction (a seller's ideal negotiating environment). Both a strategic and a financial buyer bid against each other to acquire this company, driving the final offer 75 percent beyond this seller's expectations. When the seller selected the strategic buyer, the financial buyer was very disappointed and wanted to continue negotiations. The seller rejected this plea and sold to the strategic buyer because he believed that his employees would respond more favorably to the strategic buyer and that they would enjoy greater career opportunities.

During times when the economy is slow and multiples are low, financial buyers may be a seller's best (and only) alternative. Unlike strategic buyers whose immersion in the day-to-day operations of a business often cause them to ignore their acquisition activities, financial buyers are focused on return on investment and on identifying new acquisition opportunities. Their job is to place their investors' money in companies yielding rates of return nearing 35 to 40 percent. Your investment banker should identify and include financial buyers on your list of possible buyers.

Question 19

What factors prompt buyers to enter the marketplace?

*B*efore potential buyers evaluate whether your particular company meets their acquisition requirements, they will compile a shopping list of attributes that they are seeking. This list includes:

- *Strategic fit with the buyer's business objectives;*
- *Timing of the sale and industry cycles;*
- *Current condition of the merger and acquisition market;*
- *Availability of capital;*
- *Financial synergies; and*
- *Geographic location.*

Let's look at each.

STRATEGIC FIT

Buyers look for companies that fit their objectives. If a buyer wants to enter your industry or expand into a market you control, his choice is to buy your company or start his own operation to compete against you. Buying your company may cost more initially but it should reduce his risk in the long run. If your company has a proven track record, strong management, and a solid customer base, a savvy buyer will prefer paying a premium price to competing head to head with you in the marketplace. Of course, if your company does not match a buyer's objectives, it will hold little to no value for that buyer. (See Question 16 for more information on strategic buyers.)

TIMING

Most buyers look for companies on their way to, but not at, the peak of their growth potential. More specifically, the ideal time to sell is when you can demonstrate that your company's earnings stream has steadily increased over several years and is projected to continue. If your company's earnings are flat, you can either hold on until you achieve a positive trend or be willing to accept a lower purchase price. Because buyers pay for future cash flow, they want some assurance that the future holds upside potential. Sellers who can demonstrate this potential are rewarded with higher sale prices.

If, like most industries, your industry predictably cycles from great to marginal and back again, the best time for you to sell is as close to the beginning of the upswing as possible. Doing so enables buyers to envision sufficient time to recover their investment and to enjoy the upside potential remaining in the cycle. Keep in mind that selling makes sense only if the buyer's offer meets or exceeds your definition of financial independence.

CONDITION OF THE MERGER AND ACQUISITION MARKET

Between 1993 and the third quarter of 2000, there was an unprecedented boom in the mergers and acquisitions (M&A) market. Each year far exceeded the prior year's record for the quantity of mergers and acquisitions completed and the total dollars paid. During this period, many owners of middle market companies sold their companies for amounts never before seen in their industry sectors. Companies with histories of outstanding performance commanded extraordinary prices. Companies that performed reasonably well sold for excellent multiples, thanks to the robust M&A market. A market fueled by a record high stock market and a strong economy made lenders eager to do deals.

Even companies with mediocre records were acquired at respectable prices by industry consolidators eager to boost their performance in the public markets. Business owners who recognized this window of opportunity sold their companies and were richly rewarded for their good timing.

In 2001, we saw a precipitous decline in M&A activity. The factors that led to the robust market changed dramatically. The stock market dropped, the recovery of the economy became uncertain at best, and lenders became increasingly cautious. During 2002, the M&A market halted its decline and readjusted to levels more consistent with those of the pre-boom period. While some observers have characterized the current market as anemic, it is, in fact, consistent with historic activity levels.

"Keep in mind that buyers, regardless of market conditions, are always looking for the right company to buy."

That said, two factors remain constant: buyers are still looking to buy and owners (if the deal is reasonable) are willing to sell. Sellers must decide whether to sell at present for reasonable multiples or to continue to operate in a sluggish economy hoping that their earnings and/or multiples will improve. Owners wishing to sell today do well to focus exclusively on one factor: Will a sale today meet my definition of wealth and freedom?

Many owners that I have counseled subsequent to the boom are frustrated because their industry peers sold at the top of the market. These sellers received unprecedented prices for their companies. I frequently hear, "Three of my friends sold their companies between $25 million and $30 million. Why didn't I sell then?" Before I allow too much crying over spilled milk, I ask, "If the multiples being paid today in your industry will yield a purchase price of $15 million (for example), does $15 million satisfy your need for wealth and freedom?" When the owner answers affirmatively, I guide him through a discussion of the questions contained in this book in an effort to crystallize his objectives on exiting his business.

I recommend that you continuously monitor the fair market value of your company. Keep in mind that buyers, regardless of market conditions, are always looking for the right company to buy. Year in and year out the number of buyers far exceeds the number of available sellers. Certainly, market conditions influence purchase price and terms, but buyers continue to pay premiums for companies that are well-positioned and which help the buyer to reach its acquisition objectives.

AVAILABILITY OF CAPITAL

Interest rates, or the cost of capital, have a direct and profound effect on whether buyers can afford to make acquisitions. If credit markets are tight, buyers have greater difficulty borrowing money to make purchases. These buyers tender lower offers in order to reduce the risk to themselves and to their lenders. During tight credit markets, sellers are often asked to carry back greater portions of purchase prices. Capital intensive companies fare better during these markets because they have hard assets that make lenders more willing to extend credit. Having said this, motivated buyers usually find ways to arrange financing for the companies they are committed to buying. This process of raising acquisition capital requires you, the seller, to be patient.

FINANCIAL SYNERGIES

Financial synergies are the cost savings or increased sales that can result when two companies become one. When calculating what a company is worth, buyers will project future cash flow as influenced by these synergies. The potential for financial synergies motivates strategic buyers to pay more for your business than either financial or entrepreneurial buyers. (See Question 16 for more information about the value of financial synergies to the strategic buyer.)

GEOGRAPHIC LOCATION

Buyers are often motivated to enter the market in order to establish a presence in a particular part of the country or metropolitan area. How well your company satisfies that desire influences how much the buyer is willing to pay.

Obviously, the better your company meets these criteria, the greater the probability that it will attract interest from buyers. Once interested, a buyer will pay more for your company if it possesses the Value Drivers discussed in the next Question.

Question 20

What factors prompt a buyer to pay more for a company?

*O*nce a buyer has decided to enter the marketplace in search of a company that meets its criteria (see the previous Question), it evaluates potential candidates based on the presence of "Value Drivers." Value Drivers are those characteristics that influence a buyer's decision about how much to pay for a company. Those Value Drivers common to all industries include:

- *A stable, motivated management team;*
- *Good and improving cash flow;*
- *Operating systems that improve sustainability of cash flows;*
- *A solid, diversified customer base;*
- *Effective financial controls;*
- *A realistic growth strategy; and*

• *Facility appearance consistent with asking price.*

As you may have guessed, Value Drivers are so named because they drive up the value of a company.

> "Installing or enhancing the Value Drivers in your company are actions you can take now to improve the quality and profitability of your company."

In addition to their role in a sale context, Value Drivers are also important when market cycles, personal objectives, or other objective circumstances prevent you from pursuing a sale to a third party. Installing or enhancing the Value Drivers in your company are actions you can take now to improve the quality and profitability of your company. Once the cycle swings back in your favor, your personal objectives are met, or circumstances change, your company will be well-positioned to sell.

MANAGEMENT TEAM

One of the most important Value Drivers in any business is its management team. This team is composed of those people who are responsible for setting company objectives, monitoring its activities, and motivating workers. In many small companies, this "team" consists of one person, generally the owner. To build a championship caliber organization, however, the management team should include people with a variety of skills. Surrounding yourself with quality people whose skills are different than and complement yours is a necessary prerequisite to a successful sale.

In addition to talent, you need a management team with staying power. One of the first questions prospective buyers ask is, "Who runs the company and are they willing to stay?" If the answer is, "The owner is in charge, does not have a successor, and wants to leave soon after closing," the value of the company plummets and most buyers (strategic or entrepreneurial) will look elsewhere. If you sell to a financial buyer who has assembled his own management team, you might get away with not having your own team, but you still won't maximize the value of your company.

If a company has a solid management team committed to staying and running the company, a buyer will likely assume the following:

- *business will continue as usual;*
- *customer relationships will be maintained;*
- *the company's reputation will remain intact;*
- *rank and file employees will remain in place;*
- *vendors and lenders will feel secure;*
- *the company will continue to grow; and*
- *future cash projections are attainable.*

When confident about these assumptions, buyers are willing to pay a higher purchase price. (See Question 21 for ways to retain a talented management team.)

STABLE AND INCREASING CASH FLOW

Ultimately, all Value Drivers contribute to a stable and predicable cash flow. And in the end, it is the cash flow that determines what a buyer will offer to pay. Buyers pay top dollar for cash flow that they expect to increase after they buy a company. The best time to sell based upon cash flow is when you can demonstrate a positive upward trend for two, if not three, consecutive years. The worst time to sell is when cash flow is flat or declining.

OPERATING SYSTEMS

Owners must also build reliable operating systems that can sustain the growth of the business. Operating systems include the computerized and manual procedures used in the business to generate revenue and control expenses (i.e. create cash flow), as well as the methods used to track how customers are identified and how products or services are delivered.

Additional operating systems include:

- *Personnel recruitment, training, and retention;*
- *Human resource management (an employee manual);*
- *New customer identification, solicitation, and acquisition;*
- *Product or service development and improvement;*
- *Inventory and fixed assets controls;*
- *Product or service quality controls;*
- *Customer, vendor, and employee communication;*
- *Selection and maintenance of vendor relationships; and*
- *Business performance reports for management.*

Obviously, appropriate systems and procedures vary depending on the nature of a business. The more effective systems you have in place, the greater your purchase price is likely to be.

ESTABLISHED CUSTOMER BASE

The ability to document an established customer base in which customer turnover is low and no single client (or clients) dominates total sales is a strong Value Driver. Because a diversified customer base helps to insulate a company from the loss of any single customer, buyers will be wary if only a few customers account for the bulk of your sales. If this is the case, you may be required to stay after the closing in order to properly transition customer relationships to the buyer. The buyer may also require a post-closing reduction to the purchase price if the revenues from the key customers fall below a negotiated dollar threshold during a stated timeframe after the closing date.

EFFECTIVE FINANCIAL CONTROLS

Another key Value Driver is the existence of reliable financial controls that are used to manage the business. Financial controls are not only a critical element of business management, but also safeguard a company's assets. Most importantly, however, effective financial controls support a claim that a company is consistently profitable.

At some point during the sale process, the buyer will perform some level of financial due diligence. If the buyer's auditors are not completely comfortable when reviewing your company's past financial performance and you cannot make them comfortable, the sale process will come to a halt.

The best way to document that your company has effective financial controls and that its historical financial statements are correct is through a certified audit by an established CPA firm. A lack of financial integrity is one of the most common hurdles encountered during the sale process. The audit provides such integrity.

Business owners universally perceive financial audits to be an unnecessary expense, or at best, a necessary evil required by their banks. In reality, an audit is an investment in the value and the marketability of your business. *The best way to demonstrate the sustainability of earnings is to have your historical financial statements audited by an independent certified public accountant.*

When should financial audits of your company begin? The answer depends on the likely sale price of your company and when you plan to sell.

The greater the purchase price you are asking, the greater the likelihood that audited financial statements will be necessary. If you plan to sell your company within the next two to three years, begin having your statements audited now. It is very important to engage the services of a recognized, reputable CPA firm to begin a review of your current financial statements and practices so that any financial irregularities or inadequacies are discovered and immediately corrected.

As you know, there are three levels of accountability. The first is *unaudited* financial statements that your company's CPA prepares for you and perhaps for your bank. The CPA firm makes no representations as to the accuracy of those financial statements.

The next level is a *reviewed* financial statement by your CPA firm. This means that the CPA firm has reviewed the financial information and has determined that it is accurate based on your representations to the CPA firm. It is not uncommon to see sales of mid-market companies in which the buyer requires only reviewed statements.

The final level is an *audited* financial statement. In an audited statement, a CPA firm verifies that the information contained in the financial statements is accurate based upon its own investigation.

Know that the investment you make to deliver proper financial statements will pay huge dividends when you sell your company.

REALISTIC GROWTH STRATEGY

Buyers pay premium prices for companies that have realistic strategies for growth. Growth strategies must be communicated to a potential buyer in such a way that a buyer can see specific reasons why cash flow, and the business, will grow after being acquired. Pro forma statements illustrating this growth are used by buyers when formulating a discounted future cash flow valuation of your company. This valuation typically determines what a buyer will pay for your business. Growth strategies can be based on:

- *Industry dynamics;*
- *Increased demand for the company's products;*
- *New products and new product lines;*
- *Marketing plans; and/or*
- *Growth through acquisition plans (See Question 11).*

Be prepared to articulate why you believe that a buyer will be able to implement your growth strategy successfully. Failure to do so may result in a lower purchase price and/or require you to remain longer after closing than you desire.

APPEARANCE OF FACILITY

Buyers do judge books by their covers. I am often amazed when a successful owner (whose plant resembles the chaos of a teenager's bedroom) expects to put his company on the market without even cleaning it up. A rundown, disorganized-looking facility creates doubt in buyers' minds about what else might be disorganized. A good-looking facility shows buyers that you are proud of your business in every respect and that you have made the necessary investments to keep it operating in peak condition. It also indicates that you have not deferred capital investments that the buyer may ultimately have to make. A clean, well-organized office communicates the message that the business itself is clean and well organized. A few thousand dollars of superficial improvements can markedly improve the marketability of your business and increase the interest of potential buyers.

Receiving a premium price for the sale of a business depends, in large part, upon an owner's efforts to adopt and to implement Value Driver techniques. These Value Drivers are characteristics that professional, sophisticated buyers seek in closely-held businesses. You can command a higher price for your business by developing and enhancing each Value Driver described here.

Question 21

What is an Employee Incentive Plan?

A Key Employee Incentive Plan (or Bonus Plan) is one of the best ways for owners to build value in their companies. Handcuffing talented key employees to a company not only drives up value but it is a critical factor in whether an owner can exit his company at all. Whether an owner plans an eventual sale to a third party, to a family member, or to the employees participating in the Bonus Plan, it makes good sense to hang on to and to motivate top performance from the employees who give the company much of its value.

For example, a third party buyer will place great value on the team that created a successful company and will usually depend on that team to take the company forward. In family succession situations, few children (no matter how bright or motivated) are prepared to assume, without the assistance of other key employees, the management of a successful enterprise. Similarly, the owner who plans to sell his company to key employees must first make sure that these employees exist; second, that they have confidence in their ability to maintain the company's success once the owner exits, and third, that they have sufficient cash to purchase the company. In all three cases, a properly designed Employee Incentive Plan makes a company more valuable. Let's look at how that is accomplished.

Which employees are key to the success of your business?

This is the first question an owner faces when designing a Bonus Plan. The easiest way to identify key employees is to determine which ones think and act like you do. Ask yourself which employees want more challenges. Which ones want to prosper as the company grows and are willing to put in the additional effort to make that growth happen? In short, which employees behave as you do?

Some owners find it easier to identify *key positions* in their companies and then determine if the people filling those positions meet the criteria outlined above. If the folks filling key positions do not possess the characteristics of key employees, you may wish to make some personnel changes.

Once key employees are identified, you can begin to motivate this important group.

What are the characteristics of an Incentive Plan?

A well-designed Plan has six characteristics that are key to its success.

- *First, as the employee makes more money under the plan, the company must make more money.*
- *Second, the bonus earned by the employees must be large enough to motivate those employees to improve their performance.*
- *Third, the performance standards that you set must be specific and measurable.*
- *Fourth, whatever objective standard you set for employee performance must be tied directly to the net income of the company. If net income does not increase, the employee does not receive a bonus.*
- *Fifth, as an employee earns his bonus, part of that bonus is deferred until a future date. If the employee leaves employment prior to that future date, he or she forfeits that part of the bonus. (This deferral characteristic of Incentive Plans is referred to as "golden handcuffs.")*
- *Sixth, for any plan to work, an owner must communicate it, in writing, to those involved. Additionally, the Plan must be simple, easy to read, communicated face-to-face, and ideally, have a summary for convenient reference.*

Let's now examine what types of plans are on an owner's menu.

EQUITY-BASED PLANS

In an equity-based plan, owners make available to key employees stock ownership. Usually, they do so because offering ownership is one of the most powerful retaining factors that an owner

"...offering ownership is one of the most powerful retaining factors that an owner of a closely-held company can offer."

of a closely-held company can offer. In addition, stock ties key employees to a company by making them part of it. Some owners choose to require employees to pay for ownership so that these employees are invested (literally) in the company. Paying for stock also demonstrates an employee's dedication and commitment to the company. Finally, an employee who owns stock sees a direct link between his performance and the value of the company. As perform-ance and value increase, so does the value of his benefit (stock).

On the other hand, a stock bonus is not an ideal motivator if an owner fails to consider carefully who is eligible to receive stock. For example, the owner who bonuses a small percentage of stock to an employee as a reward for his or her efforts during startup or for per-forming a task integral to one facet of the company, can find that his largesse backfires. The person so valuable at startup may not have the necessary skills to manage others once the company has become estab-lished. Or the employee so integral to the owner's early efforts becomes less important once the organization has grown. In either case, that employee (now shareholder) has been given, along with the stock, certain privileges. Namely, that employee has the right to access company books and records, the right to be informed about the finan-cial condition of the company (including your salary and "perks"), and often, a right to be consulted and given the opportunity to vote on major decisions. If one of your future corporate decisions includes a sale, be aware that law, your company's articles, and/or bylaws may require you to consult this minority shareholder.

If, after these caveats, you believe that stock is the best motivator for your key employees, I suggest that you look at the timing of this award. First, have your employees been with your company at least two years? Second, would this employee be more motivated by stock than by cash? Third, are you prepared to award a meaningful amount of stock? And fourth, are you willing to bring this employee into your confidence (including access to all financial information)?

Once you have answered these questions satisfactorily, there are several other elements to consider, such as:

- *What type of stock is to be awarded?*
- *How much stock will be awarded at the outset and in the future?*
- *What valuation formula will you use when awarding and re-acquiring stock?*
- *When will payments be made?*
- *What agreement will govern the buy back of the stock should the employee leave?*

If you wish to seriously consider a stock-based bonus plan, I suggest that you meet with your attorney to discuss these as well as other issues. Or I encourage you to order a copy of *The Completely Revised How To Run Your Business So You Can Leave It In Style*. My law partner, John Brown, wrote this book and in it describes exit planning techniques, such as this one, in much greater detail than is possible here. (To order a copy, go to *www.exitplanning.com* or to any bookstore.)

CASH-BASED PLAN

Most of the key employee incentive plans that my firm prepares are cash-based rather than stock. Many owners, for the reasons discussed above, are simply uncomfortable granting ownership to key employees and instead provide cash or rights to appreciation in stock through a non-stock incentive plan. The most common cash-based incentive plans are:

- *The Non-Qualified Deferred Compensation plan;*
- *A Stock Appreciation (SAR) or "Phantom Stock" Plan; and*
- *A blended plan combining current cash bonuses with deferred benefit.*

In Question 22, we discuss the Non-Qualified Deferred Compensation plan. We'll complete our discussion of Employee Incentive Plans with a quick review of SARs and blended plans.

An employee who receives a bonus through a Phantom Stock Plan receives something that looks like stock, grows like stock, and can be turned in for cash just like stock, but is not stock. These phantom shares correspond to shares of stock, in that as the company becomes more valuable, so do the phantom shares. Phantom shares are allocated to an employee's account and any dividends paid are credited to that account. When the employee terminates his employment, the company typically pays him (on a deductible basis) the per share equivalent value of each of the phantom shares vested in his account.

Similarly, in a Stock Appreciation Rights (SAR) Plan, the value of benefits in the Plan is tied to the value of the company's stock. Unlike a Phantom Plan, however, the participating employee is only entitled to receive appreciation on a certain percentage of SAR units valued against the corporation's stock, not the entire principal value of the stock. When an employee terminates his employment, the units in his account are re-valued to reflect the current market price, or formula price, of the stock. The payment to the employee is made either in a lump sum or in a series over several years, depending upon how the plan was designed.

A "blended plan" is simply an incentive plan that uses a cash bonus coupled with a deferral of benefits to a later date. Members of your Advisory Team can help you determine if a "blended plan" will help you to achieve your ownership objectives.

No matter the type of plan, stock-based or cash-based, there are several design features that you should understand when determining what type of plan will work best for your company. Those features include:

- *Benefit formula;*
- *Forfeiture;*
- *Payment schedules; and*
- *Funding devices.*

All of these features are described in the context of a Non-Qualified Deferred Compensation Plan in the following Question.

Question 22

What is a Non-Qualified Deferred Compensation Plan?

A Non-Qualified Deferred Compensation Plan (NQDC) is a cash-based incentive plan designed to motivate key employees to increase the value of your company. Properly designed and implemented, the NQDC can be a great way not only to motivate and retain your key employees, but also to put cash in your employees' hands to buy you out. Let's look at how the NQDC accomplishes the first task before we look at it in the context of your eventual exit.

An NQDC is a promise to pay benefits in the future based upon a key employee's (or group of key employees) current or past services. "Non-qualified" simply means that as long as certain requirements are met, the plan does not have to meet requirements of the

> "...the objective of the NQDC Plan is to tie the employee to the company and to motivate the employee to make the company more valuable."

Employee Retirement Income Security Act. With the exception of with-holding for FICA taxes, in certain situations, the benefits awarded to an employee under an NQDC are not taxable until the date when such benefits are actually paid to the employee.

Like other incentive plans, an NQDC has several features that make the plan more effective in reaching an owner's objectives. Keep in mind that like all incentive plans, the objective of the NQDC Plan is to tie the employee to the company and to motivate the employee to make the company more valuable.

BENEFIT FORMULA

The benefit formula is the formula you and your advisors create that motivates the employees to increase the profitability of your company. You and your advisors carefully set performance standards so that unless the business meets its profitability objective, the employee cannot meet his objective (i.e. does not earn a bonus). For example, you might decide to make 30 percent of your company's taxable income in excess of $100,000 available for bonuses. If your company's taxable income is $300,000, the benefit formula would look like this:

$300,000	taxable income
< $100,000 >	your baseline amount
$200,000	
x 30%	
$ 60,000	funds available for key employee bonuses

If we assume that you have two key employees, you may decide to award half of the bonus ($30,000) immediately in cash or stock and to award the other half ($30,000) as non-qualified deferred compensation subject to vesting. Those decisions are part of your benefit formula.

VESTING

As mentioned, vesting is part of any well-designed bonus plan. It handcuffs the employees to the company for a pre-determined time period necessary to become entitled to the benefits that have accrued to them under the benefit formula. There are a number of ways an owner can vest his employees' benefits, one of which is a continual or "rolling" vesting schedule. In this case, a single vesting schedule is applied separately to each year's contribution. For example, in our illustration above, the part of the award subject to vesting ($30,000) is allocated $15,000 to each of two employees. If you have chosen a five-year vesting schedule and the award is earned in 2003, here's how vesting handcuffs that employee to your company:

	0%	20%	30%	40%	60%	100%
2003	. . . . .					
2004	. . . .					
2005	. . . .					
2006	. . . .					
2007	. . . .					
2008	. . . .					

Only in the year 2008 is the employee fully vested in an award earned in 2003. The owner who chooses this type of vesting schedule handcuffs the employee to the company for a long period of time because that employee is never fully vested in the most recent contributions.

FORFEITURE PROVISIONS

Successful incentive plans include forfeiture provisions which enable the owner to terminate an employee's otherwise vested rights in the benefits of the plan. Should an employee leave your company and violate his agreement to: (1) compete; (2) take trade secrets; or (3) take vendors, customers, or company employees, he loses *all* deferred compensation. As you might guess, forfeiture provides a strong incentive to former employees to live up to the promises they made to the company.

PAYMENT SCHEDULES

Owners combine payment schedules with forfeiture provisions to prevent recently departed employees from competing using funds earned through the deferred compensation plan. The payment schedule determines when payments of vested amounts commence and how long they continue after the employee leaves.

FUNDING DEVICES

To successfully motivate employees, a plan must be funded so that cash is available when it is needed. Your employees must be confident that the funds exist. Your banker, financial planner, or CPA can help you with your choice of funding vehicles.

USING AN NQDC TO BUY YOU OUT

As mentioned, installing an NQDC is a great way to motivate key employees but it is also one way to put cash in your employees' hands for an eventual buyout. If your objective is to sell your company for fair value, the Modified Buyout can help you meet your objective.

The Modified Buyout is accomplished in two steps: (1) the initial sale of a minority interest and (2) the sale of the balance of your ownership interest.

STEP ONE: SALE OF INITIAL MINORITY INTEREST

In the first step, you make available a pool of stock (generally non-voting) to employees as an incentive benefit. Rather than giving stock to the participating key employees, you make a percentage available at a price determined by a valuation formula set by you and your advisors. Usually, this initial value is set lower than fair market value to make the purchase affordable by the employees – as well as to provide them an incentive.

Your employees will pay cash for these initial shares. Should an employee need to borrow funds to make this purchase, your company can guarantee that employee's promissory note to a bank. Obviously, you will have to communicate this plan and your objectives to your banker.

There are a number of advantages to the employee who purchases non-voting stock. Among the most important are that employees:

- *Enjoy actual stock ownership in your company and an ability to receive any appreciation in the stock;*
- *Participate (pro rata based on their stock ownership) in any "S" distributions your company makes and more directly in day-to-day operating decisions;*
- *Would receive fair market value for their percentage of stock if your company was to be sold to a third party;*
- *Would be appointed as directors to serve under the terms of the bylaws (such positions not being guaranteed);*
- *Participate in any future conversion of non-voting stock to voting stock; and*
- *Participate in determining which additional key employees are offered stock from the pool and in what amounts using established criteria.*

As employees purchase stock, they execute Stock Purchase Agreements with your company to provide for the repurchase of their stock in case of death, long-term disability, or termination of employment. After a set amount of time (several years, at least), your company will be re-valued to reflect the sale of the majority interest of the stock (a valuation that will be based on a fair market formula driven by an earnings stream formula).

STEP TWO: SALE OF BALANCE OF OWNERSHIP INTEREST

Once you have completed Step One, you still retain a remarkable amount of flexibility. You have three possible options:

1. *Sell the balance of the company to the key employees, at true fair market value;*

2. Sell to an outside third party; or

3. Continue to own the company and be actively involved in its operation and management.

At this point, your decision about whether (and to whom) to sell the balance of your stock will depend on:

- *Your analysis of your key employees' ability to move the company forward* while paying you full fair market value for your remaining ownership interest. You must assess their readiness to move on without you, the adequacy of the cash flow to pay you, and whether there are outside influences (economic or lending climates) that might jeopardize your buyout.

- *The ability of the key employees and of the company to obtain financing* to pay you the remaining purchase price. Again, if you have cultivated a good relationship with your banker, he will not only understand the financial capabilities of your company, he will likely know the competencies of your key employees and will be a likely source for any financing.

- *The marketability of your company.*

This Modified Buyout technique works in situations in which:

- *Your key employees will eventually be capable of running and managing the company without you;*

- *You have time (five to seven years) before your desired exit date;*

- *You are willing to accept less than true fair market value for a portion of your stock (assuming that your stock is even saleable to an outside third party for cash); and*

- *You are willing to accept a fair value for your company.*

I must add that the Modified Buyout technique also works best for owners who have a skilled Team of Advisors to guide this process to a successful conclusion. You need an attorney who is experienced drafting NQDCs in the context of an owner's overall exit plan. Your accountant must be skilled in valuation and in placing value on minority interests. You need to cultivate a relationship with your banker so that your bank will loan your employees the money they need at the initial purchase and loan the company the cash it will need to fund your eventual buyout.

Question 23

What is an Employee Stock Ownership Plan (ESOP)?

*A*n Employee Stock Ownership Plan (commonly referred to as an ESOP) is a tax-qualified retirement plan, typically a profit sharing plan, which must invest primarily in the stock of the sponsoring employer. ESOPs are governed by law so there are a number of requirements, including:

- *All full time employees eventually participate in the plan;*
- *Each participant participates in proportion to that employee's compensation;*
- *Full vesting of benefits cannot exceed six years from date of participation;*
- *Upon termination of employment, the plan must give the participant the right to receive his or her account balance in cash over five years; and*
- *Contributions to the plan by the company are tax deductible and the plan does not pay income tax on the income it earns. Eventually, participants pay an income tax when they terminate employment and receive a cash distribution from the ESOP (unless rolled over into an IRA).*

Because of these and other legal requirements, owners who choose a sale to an ESOP as an exit strategy do incur significant legal and administrative fees. In my experience, however, these fees are generally no more than those incurred in a sale to a third party. If you are unable to locate a third party or the interested third parties are unacceptable to you, an ESOP may be a most attractive buyer. With that in mind, let's look briefly at the characteristics a company must possess for an ESOP to work, the basic operation of an ESOP, and the advantages and disadvantages to you, the owner.

Company Characteristics

ESOPs do not work for every owner, nor do they work in every company. There are several characteristics that should be present as a foundation for an ESOP. The company should have:

1. *Strong cash flow;*
2. *A good management team to carry on after you, the owner, leave;*
3. *Little or no permanent debt;*
4. *A relatively large payroll base;*
5. *An alignment of shareholder and employee interests; and*
6. *Adequate capitalization to sustain future company growth.*

If your business lacks any of these characteristics, an ESOP may not be the best exit path for you.

Basic Operation

In its simplest form, a sale of your stock to an ESOP proceeds as follows:

1. *Your company contributes cash to its ESOP.*
2. *The ESOP uses these tax-deductible contributions (usually along with proceeds from a bank loan) to acquire your stock.*
3. *You transfer your stock to the ESOP in return for cash. If this transaction meets certain qualifications (see below), the cash*

you receive is tax-deferred and the company's cash flow can be contributed on a tax-deductible basis to the ESOP.

4. *Your company's bank loans money to the ESOP, which, in turn, uses the loan proceeds to acquire your stock.*

5. *The bank loan is repaid from the company's future contributions to the ESOP.*

OWNER ADVANTAGES

First, the payment of both principal and interest to fund a purchase by the ESOP can be accomplished with pre-tax rather than after-tax dollars because the company can make tax-deductible contributions to the ESOP (or as a "C" corporation, pays dividends on stock owned by the ESOP).

Second, if your company is organized as a "C" corporation and the ESOP purchases stock from you, and if, after the sale, the ESOP owns at least 30 percent of the outstanding stock of the corporation, you will not be taxed (generally speaking) on the proceeds as long as you invest those proceeds in U.S. stocks and bonds.

When you sell those replacement securities, however, you will incur a capital gain depending on your basis in the stock sold to the ESOP. To avoid these capital gains taxes, you can hold on to those replacement securities until your death (when they receive a step-up basis and can be sold free from capital gain) or you can invest your proceeds in high-quality floating rate bonds. As long as you don't sell these bonds, you incur no capital gain. You can use these bonds as collateral to obtain a loan from a brokerage house or financial institution. The interest rate on this loan will likely be less than 100 basis points greater than the interest paid by the bonds. You can invest the proceeds from this loan in a variety of stocks and bonds or you can spend the proceeds without any tax consequence. (I hope this very cursory discussion of tax ramifications demonstrates how important it is to have a competent attorney and accountant on your Team of Advisors.)

Third, surveys indicate that companies with ESOPs report improvements in their financial figures and productivity after installation of the ESOP.

> "Other than a sale to a third party, the ESOP may be the best way to maximize the amount of cash you receive at closing."

Fourth, the leveraged ESOP buyout puts cash in an owner's pocket. Other than a sale to a third party, the ESOP may be the best way to maximize the amount of cash you receive at closing.

Finally, the tax benefits associated with a leveraged ESOP buyout mean that the company's cash flow is captured before it is taxed and used to finance the purchase of your stock. A combination of ESOP pre-funding and borrowing from a bank (or other financial institution) puts you in much the same position as if you had sold to a third party for cash (except that the employees are the new owners). Once again, early and active involvement of your banker is key to the success of the ESOP exit strategy.

OWNER DISADVANTAGES

As I mentioned earlier, one of the primary disadvantages to an owner is that an ESOP is costly to establish and relatively costly to maintain over the years but no more costly than a sale to a third party. Costs include the original arm's-length appraisal as well as annual update appraisals.

ESOPs are more complex than third party transactions primarily because of fiduciary requirements of the Employee Retirement Income Security Act. These requirements call for independent legal and financial professionals to advise ESOP trustees on the structure and appropriateness of the purchase of your stock.

Second, ESOPs carry a "repurchase liability" that requires the ESOP to repurchase the stock of a departing participant over a five-year period. As employees retire or leave, this liability must be funded through cash contributions from the company to the ESOP or through the company buying back stock directly from the departing participant.

Third, banks do not lend 100 percent of an owner's purchase price to an ESOP. With a strong balance sheet, you might expect to find a bank willing to lend 60 to 70 percent of your purchase price. (A good relationship with your banker can push that percentage to the higher end of the range.) Your company will likely have to pre-fund the ESOP in the years prior to the stock transaction. Of course, the same funds that serve as the bank's equity are funds that could have been bonused directly to you.

> "...key employees often view the ESOP as a disincentive because they must run the company and assume the responsibility of ownership without reaping 100 percent of the reward."

Fourth, key employees often view the ESOP as a disincentive because they must run the company and assume the responsibility of ownership without reaping 100 percent of the reward. As part of your ESOP design, therefore, it is wise to create an equity or cash incentive program for the management group. Doing so allows this group to acquire equity outside of the ESOP as a reward for its continued effort.

Fifth, your replacement securities (see discussion above) will likely be held as collateral by the financial institution making the loan to the ESOP. (How long these securities are held is a matter of negotiation between you and your banker.)

Finally, your company's ability to grow will likely be hampered when most or all of the available cash flow is allocated to ESOP contributions in order to repay the financing costs of acquiring your stock.

CONCLUSION

For all of the reasons described above, an ESOP is not for every owner or for every company. It is, however, a possible exit path for the owner who wants fair market value for his company and whose employees are able and willing to continue running the company profitably once the owner has left the scene. Once again, the ESOP demonstrates how valuable key employees are to an owner's successful exit.

PART 4 | ASSEMBLING YOUR ADVISORY DREAM TEAM

After you have made your decision to sell, selecting the right Team of Advisors is critical. Most likely, your company already has a CPA and an attorney. You also may be working with a financial advisor. It is your job to determine if these advisors are the appropriate ones to guide you through the sale process.

In the selection process, objectivity is key. If you have longstanding relationships with one or more advisors who have significant expertise in orchestrating sales of businesses, you are fortunate. If you aren't sure if your advisors have experience in selling companies, you must ask. I suggest that you engage each of your advisors in candid discussions about their experience in orchestrating transactions. If an advisor has never broached the subject of your eventual exit, I would question whether that advisor has the experience necessary to guide you through the sale process.

Should you find that one or more of your advisors lacks the experience a successful sale requires, I urge you to consider their participation carefully. Try not to let personal loyalties cloud your judgment. This is the most important transaction of your career. It is not an occasion for on-the-job training.

The answers in Part Four will help you through the Advisory Team selection process.

Question 24

Who should be on my Advisory Team?

Transaction Attorney
Investment Banker/Business Broker
Financial Advisor
Existing Banker
Certified Public Accountant

Transaction Attorney

The attorney should be one of your key advisors in the sale process. As a transaction lawyer, I am typically the first advisor retained by an owner. If an owner is still analyzing whether to sell, we discuss his specific doubts, goals and concerns as well as the ins and outs of the process. These discussions can progress quickly or take several years. In the end, an owner must reach a comfort level that enables him to sell and walk away from the company. I hope this book will guide you through some of these issues and help you to achieve the level of comfort that allows you to move forward.

A transaction attorney should, at a minimum, be able to answer all of the technical questions that sellers typically ask regarding deal structure, valuation, and tax ramifications. In addition to possessing accurate information based on years of experience, a transaction attorney must have a keen sense of empathy for what sellers experience.

Empathy is critical. A transaction attorney must have a "feel" for the deal itself, as well as for his seller/client. An attorney who fails to understand your goals, objectives and concerns will likely misread, or

> "It is the transaction attorney's job to keep all the players focused...and to move the process toward the closing as quickly as is reasonably possible."

worse yet, fail to heed your signals. A lack of empathy is usually not fatal, but it can cause embarrassment, delay and an unnecessary level of frustration on your part. If you perceive that your transaction attorney is purely a technician and lacks this empathy, you may need to over-compensate in your efforts to be understood.

Every transaction involves numerous players and "moving parts." It is the transaction attorney's job to keep all the players focused on the task at hand and to move the process toward the closing as quickly as is reasonably possible. As explained in Question 26, the investment banker will bring the buyer to the table and negotiate the economic terms and conditions of the deal. Although the transaction attorney frequently partners with the investment banker in negotiating price and terms, he really takes over at the Letter of Intent stage and drives the deal toward its closing.

Investment Banker / Business Broker

If you are selling your company to an outside third party (someone other than a family member or employee), I highly recommend that you use a transaction intermediary such as an investment banker or business broker. These professionals, in addition to performing the services discussed in Questions 26 and 27, conduct the sale process so that you can focus on running your company.

Financial Advisor

Early in the sale process, sellers often approach their financial advisors (financial planners, stock brokers, wealth management professionals and life insurance agents) with questions about selling their businesses. This topic inevitably arises during periodic financial reviews, when the business owner and advisor are defining financial and estate planning goals. To determine these goals, an owner should assess the company's present market value and add to this amount the value of his existing income-producing assets. If the combined total of these assets is sufficient to generate personal financial independence, the time is ripe to address the question of selling.

If an owner's total assets are not sufficient to generate personal financial independence, he should focus on creating additional business value while the financial advisor focuses on increasing the value of the owner's investment portfolio.

Another task assigned to the financial advisor is to prompt the owner to consider various post-closing investment strategies. Many sellers find it difficult to make such plans without their sale proceeds in hand. Often, sellers are so focused on running their companies and on the sale process itself that they don't feel they can allow themselves the luxury of thinking about the funds they will receive at closing.

While I commend sellers for their attention to the sale process, I do suggest that they spend some time considering their future investment strategies. Sellers often respond to this suggestion with the old adage about the wisdom of counting chickens before they are hatched. They prefer to postpone any investment discussions until the money is in the bank.

Please don't wait until after closing to start working with your financial advisor. You should arrive at the closing table with a well-thought-out investment strategy that can be implemented immediately. That strategy can (and most likely will) be modified as you move forward to the next phase of your life: that of a wealthy individual who has time to manage and monitor his holdings.

I strongly encourage you to make a financial advisor an integral part of your Advisory Team.

Existing Banker

Sellers rarely consult their existing bankers about a pending sale for two reasons: (1) They don't perceive the banker to be an advisor who can contribute to the process and (2) They are afraid that the banker may react negatively with regard to the underlying loan arrangement. Instead, sellers wait until just before closing to notify their banks that existing debt is about be paid off. If you have a legitimate reason (seller's paranoia is not considered legitimate) for not consulting your banker, then don't. But I hope to convince you that cultivating a relationship with your banker well before closing can help create value and establish a useful ally during and after the sale process.

> "Your banker can help you grow your company and is the logical lender for your buyer should that buyer need to finance part of the purchase price."

Unfortunately, few bankers forge close relationships with their business owner customers. It is not surprising, then, that few owners are comfortable disclosing a potential sale to their bankers. An astute banker will tell you early in your relationship that he knows you will eventually exit your business. Until that time, the bank will provide you with products and services that will help you to create value.

Similarly, too few sellers recognize the value of initiating close working relationships with their bankers. Your banker can help you grow your company and is the logical lender for your buyer should that buyer need to finance part of the purchase price. Your banker knows your company, your management team, your customer base, and your industry. In tight credit markets, this familiarity can be crucial in a buyer's attempt to obtain the financing necessary to buy you out. Additionally, your banker's understanding of your company usually pays off when the financial due diligence process that your bank performs is far less intense than that of a new, unfamiliar lender.

If your banker is not yet an active member of your Advisory Team, I suggest that you initiate a conversation that includes the following points. Tell your banker that your goal is to create value so that you can someday sell your company for the maximum purchase price. Let him know that you view him (and his bank) as a partner in this process, and you expect him to provide you with the products and services that will facilitate achieving your goal.

Next, express your hope that when the time comes, the bank will take an active interest in financing the buyer. Now that you're on a roll, throw in the fact that you would like to explore the banker's ability to invest part of your sale proceeds. At this point, your banker will be salivating. In this day of multi-service banking, most banks are looking to dazzle their former business owner clients with their financial planning, wealth management, and investment expertise. Your banker will also be anxious to fund your new entrepreneurial ventures.

I guarantee that you will have your banker's full attention. You have just done the sales presentation that, if he hasn't done, he should have. Your banker is a critical ally to your success – both before and after the sale. Bring him on board early in the process.

(For more information about how your banker can help you orchestrate a sale to employees or of your stock to an ESOP, please see Questions 22 and 23.)

CERTIFIED PUBLIC ACCOUNTANT

Your CPA is a critical member of your Advisory Team. He typically knows more about the financial history of your company than anyone, except you.

You can expect your CPA to perform or help in the valuation of your company, and help your investment banker (and eventually the buyer's financial team) to conduct financial due diligence. He will analyze the personal and business tax implications of the sale and will assist in structuring the transaction to minimize taxes. See Questions 20 and 32 for more information about your CPA's role.

CONCLUSION

Let me inject one note of caution. Sometimes, your advisors can be overly-cautious and conservative. They behave this way in an effort to protect you and your interests. If you find that your advisors are suffocating you and are more adept at raising barriers than at removing them, inform them that although you appreciate their concern, they must adopt a deal-making mentality if you are to overcome the financial issues and challenges that every deal generates.

Finally, it is your job to monitor your Advisory Team's progress and results. The information in this book will help you to do exactly that. As a successful owner, you have spent years managing people and dealing with professional advisors. Your task is not to micromanage your advisors nor to infringe upon their activities; rather, it is to insist upon clear and frequent communication, the timely attainment of deadlines, and adherence to the agreed upon game plan. It is very difficult to replace an advisor once the process is under way, so select each carefully. If you understand your role (see Question 39) and play it consistently, you should arrive at closing with your original team intact.

Question 25

What is a business broker?

Most business brokers focus on transactions significantly smaller than those handled by investment bankers. "Smaller" generally means a sale price in the range of $1 to $2 million.

There are, however, brokers who routinely handle transactions with values as high as $10 million. Much of the information in Questions 26, 27, and 28 regarding investment bankers applies to business brokers, as well.

Across the United States there are many capable business brokers who can help you sell your business. Successful business brokers generally have years of business experience, formal training, and professional designations. Their business experience and professional training enable them to understand the complexities of your business and to position your business to maximize its value to an outsider.

The broker you choose for your Advisory Team has two primary roles. His first task is to perform a valuation on your company. Second, your broker will seek a buyer for your business.

VALUATION

Brokers can employ one or more of several valuation techniques. These techniques are described in Question 33.

MARKETING YOUR BUSINESS

To locate a buyer, brokers will: (1) advertise in the business opportunities section of various newspapers and publications, (2) send direct marketing pieces to potential buyers, and (3) coop (share his fee) with other brokers.

Established business brokers maintain lists of qualified buyers and are often connected to other brokers both locally and nationally. Once the broker finds a buyer, he may take an active role facilitating negotiations, coordinating buyer due diligence, and working closely with your attorney and CPA until closing.

Your job in assembling your Advisory Team is to choose the advisors who are most qualified to help you reach your exit objectives of wealth and personal freedom. Keep that goal in mind as you select a business broker for your Team. Interview a number of them.

Ask:

- *What is the dollar range of his average deal?*
- *What are his qualifications for performing valuations?*
- *How much experience does he have performing valuations?*

Then ask for a list of attorneys, CPAs, and clients with whom each broker has worked. Interview these references. Include in your interview these questions:

- *How did the broker market each client's company?*
- *Did he know the prospective buyer prior to the sale?*
- *Was the broker a skilled negotiator?*
- *Did he understand deal structure, tax structure, and the sale process?*
- *Did he keep all parties informed on a timely basis?*
- *Did he negotiate the maximum purchase price or did he encourage sellers to take the first offer?*

BROKER FEES

Business brokers generally charge a minimal fee for preparing a business valuation. The bulk of their compensation is in the form of a commission that is based upon the sale price delivered at closing. The broker's commission is a sliding percentage based on sale price and on local market rates. For example, a broker may charge ten percent for the first million dollars in sale proceeds, nine percent for the second, eight percent for the third, six percent for the fourth, etc.

Discuss the broker's fees with your attorney and CPA. These advisors may be able to offer valuable input. If they have worked with other brokers, they will know what fee structure is competitive in the market. They may also have some ideas on how to use the fee structure to motivate the broker to seek the highest possible sale price (rather than to take the first offer). Again, your goal is not to negotiate the lowest fee but to motivate the broker to bring you the best possible deal. If he does so, he has earned his fee and you should be happy to pay it.

LISTING AGREEMENT

I strongly recommend that you ask your attorney to review the broker's Listing Agreement before you sign. Your attorney will alert you to items in the broker's Listing Agreement, such as "tail" provisions, that can affect you long after your Agreement with the broker has expired. Tail provisions state that if, up to an agreed upon date (a date often 24 months after the expiration of the Listing Agreement) you sell your company to a buyer originally contacted by this broker, you will owe the broker his stated fee. Allowing your attorney to review the Listing Agreement before you sign it gives you the opportunity to negotiate tail (and other important) provisions in the Agreement.

Question 26

What is an investment banker and what does he charge?

WHAT IS AN INVESTMENT BANKER?

For purposes of our discussion, investment bankers are individuals who represent a seller in the sale or merger of the seller's business. Their resumes typically include the following items: post-graduate degrees (CPA, MBA or both); work experience in large national (Wall Street) or regional investment banking firms; knowledge and understanding of accounting, corporate finance, and basic securities laws; and experience handling multiple transactions with regional, national, and international buyers.

Investment bankers often are thought of as people in fancy suits who put together multi-billion dollar mergers and acquisitions, live only in New York, and don't have an interest in smaller, privately-held companies. While it is true that many of the best known New York-based and large regional investment banks are not interested in transactions valued at less than $100 million, there are many other high quality investment bankers throughout the country who specialize in smaller transactions (known as the "middle market"). In fact, many local and regional investment banks are led by people who received their training at larger, well-known firms before starting their own boutique firms.

> "The investment banker you choose should have a reputation for objectivity and professionalism as well as exceptional analytical and marketing skills."

As you select this member of your Advisory Team, it is vital to ask for and contact references. The investment banker you choose should have a reputation for objectivity and professionalism as well as exceptional analytical and marketing skills. Your investment banker must also be connected to a large pool of potential buyers and must understand the dynamics of the transaction process. In addition, a good investment banker will have the resources necessary to identify and seek out the buyers who will be most interested in your business.

An investment banker may also be able to provide alternatives if your business is not quite ready to be sold. An investment banker can assist you in:

- *Raising capital to further the growth of your business;*
- *Arranging a transaction that enables you to withdraw cash from the company while still retaining control of the business;*
- *Coordinating an initial public offering;*

• *Recommending consultants who can improve the operations of the company; or*
• *Facilitating the implementation of a wide variety of financing options.*

INVESTMENT BANKER FEES

Investment bankers who represent middle-market companies in sales transactions are typically compensated on a commission basis. It is accepted practice for investment bankers to charge an up-front or monthly retainer fee, as well. This retainer fee is generally not large enough to cover all costs, but is sufficient to enable them to determine that a seller is committed to the process. In addition, the retainer fee is typically credited against the ultimate commission.

The following fee schedule is typical. The commission on a business with a $5 million to $10 million value will be about five percent. For businesses with values greater than $10 million, the commission will generally be less than 5 percent with the percentage declining as the value of the company increases. Again, you should consult your attorney when negotiating the fees and other terms described in the investment banker's engagement letter.

"The best fee structure for a seller is not necessarily the one with the lowest fee."

I encourage you to have a frank and comprehensive discussion about fees with every investment banker you interview. Realize, however, that it may not be in your best interest to drive your hardest bargain. The best fee structure for a seller is not necessarily the one with the lowest fee. As a seller, the best fee for you is the one that motivates the investment banker to seek the highest possible price for your company. The best fee is the one that rewards him as you are rewarded. Avoid the fee structure that prompts the investment banker to accept the first offer. You want to provide the investment banker the financial motivation to bring every possible dollar to the closing table.

I was recently involved in a transaction in which the owner's goal was to sell his company for $x million. The investment banker's fee was structured so that for any $500,000 amount in excess of a $x million purchase price, the investment banker's fee increased.

The investment banker orchestrated a controlled auction for this seller. One suitor was a strategic buyer, the other a financial buyer. When the bidding had reached several million dollars above the seller's expectations, the seller selected the strategic buyer and told the investment banker to halt the bidding. Convinced that there was still money left on the table, this banker asked the seller to give him 24 hours to continue negotiating with this buyer. Indeed, the strategic buyer offered to pay an additional $1.5 million. At this point, the investment banker advised the other suitor, the financial buyer, that the auction was complete and that the other suitor had won. The financial buyer pleaded with the investment banker to allow him to meet the seller face to face. The banker politely refused and the deal with the strategic buyer was completed.

The lesson here is that sellers do well to give their investment bankers the incentive and the room to be creative and aggressive. Make sure that the fee structure you negotiate motivates your investment banker to work in your interest as well as in his own.

Finally, be aware that your investment banker's engagement letter will include items, such as "tail" provisions, that can affect you long after your engagement with the investment banker has expired. These tail provisions state that if, up to an agreed upon date (a date often 24 months after the expiration of the engagement letter) you sell your company to a buyer originally contacted by this investment banker, you will owe the banker his stated fee. Allowing your attorney to review the Listing Agreement before you sign it gives you the opportunity to negotiate tail (and other important) provisions in your engagement.

THE ROLE OF THE INVESTMENT BANKER

The investment banker's role is to sell your company in a way that meets your stated objectives. To do this successfully, the investment banker will:

- *Perform a valuation of your company;*
- *Identify and qualify buyers;*
- *Negotiate the economic terms and conditions of the transaction; and*
- *Facilitate the closing process.*

VALUATION

The actual sale process starts with a thorough and comprehensive valuation of your company. The investment banker will conduct exhaustive due diligence of the company's financial information (going back at least five years). Once assured that the numbers are reliable, the investment banker will apply various valuation formulas to establish a range of value. (For an explanation of various valuation methods, please see Question 33.) Critical to this valuation process is a comprehensive search and analysis of purchase prices paid for comparable companies. Armed with this range of value, the investment banker will ask if you are willing to sell at a price on the conservative end of the range. If so, the investment banker proceeds to the next step. If not, the investment banker will identify areas of your company (or "Value Drivers") that need improvement in order to increase the value of your company to your desired level. (For a description of various Value Drivers, please see Question 20.)

Don't allow the cost of the valuation to become a stumbling block in your decision-making process. Often, investment bankers will credit the cost of the valuation against their commission for selling your company. The cost of the valuation often depends upon the size and complexity of your business. For example, a valuation for a middle-market distribution company should be less expensive than one for a manufacturing company with multiple locations. You should expect to pay between $5,000 and $15,000 for a comprehensive valuation. Don't be timid about negotiating the cost. Again, when you successfully complete a transaction and achieve wealth and freedom, your out-of-pocket costs will be negligible.

IDENTIFYING BUYERS

Identifying buyers is an obvious and critical function of your investment banker. Once the investment banker has a thorough understanding of your company and industry, he will search his proprietary database and other databases for logical buyers. He will also ask you for a list of buyers that you have identified. The good investment banker is then creative and looks outside the box for not-so-obvious logical buyers who, if properly educated, could become highly-motivated buyers.

Once a complete list of buyers is compiled, the investment banker determines which ones have the financial capability to complete the transaction. Expect the investment banker to review this shorter list of *qualified* potential buyers with you. Take this opportunity to offer input about how specific buyers might best be approached and to tell your investment banker if there are buyers that you do not want contacted.

> "The best investment banker is one who knows how to sell."

NEGOTIATING ECONOMIC TERMS

Negotiating the economic terms and conditions of the transaction is where the investment banker truly earns his fee. The best investment banker is one who knows how to sell. He knows your company inside and out and can anticipate and answer every conceivable question that a buyer might pose in an effort to knock the price down. To respond effectively, the investment banker must be fluent in the tax, operation, and valuation aspects of your company. He will have to defend his valuation of your company against the buyer's financial experts' vigorous attempts to reduce it.

FACILITATING CLOSING

Facilitating the closing process is a function that many investment bankers perform inadequately. I have worked with investment bankers who, once the Letter of Intent is signed, fade into the background while we, the transaction attorneys, assume the role of lead negotiator. Although my preference is to assume the lead at this point, my job of completing the sale process and guiding the parties to the closing table is much easier and more efficient when the investment banker stays actively involved and we work as a team. The engaged investment banker is a source of information about the inner workings of the seller, is a sounding board on tax issues, and is a catalyst who can get the buyer on track when the buyer's advisors slow the process. To determine if your advisors understand the necessity of teamwork, ask both your attorney and investment banker if they have ever worked together. Ask if their relationship and the deal process both proceeded smoothly. If you sense any friction, choose a replacement for one or the other or live with their reassurances that they can work together productively for you. A cohesive Team of Advisors is critical to the success of your exit.

Question 27

How do I choose an investment banker or broker?

As discussed in the two preceding Questions, there are differences between an investment banker and a business broker. You must select the type of transaction intermediary – investment banker or business broker – appropriate to your transaction. No matter which type of transaction intermediary you choose, you must find an individual with whom you can work well, and with whom you are comfortable discussing the most confidential details of your business. Consider these six key attributes in selecting your transaction intermediary.

> "...you must find an individual with whom...you are comfortable discussing the most confidential details of your business."

- First, they must adhere to the highest levels of *professional integrity* and put your interests ahead of their own so that you can trust them to give you honest, objective advice. You can determine this by speaking to references, preferably former owners, from several completed transactions.

- Second, they have the exceptional *oral and written communication skills* necessary to present your company in the most favorable light and to conduct effective negotiations. Analyze these skills as you interview the candidate and also as you review at least three Confidential Information Memoranda prepared as part of prior sales.

- Third, they must have a keen *understanding of accounting and financial matters*, because every negotiation regarding price and transaction structure hinges on a fair and accurate discussion of your business's historical financial performance and future projections. If you aren't comfortable analyzing this skill, have your CPA join you when interviewing a potential transaction intermediary.

- Fourth, their *creativity* should enable them to develop imaginative strategies for marketing your business and to find win-win solutions to problems that arise during negotiations with buyers. In evaluating the three prior characteristics, you will gain some insight into the investment banker's (or business broker's) creative capacity. You should be convinced that your transaction intermediary will not take a "cookie cutter" approach to the sale of your company.

- Fifth, your transaction intermediary must be *responsive*. The sale of your business is an emotional roller coaster. An extra layer of anxiety is created when you can't get your investment banker or business broker to return your phone calls. Make it clear that you do not intend to spend your time making repeated phone calls. When you initiate a call, you expect a response within a reasonable timeframe. If, during the process, you must constantly request status reports, the investment banker or broker is not being responsive. You should not tolerate unresponsiveness for a moment. Advise your transaction intermediary how and when you can most readily be reached and insist on being kept current on material developments.

If poor communication persists but your transaction intermediary is otherwise doing a good job, remind him that your future referrals are at stake. Letting him know that you are not happy with the current state of affairs usually reinvigorates the flow of information.

- Finally, successful transaction intermediaries understand that selling your company is a specialized process. They must be very *persistent and methodical* and pursue the transaction process in an organized manner until all reasonable alternatives are exhausted. Again, review references, check their reputations, and trust your "read" as you interview brokers and investment bankers.

The transaction intermediary who is right for you depends on the size and nature of your business, his ability to work productively with a skilled transaction attorney as well as the level of complexity of the potential sale. As with most important business decisions, I recommend that you consult with your CPA and transaction attorney when considering the selection of a transaction intermediary.

Question 28

When selecting an investment banker, should I chose an industry expert?

*A*t first glance, the answer to this question is, "Of course." There is a certain logic to hiring someone who can identify all potential buyers within your industry, probably knows many of the key players in these companies, and has likely sold companies to many of these buyers in the past. I have worked with many investment bankers who were "industry experts" who fulfilled all of these expectations. (Business brokers are less likely to carve out a niche as industry experts.) Some industry experts, however, fall victim to a number of common pitfalls.

It is likely that you will run across the industry expert who prefers a cookie cutter approach to deals and fails to look at a company's unique characteristics. These industry experts may not be willing to play hardball on your behalf because they are reluctant to ruffle the feathers of the same buyers who they want to sell to in the future. When hardball is exactly what your deal requires, this deficiency may cost you a significant number of dollars. For this reason, if you are contemplating hiring an industry expert, ask references how this person behaved in situations when a deal hung in the balance.

> "I believe sellers should look for investment bankers who are experts...in negotiating and orchestrating a sale."

You want an investment banker whose first allegiance is to you. If pulling a deal from the table is necessary to convince a buyer that his offer does not meet your expectations, you must have an investment banker (industry expert or not) who will play that card.

I believe sellers should look for investment bankers who are experts, but experts in negotiating and orchestrating a sale. Industry expertise can be acquired. In reality, all deals follow a similar pattern. Certainly, industries differ from one another in various ways but your investment banker can be brought up to speed on these variations with your expert tutoring. Once you share your insights with your investment banker, he is prepared to do battle with one goal in mind – meeting your objectives. His ability to represent your interests professionally, combined with a "take no prisoners" attitude, is exactly what you want.

Question 29

Are my current attorney and CPA the right advisors to help me sell my company?

*A*fter reading this book, you will have a much clearer perspective of the sale process and the roles your advisors play in it. You will be eminently qualified to determine whether your current advisors are capable of guiding you through this process.

ATTORNEY

You may be surprised that many business attorneys and CPAs simply lack hands-on experience in selling companies. A well-trained business lawyer may not be an experienced "deal" lawyer. There is a difference.

In my practice, 85 percent of the sellers I have represented come to me for the first time in order to sell their companies. They have long-term relationships with their lawyers but come to my law firm because we focus on transactions.

If an owner's understandable feelings of loyalty cause him to struggle with his decision to bring my firm into the mix, I suggest that he ask his lawyer if he considers himself to be a transaction lawyer. As an objective measure, sellers can ask "How many sale transactions have you handled in the last two years?" "Did they close successfully?" If the answer is between eight and ten *and* the deals closed, I suggest to the owner that he stay with that attorney. If the response is less than five, continue to interview. I suggest that you ask your attorney these same questions. Having known your attorney over a period of years, you are the best judge of whether he possesses the necessary level of skill and empathy discussed in Questions 24 and 30. You deserve a specialist to handle the biggest financial deal of your career.

While the number of transactions completed is somewhat arbitrary, if an attorney works on only two deals each year, he is spending the vast majority of his time on matters other than transactions. An attorney who spends the majority of his time in transactions will be better equipped to handle your deal successfully.

When a business owner first meets with me regarding the sale of his company, we also probe the experience of his other existing advisors. If the existing advisors are not experienced in transaction work, I suggest bringing in advisors who are. Don't be afraid (due to misplaced loyalty) to assemble an Advisory Dream Team to handle the biggest deal of your life. Your existing advisors may have to assume supporting roles. You have compensated them fairly for their past work, and you may wish to continue using them for future projects, but don't limp through the sale process depending on an inexperienced advisor. Remain focused on your goal: selling your company to achieve wealth and person freedom.

CERTIFIED PUBLIC ACCOUNTANT

Whether your CPA is competent to join your Advisory Team depends on the role you assign to him. (See Question 32.) If you plan to retain an investment banker, your CPA will provide a wealth of insight, historical information, and data about the company that facilitates the due diligence and tax planning processes. If, on the other hand, you do not plan to retain an investment banker, you must evaluate whether your CPA has, in addition to the requisite financial skills, the negotiating skills necessary to close the sale.

If any one of your advisors proves to be unresponsive, if his ego obstructs progress, or if he dismisses your input, you have a serious problem that you must deal with immediately. Your future is riding on this deal and you deserve the best advisors possible.

Question 30

What role does the transaction attorney play?

The transaction attorney's role in the sale process can be divided into the following parts:

1. *Counseling*
2. *Assembling the Advisory Team*
3. *Initiating the Due Diligence Process*
4. *Negotiating the Confidentiality Agreement*
5. *Structuring the Deal*
6. *Negotiating the Letter of Intent*
7. *Negotiating the Definitive Purchase Agreement and miscellaneous agreements*
8. *Tax and Estate Planning*
9. *Maintaining Momentum*
10. *Conducting the Closing*

COUNSELING

One of the things I enjoy most in my career is counseling business owners through the process of deciding to sell a business (hence, the title of this book). For most owners, this process is a challenge – for reasons you all too well understand. Your business (your baby, your life, your identity, your platform in the community) is the source of personal inspiration, creativity, productivity, personal and financial achievement, and personal growth. Hiring, firing, and maintaining customer, vendor, creditor, landlord, lender, and professional relationships generate personal growth, fulfillment, frustration, and disappointment. Some owners can easily make the decision to walk away from all of this. The majority, however, make the decision to leave in fits and starts. Once an owner reaches his decision, however, his desire to exit begins to gain urgency.

Business owners don't typically discuss their ideas and feelings about exiting with anyone – certainly not with key employees or minority shareholders. Owners may discuss their plans with their spouses but unless the spouse is meaningfully involved with the company, their insights usually have limited value. As the spouse of one of my sellers stated after hearing that her husband was planning to sell, "I married you for better and for worse, but I did not marry you for lunch!"

> "When representing a seller, my job is to help him focus on the issues that are most important to him and to help him make the best personal decisions."

In an effort to get out of their spouses' hair, many sellers pick their new offices before they've even closed on the sale of their companies. These sellers benefit from going to an office (outside of their homes) to conduct whatever business they have. This new business may be nothing more than spending a few hours each day checking investments, reading, reviewing mail, or exploring new business opportunities. Both you and your spouse will be happier if you continue to be productive – however you define that term.

When representing a seller, my job is to help him focus on the issues that are most important to him and to help him make the best personal decisions. If my client/seller has identified and understands his fears, I am better able to prepare that seller for the inevitable ups and downs of the sale process.

Expect your transaction attorney to continue counseling you throughout the sale process. When we encounter high and low points, it is my job to keep the seller balanced and focused on the ultimate goal – closing the deal. Because there is no such thing as an easy deal, I warn sellers that deals take time and to expect a roller coaster ride. I remind them that patience is essential. No matter the present frustration, it will pass. A good transaction attorney with a deal-making mentality will find a way to get the deal done.

ASSEMBLING THE ADVISORY DREAM TEAM

With the help of the seller, I can predict if his existing advisors will aid or hinder the process. The seller can then make personnel decisions accordingly. It is critical that you employ a strong Team of Advisors who knows how to close transactions efficiently.

INITIATING DUE DILIGENCE

The fact-finding process, known as due diligence, is discussed thoroughly in Question 46. I commence this process as soon as an owner tells me he is ready to sell. Giving your advisors ample time to assemble and digest all of a company's financial, legal, and operational information for a buyer's review is critical to successfully closing your transaction.

NEGOTIATING THE CONFIDENTIALITY AGREEMENT

This Agreement is drafted by your attorney and should not be the subject of extensive negotiation. If the buyer's attorney is over-negotiating the Confidentiality Agreement, this may foreshadow difficult times.

As a lawyer, I am ethically prohibited from communicating with the opposition when that opposition is represented by counsel. I simply cannot advise a buyer that his attorney is creating unnecessary obstacles. Your transaction intermediary, however, is under no such restriction and can speak directly to the buyer. If the buyer's counsel is over-negotiating the Confidentiality Agreement, or subsequent agreements, your investment banker can gently advise the buyer that the deal is starting on the wrong foot. Your investment banker won't throw the buyer's attorney under the bus at this point but a gentle nudge usually puts the deal back on track. If obstructionist behavior continues, the investment banker can argue that the deal-breaking mentality of the buyer's counsel has been a problem from the outset and that the buyer must take control of his team if he wants to consummate the deal. (See Question 44 for a full discussion of Confidentiality Agreements.)

STRUCTURING THE DEAL

The decision whether to pursue an asset sale or a stock sale will be made by you and your Team of Advisors. (See Questions 34 and 35 for the differences.) Of course, the buyer will have a say in this decision but it is imperative that you, as an owner, know which type of sale is in your best interest and rely on your advisors to negotiate accordingly.

NEGOTIATING THE LETTER OF INTENT

Letters of Intent are fully discussed in Question 45. For our purposes here, remember two things. First, don't sign a Letter of Intent without the assent of your transaction attorney. And second, with very few exceptions, do not sign a binding Letter of Intent.

NEGOTIATING THE DEFINITIVE PURCHASE AGREEMENT

After the Letter of Intent is signed, the buyer's accountants will complete their financial due diligence. The buyer's attorney will simultaneously launch the legal due diligence process and the drafting and negotiation of the definitive purchase agreement and all other legal documents. It is your attorney's job to cooperate with the buyer's advisors, while at the same time negotiating terms and documents that are fair and reasonable for you.

Some sellers believe that they can save money if their attorneys draft the deal documents. Not only is this untrue, but buyers nearly always insist on drafting the documents. In fact, I prefer letting the buyer's attorney take his best shot; then I begin negotiating from that point.

TAX AND ESTATE PLANNING

Your goal is to take home, after-tax, as much money as possible. Your CPA, transaction attorney, and investment banker should weigh all available options to help you to achieve this goal. Similarly, once you decide to put your company on the market, your advisors should analyze the impact a sale will have on your estate planning objectives. Certain estate tax planning techniques can only be employed prior to the sale. Remember, Uncle Sam should only get that to which he is legally entitled. Not one penny more!

> "Uncle Sam should only get that to which he is legally entitled. Not one penny more!"

MAINTAINING MOMENTUM

A seller's transaction attorney must take the lead in pushing a sale to closing as quickly and as efficiently as reasonably possible. Remember, "Time kills deals."

Your transaction attorney is maintaining momentum if he is:

- *setting the pace,*
- *providing your advisors (and the buyer's advisors) the information they need on a timely basis,*
- *turning around documents quickly,*
- *keeping egos from derailing the process,*
- *establishing and meeting deadlines,*
- *keeping advisors on track and focused,*

- *anticipating difficult issues and creating multiple strategies to deal with them, and*
- *keeping in perspective the "crisis of the day."*

It is critical that your attorney possess a "deal-making" vs. "deal-breaking" mentality. A good transaction attorney will keep his ego in check and constantly seek ways to anticipate and overcome obstacles, rather than becoming an obstacle himself. Your transaction attorney must remember and remind opposing advisors that they each were hired to find ways to make the deal a "win-win" situation. If you detect that your transaction attorney is more concerned with winning each point rather than facilitating consensus, remind him that you hired him to protect you and to close your deal.

Removing a transaction attorney is a drastic course of action and is rarely required. I have, however, been brought into transactions in which the parties were "hopelessly deadlocked." In this situation, my task is to devise a strategy that moves the deal forward. If I can convince both sets of advisors that they have overestimated the amount of risk involved and that a middle ground for compromise exists, the deal can progress.

I remember one case in which a buyer's counsel assumed a hard stance regarding his client's exposure to liability for potential environmental issues. This attorney argued that, because the actions causing this potential liability occurred prior to closing, the seller should indemnify the buyer indefinitely. Seller's counsel countered that after a certain date, the seller should be released from this duty to indemnify. Both sides had drawn a line in the sand, and as a result, the deal was in jeopardy.

It was at this point that I was consulted. To the seller's attorney I argued that if the seller was ultimately determined to be liable for violating the law, he would be considered liable regardless of whether he sold the company or continued to own it. Given that, I suggested that the seller would be better off selling the company today, taking his purchase proceeds now, and fighting a claim, if necessary, in the future. If the seller failed to sell today, his potential liability would remain unchanged but he would have no sale proceeds and his company would be difficult to sell to another buyer. After careful consideration and consultation with his client, the seller's attorney allowed his client to indemnify the buyer indefinitely and the deal closed. To this date, the potential environmental issue has not surfaced.

If you feel that your transaction attorney is failing to maintain the deal's momentum, convene a team meeting to assess the situation. You are the customer. Employ your CEO skills to keep the sale process (and your Advisory Team) on track.

Conducting the Closing

The ideal closing is anti-climactic. Most of our deals close via facsimile machine with principals and advisors seated in different cities in their respective conference rooms. This scenario can only happen if there are no outstanding unresolved issues – the goal of every closing. On the other hand, if unresolved issues remain at closing, emotions may be running high and patience thin. When this occurs, remain calm. As you sign document after document, remind yourself how close you are to the finish line and that patience wins the day. If your Team has done its job well, you and the buyer will leave the closing smiling even though a severe case of writer's cramp has temporarily seized your signing hand. I've found that writer's cramp can always be remedied with a few sips of celebratory champagne.

Question 31

What are the legal fees for this process?

*U*nlike the fees you will pay a broker or investment banker, the fees that attorneys charge are not based on the purchase price but on an hourly rate. The services that an attorney performs for a $1 million deal are remarkably similar to those he provides for a $10 million deal. In both cases, the attorney's goal is the same: protect your interests while helping you to achieve your exit objectives.

Basically, the four items that determine the fees you will pay for a transaction are:

- *Your transaction attorney's experience level;*
- *Your deal sophistication as well as that of the buyer and the buyer's Advisory Team;*
- *The organization of your due diligence; and*
- *The composition of your Advisory Team.*

ATTORNEY EXPERIENCE

As you interview attorneys to represent you in the sale or purchase of a business, you will quickly discover that more experienced transaction attorneys charge higher rates. This might lead you to assume that hiring an attorney with a lower rate will reduce the overall fee. This assumption could be an expensive error. Typically, the less experienced attorney (with the lower hourly rate) will spend more time working through issues that a more experienced attorney will quickly dispatch. Ask for names of sellers an attorney has represented in the past and check those references.

This might be a good time to refer back to Question 30, "What Role Does the Transaction Attorney Play?" Ideally, you should choose an attorney with whom you are comfortable, and who has a proven track record of successfully closing transactions. You should also make sure that your attorney has an adequate support team (junior associates) who bills at lower hourly rates and can keep the deal moving forward until the lead attorney is needed.

BUYER AND SELLER SOPHISTICATION

If you are selling to a strategic or financial buyer, you can anticipate that they are more sophisticated about the sale process than you are. Why? Because they make their living buying and selling companies. For that reason, it is crucial to arm yourself with information about the process and your role in it.

In Question 39, we will discuss your role in the sale process. We will identify six tasks to be performed by a seller. Namely:

- *Selecting Advisors;*
- *Acting as a Resource;*
- *Acting as a Spokesman;*
- *Determining Who Knows;*
- *Stepping Away; and*
- *Maintaining Confidentiality.*

The most crucial of these – as related to their impact on fees – are acting as a resource/spokesman and stepping away. Buyers or sellers who assume roles that are better played by their advisors typically introduce inefficiencies and miscommunication into the process that may endanger a successful close. For example, when buyers and sellers communicate regarding deal points in the absence of their advisors, the version each attorney subsequently hears is often quite different. Subsequently, confusion reigns supreme. These miscues by the principals will unequivocally lead to greater attorney fees due to unnecessary drafts and revisions to documents, legal research, and a host of telephone calls between the attorneys. Don't talk to the buyer without your attorney's consent and unless you and your Team of Advisors have agreed that doing so will achieve a specific objective.

In summary, you have control over your own activities as they relate to legal fees but no control over the sophistication or activities of your buyer. Similarly, you have no control over the sophistication level of the buyer's advisors. If they are inexperienced, expect the fees you pay to increase as your advisors spend time educating the buyer's advisors.

SELLER'S ORGANIZATION OF DUE DILIGENCE

All else being equal, sellers who enter the sale process with their corporate houses in order will pay less in legal fees than those who do not. In other words, sellers who locate minority shareholders and their stock certificates, complete their corporate records, clean up pending or threatened litigation, organize permits, licenses, contracts, leases, etc., reap the rewards of their efforts during the sale process. Their expenses are lower and by removing potential obstacles, the deal progresses more efficiently. (For a complete list of items that will be reviewed by a buyer, please see Appendix B.)

COMPOSITION OF ADVISORY TEAM

The amount you pay in legal fees is also related to the mix of players you have drafted for your Advisory Team. If you have retained a broker or investment banker to negotiate the financial terms and conditions, you will incur minimal legal fees during this first phase of the sale process. If, however, your Advisory Team is composed of a CPA and a transaction attorney (no broker or investment banker), expect to incur greater fees while your attorney helps negotiate the financial terms of the deal.

Whether a transaction intermediary is part of the game or not, legal fees will escalate as the deal progresses. Your attorney will negotiate the Letter of Intent, develop strategies, counsel you and the opposing party's advisors through the due diligence items, and negotiate the terms of the definitive purchase agreement. As a seller's general rule of thumb (and for your own cash flow purposes), you will incur the bulk of your legal fees during the period beginning with the Letter of Intent and ending at closing.

Usually, attorneys charge on an hourly basis (rather than as a percentage of the deal). You should ask for and expect to receive an estimate of the fees. Your attorney should be able to tell you, within a range, what he anticipates the fees to be. Because quoting a fee range is based on experience, inexperienced attorneys may hesitate to do so. Insist on a range from any attorney you interview.

You should understand that quoted ranges do change should unforeseen issues arise and require attention. For example, are there minority shareholders or items in your operational activities that could create impediments to closing? In privately-held companies, it is not uncommon for owners to lose contact with minority shareholders. Locating, and, if necessary, cashing out, these shareholders can take time and money. (See Question 34.) Your attorney should let you know when issues arise that will push the fees beyond the range quoted.

Ask your attorney to bill you on a regular basis. My firm sends a bill to the client every two weeks. From our perspective, doing so minimizes surprises and prevents unpleasant cases of sticker shock. From an owner's perspective, the invoice gives him a good indication of where he is in the process. He can see, in print, what has been done to date. An invoice is also a tool the owner can use to spot inefficiencies. For example, if he sees multiple phone calls requesting information, he may need to alert his management team that its failure to provide information on a timely basis is costing him money. Periodic invoices serve as both a management tool and a barometer of the sale process.

Question 32

What role does the CPA play and what are the fees for this process?

The role the Certified Public Accountant plays in the sale process depends on whether or not a transaction intermediary is involved.

If an investment banker or business broker is involved in the transaction, the CPA's role includes structuring the sale to minimize taxes and helping the transaction intermediary to pull together and deliver all financial information a potential buyer requires to evaluate your business. The CPA plays a vital role throughout the process because the CPA knows and understands all of the historical financial and operational data of your business, knows your personal tax objectives, and can provide a great deal of support to the transaction intermediary and attorney.

If no transaction intermediary is involved in the transaction, the CPA plays a more visible role. The CPA will perform the business valuation, justify and defend that valuation to the buyer's financial advisors, and in conjunction with your transaction attorney, often lead negotiations about purchase price, valuation, and structure.

Over the years, I have worked with CPAs in many successful transactions, even though the CPA may not have had a great deal of transaction experience. In these transactions, the seller typically has chosen not to retain a transaction intermediary and to proceed with only one buyer. In this case, I coach the CPA about the overall sale process, develop strategies, and jointly negotiate the deal. If you are in this situation, it is critical that your transaction attorney and CPA share a focus that puts your deal ahead of their individual egos. Should you sense friction or a lack of communication between the two, remind them that this is the most important transaction of your career. If matters do not improve, step in and make their cooperation a requisite of continued employment.

FEES

Like your attorney, the Certified Public Accountant will charge for his services on an hourly basis.

What you pay an accountant typically depends upon what role you ask him to play in the deal. At a minimum, the CPA provides tax analysis, gathers historical and current financial information, and may be asked to create audited financial statements (if he hasn't already done so). If you have retained a transaction intermediary, your CPA will turn this information over to him so he can perform a valuation. If you have no transaction intermediary, the CPA will perform (and you will pay for) the valuation. He may also negotiate the financial terms of the deal. In this situation, his fees will be significantly greater than if you had a transaction intermediary negotiating the financial terms.

Your CPA is, of course, the advisor most familiar with your personal and business financial history. For that reason, he is perhaps best suited to calculate the amount of money you will have available, after taxes, post-closing. Armed with this information, your CPA will also assist your financial planner/wealth management expert in structuring your newly burgeoning investment portfolio.

As with your attorney, you should seek an estimate of the fees at the outset. If your CPA will assume a limited role in the transaction, this range should be fairly easy to project. If you expect your CPA to assume roles more often played by a transaction intermediary, the quoted range will be higher. No matter which role he plays, use your accountant to provide accurate information and guidance throughout the sale process.

PART 5 | VALUATION AND DEAL STRUCTURE

With the decision to sell made and your Advisory Team in place, the final preparations for the sale process begin. Before you can sell your company, however, you must know what you have to sell. How much your company is worth and how it is organized (is it a C corporation or some type of pass-through entity?) critically affect the amount of cash you can expect to receive at closing.

In this Part Five, we take a cursory look at various valuation methods. Your transaction intermediary or CPA will develop the valuation for your business and defend it from attacks by the buyer's advisors. This valuation is the basis for your asking price and the subject of extensive negotiation. For these reasons, you should have a talking knowledge of how your advisor arrived at the assigned value. I thank Joseph Durnford of JD Ford Investment Bankers, LLC, for his contribution to this Question.

When you started your company and picked an entity form (C corporation, S corporation, etc.), you may have given little thought to the day you would eventually sell. If so, I encourage you to spend some time now on Questions 34 and 35. Your company's entity form has huge tax ramifications for both you and your buyer.

Finally, sellers often ask if they will be required to carry promissory notes for their buyers. Look for a discussion of promissory notes in Questions 36 and 37.

Question 33

What are the different ways to value my business for a sale?

*T*ransaction intermediaries generally employ one, or a combination, of four approaches to assigning a value to a company for the purposes of a sale:

- *Market*
- *Income*
- *Cost*
- *Rules of Thumb*

Let's look at each briefly.

MARKET APPROACH

Using the Market Approach, an analyst will compare the subject company to external objective data. This objective data can be the value of similar public companies (the Public Company approach) or it can be Recent Industry Transactions. In either case, placing a value on the company is similar to the typical real estate valuation: The subject property is compared to other properties.

Public Company Comparison. Let's assume that you have retained a transaction intermediary to determine the value of your business for a potential sale and that your company manufactures equipment for the construction industry. The transaction intermediary might start by looking at how the market values public companies that are engaged in similar activities. For example, he will analyze how John Deere's or

Caterpillar's price per share relates to its earnings, cash flow, sales, and book value. He will then apply the resulting ratios or "multiples" to your company.

In this scenario, he learns that since Caterpillar shares trade at $X each and the earnings per share are $Y, the price/earnings ratio for Caterpillar is X/Y. He then applies that ratio to your earnings to arrive at a value for your company.

Keep in mind, however, that this formula is just a starting point. Because the value of Caterpillar is expressed as the price for a single share of a publicly traded company, the transaction intermediary must apply both a control premium and a discount for marketability before applying the multiple to your company. The control premium accounts for the fact that a buyer can purchase a single minority share of Caterpillar; what you are selling however, is the entire controlling interest. The marketability discount accounts for the fact that the purchaser of Caterpillar shares can sell his shares the next day, whereas it can take many months to sell the shares of a private business. Finally, the multiple that the transaction intermediary extrapolated from a public company was an after-tax multiple. It is important to adjust your private company's earnings to reflect an after-tax rate.

Comparable Transaction. In this second type of Market Approach, the transaction intermediary compares the subject company to others like it that have sold in the recent past. Using our earlier example, he will look for information about the sale of companies similar in function and size to yours. His efforts will likely be hampered by the fact that data about the sales of private companies are difficult to obtain. If possible to obtain, the information about comparable transactions is invaluable because the best estimate of what buyers *will* pay is what buyers *have* paid. This approach will also provide insight into how acquisitions in an industry are structured.

INCOME APPROACH

The classic methods used by CPAs to value a company for sale are Income Approaches. The two variations, the Capitalization of Historical Earnings and the Discounted Cash Flow Analysis, both look to the past as a predictor of the future. Given that the purchase price of a company is the cost of the investment, the buyer's expected rate of return on that investment determines what he is willing to pay for that asset.

Capitalization of Historical Earnings. Using this method, the transaction intermediary looks back at cash flow and applies a capitalization rate. This capitalization rate is the anticipated return on investment and thus reflects the risk compared to the expected return. This method may not fully account for "blue sky" (the company's future potential) – something for which sellers always want compensation.

Discounted Cash Flow Analysis. The Discounted Cash Flow Analysis uses the same data to forecast future performance as does the Capitalization of Historical Earnings method but it accounts for the value (on a discounted basis) of blue sky. For that reason, it is much more popular with sellers than the Capitalization of Earnings approach.

As a rule, sellers want buyers to pay them for all of a company's future growth. Not surprisingly, buyers are reluctant to do so. Sellers argue that a company will continue and thus have value into perpetuity – long beyond the five to ten year period for which the buyer is forecasting income. For that reason, this formula also discounts the value of the presumed value of the company at the end of that period (the terminal value or the assumed future sale price).

COST APPROACH

The Cost Approach is generally used when the subject company is under-performing. This approach includes only the book or replacement value of the tangible assets. The Cost Approach essentially asks, "How much money would it take to buy the assets and assemble them for use in the business?" This approach assigns no value to the goodwill generated by those assembled assets.

RULES OF THUMB

In every industry, there are certain "Rules of Thumb" which deserve consideration. For example, in your industry, it may be that companies are generally bought at five times cash flow or two times book value. We don't recommend that you act solely on these rules but that you use them as guidelines. For example, during the consolidation boom of the 90s, consolidators approached owners with offers exceeding pre-existing "Rules of Thumb" and owners eagerly sold. These sellers took advantage of the market's abnormal appetite.

As you consider the various valuation approaches, remember that the value of your business changes constantly. Also, your motivation for valuation (estate planning or sale to a third party) will affect its value (low for purposes of estate planning and high for purposes of a sale to a third party). The market for your company is not static. There are windows of opportunity that fly open and slam shut. At a minimum, if you wish to stay abreast of what is happening in your industry, read its trade magazines and network with colleagues and competitors.

If you are committed to an eventual sale and want to take full and immediate advantage of what the market can bring, obtain periodic valuations. As part of these valuations, your advisor should point out improvements that can be made to your business to generate a higher purchase price. (Review Question 20.) Doing so will prepare you and your company to answer when opportunity knocks.

Question 34

Why do sellers prefer stock sales over asset sales?

TAX TREATMENT

If your business is a "C" corporation, you will prefer, for tax reasons, to sell your stock. This is so because as you sell your stock, you will be taxed only once. You will pay a Federal capital gain tax on the difference between the price received for your stock and the original cost basis in the stock. Of course, you may also pay a state capital gain tax.

If, on the other hand, you sell the assets of your "C" corporation, there will be two taxes levied. Your company will pay a tax at the corporation's regular tax rate (subject to Alternative Minimum Tax) on the taxable gain it recognizes on the sale of those assets. When the corporation then distributes cash to you, its shareholder, in the form of a dividend or in liquidation of the corporation, you will be taxed on that income at your personal income tax rate or the capital gains rate, if applicable. In this situation, you could pay a combined tax rate as high as 60 to 75 percent to Uncle Sam. In addition, Colorado, like many other states, assesses a tax on both the corporate gain and the personal gain.

If your company is organized as an "S" corporation, you can sell its assets without incurring such an onerous tax penalty. In an "S" corporation, the tax on the sale of assets by-passes the company and passes through to you, individually (therefore, you pay only one tax). The amount of the tax is based upon the type of asset sold and its cost basis.

For example, goodwill is taxed at capital gains rates while hard assets, such as inventory, are taxed at ordinary income rates. This distinction among assets results in a blended rate of ordinary income and capital gain rates. Although this blended rate is less than the double tax (incurred by a shareholder of a "C" corporation selling assets), it is still higher than the single capital gain tax on the shareholder selling stock in his "C" or "S" corporation.

For these reasons, it is extremely important that, early in your planning process, you consult your CPA and attorney to determine which sale structure minimizes your tax bill. If you own "C" corporation stock, your attorney will have to negotiate aggressively for a stock sale. If you own a highly-profitable company and are pursued by multiple deep-pocketed buyers, the odds of you selling stock are reasonably good. Some buyers want your company so badly that they will forgo the tax advantages and avoidance of liability that they would have enjoyed by buying your assets. If, on the other hand, your transaction is smaller and your buyer is an entrepreneurial buyer, you will find it difficult to sell stock. The entrepreneurial buyer needs to achieve a "stepped up" basis in the assets he seeks to acquire. This concept is more fully discussed in Question 35.

CONTINUED EXISTENCE

Another advantage to selling stock is that your entity (corporation) remains in existence and passes from seller to buyer. The buyer continues operating your entity. In most cases, the corporation's contracts and relationships stay in place, eliminating the need to obtain third party consents. In addition, there is no need to liquidate the entity after closing. If assets of the entity are sold, a dissolution of the entity will normally follow. While this may seem to be a minimal bookkeeping issue, it can prove tedious and costly.

MINORITY SHAREHOLDERS

Before we complete the discussion of selling stock, I leave you with one warning: If you have issued stock to minority shareholders, they have the power to derail your transaction. Whether your company is organized as a "C" or an "S" corporation, if you have decided to sell your company via a stock sale, most buyers will not close unless you can deliver 100 percent of the issued and outstanding stock. Absent a buy and sell agreement mandating that your minority shareholders must sell if you, the majority owner, decide to sell, they have no obligation to sell. Should they decide to hang on to their stock, your deal is probably dead.

> "If you have issued stock to minority shareholders, they have the power to derail your transaction."

If, on the other hand, you decide to sell assets, state law and your company's Articles of Incorporation define the number of votes required for approval of a sale of "all or substantially all of the assets."

Finally, you should be aware of a principle known as "Dissenters' Rights," which asserts that minority shareholders have the right to challenge certain transactions. Minority shareholders may raise other challenges as well so it is imperative that you discuss the existence of minority shareholders with your transaction attorney.

For these reasons, one of the first questions I ask a potential seller is if he owns 100 percent of the stock. If he does not, I warn him that these other shareholders (usually key employees or other family members) may, when approached about a sale, become motivated by greed. The mere whiff of a big payday often causes behavior that sellers never could have anticipated. I've seen too many situations in which relatives or otherwise good and rational people convince themselves that despite all of the seller's hard work over the years, they are somehow entitled to more than their share of his payday.

If you suspect that there may be people like this in your future, it is imperative that you develop a strategy early in the process to handle them. You do not want to be caught by surprise as you near closing, because their leverage increases as the time before closing decreases. They know that either you pay them more than they deserve or they threaten the closing. Don't let this happen to you.

Question 35

Why do buyers prefer to buy assets?

*A*s a general rule, buyers want to acquire assets for two reasons: to limit liability exposure and to obtain favorable tax treatment. In buying assets, buyers choose which assets they will acquire and which liabilities (if any) they will assume. In its purest form, a buyer picks which desks, equipment, pieces of machinery, and accounts receivable, etc. he wants to purchase. In reality, however, this rarely happens.

Instead, buyers typically acquire a seller's entire operating business and assume certain liabilities. More often than not, the assets not sold ("excluded assets") are determined by the seller. (These tend to be personal assets that are on the company's books.) Buyers typically assume certain future liabilities which include existing contracts with customers and vendors, and real estate leases.

Buyers will not assume unknown or contingent liabilities of a seller. An asset sale allows a buyer to leave the liabilities he elects not to assume in the seller's entity. Buyers look to the seller's warranties and representations and to indemnification provisions to protect them from those liabilities not assumed. In addition, a buyer may also require a seller to pay off certain unassumed liabilities at closing.

TAX TREATMENT

There are tax advantages to the buyer purchasing assets. Most important is the buyer's ability to achieve a "stepped up" basis in the assets he acquires. Let's take a fully depreciated asset as an example. If the buyer acquires that asset via a purchase of stock, he takes that asset with the tax basis as it exists in the company (i.e. carry-over basis). In other words, it is a fully-depreciated asset inside the entity bought from the seller. If, on the other hand, he acquires that same asset via an asset purchase from the seller's company, what he pays the seller for that asset establishes his basis in that asset, which, in most cases, leads to a step up in basis. The buyer then can start depreciating that asset all over again. This is a big tax advantage for the buyer.

In addition, each party will want the purchase price (the total of the money paid or payable and liabilities assumed) allocated to different assets. Given that assets are treated differently (from a tax perspective), sellers and buyers look to assign greater or lesser values to equipment, inventory, and accounts receivable. In an asset transaction, the buyer will want to allocate a greater value to ordinary assets – those which can be written off quickly such as equipment and inventory. Similarly, the buyer will desire to allocate less value to intangible assets (those that cannot be written off as quickly) such as goodwill, non-competes, client lists, and intellectual property. The seller, on the other hand, will want to allocate the purchase price to those assets that give him the best tax treatment.

Having analyzed the stock vs. asset debate, how do deals get done? It usually depends upon which party (buyer or seller) has the most leverage. If the buyer is a large publicly-traded company, it may be willing to forgo the tax advantages of purchasing your assets in order to make the acquisition. A smaller buyer, however, may not be able to afford the transaction without the tax benefits that a purchase of assets entails. If you own a highly-successful company that a buyer or multiple buyers simply must have, your advisors will be better able to structure the transaction to your benefit. If not, they will have to work diligently to secure a purchase price that will give you financial security – even after the tax bill is paid.

Question 36

Will I be asked to carry back a promissory note?

The answer to this question depends on a number of factors. If you own a good company in high demand you will probably be able to insist on an "all cash" or "all stock" closing. If your company has been struggling and there are a limited number of buyers, expect to carry back a portion of the sale price in the form of a promissory note. Similarly, if you own a small company (worth between $500,000 and $2 million) that attracts an entrepreneurial buyer, you will also likely be asked to carry back some part of the purchase price.

If the financial markets (lenders) are tough, making loans for acquisitions difficult to obtain, then you should expect to carry back part of the purchase price. As I write today, lender's loan requirements are very stringent and buyers are routinely asking sellers to carry back portions of the purchase price. Finally, when the cost of borrowed funds is high, sellers are generally asked to carry back part of the purchase price.

If the amount of risk you are required to take by carrying back a note is unacceptable, don't agree to the note. Continue to own and operate your company until the financial markets are more favorable and/or your company is performing at a level that attracts buyers capable of cashing you out. This is a far better alternative than selling your business only to return to it in the future because the buyer defaulted on his promissory note to you.

Question 37

If I carry back a note, how will my interests be protected?

A note is simply a promise to pay. Any time you carry back a note you are at risk of not receiving your money. If you have to sue to enforce the note, there is a strong probability that the buyer will assert defenses and counterclaims alleging a breach of warranties or representations. The buyer will argue that the company's post-closing cash flow proved insufficient to pay the debt because you misrepresented the company. Surely, you don't expect a buyer to admit that his leadership was in any way responsible for the company's inability to meet its financial

> "Any time you carry back a note you are at risk of not receiving your money."

obligations! This is just another reason why thorough due diligence and careful negotiation of the warranties and representations are so critical.

To protect yourself from these post-closing calamities, you must secure the note as well as possible. Recall those meetings in your banker's office when you were asked to give personal guarantees and pledge everything you and your company owned. Well, now it is your turn to think and act like a banker. You want to assume the most favorable position to access available cash or to re-take immediate control and possession of your company, if possible. Insist on the buyer's personal guarantee. Require the buyer to provide verifiable financial statements. If you have sold your company's stock, obtain a security interest in that stock and in the assets of the company. If you have sold assets, obtain a security interest in the assets of the company. In addition, negotiate a termination of your covenant not to compete if the buyer defaults. Prohibit the buyer from taking distributions until the promissory note is paid in full. Insist upon the cross-collateralization of other closing documents so that a breach of one agreement constitutes a breach of the promissory note. For example, if the buyer breaches the security agreement or the building lease (on which you are the Landlord) or your employment agreement, you should be entitled to declare a default and accelerate payment under the promissory note.

Finally, when carrying back a note, ask for the same protections other lenders do: financial covenants, annual/quarterly/monthly financial statements, tax returns, access to the buyer's books and records, reviewed or audited financial statements.

Keep in mind, however, that a buyer who requires you to carry a promissory note most likely has another lender in first position. If this is the case, expect your rights to enforce and to collect your note to be subordinated to that lender and therefore to be severely restricted. I watched a large transaction nearly collapse because at the last moment, the buyer's principal lender tried to force on my client a totally unreasonable subordination agreement. This agreement stated that the seller could not receive any note payments from the buyer until the primary lender was paid in full. After many tense sessions, we convinced the lender's counsel to amend the subordination agreement to allow the seller to receive note payments so long as the buyer was in compliance with the lender's note. This was a good solution but the emotional toll it took on the seller was heavy.

One final word of caution: Don't let your desire to sell the company overwhelm your common sense and reliable instinct about the amount of the note (less is better than more) or the buyer's financial condition (strong is better than weak). Sellers can become so anxious to close that despite evidence to the contrary, they convince themselves that the buyer is incapable of failure. They become overly-confident about the buyer's ability to pay 100 percent of the note. If you find yourself embarking on this fantasy trip, hopefully your advisors will snap you back into reality. Your worst nightmare is to sell your company only to have to litigate to obtain the payment of your note or the return of your company after the buyer has run it into the ground. Look to your transaction attorney to negotiate as much protection as possible to secure your note.

PART 6 | THE SALE PROCESS

Finally, the biggest deal of your lifetime begins.

- *Your decision to sell is fixed and well-conceived.*
- *You are comfortable in your role as a seller.*
- *You have chosen the type of buyer that is right for you.*
- *Your Team of Advisors understands your objective and is prepared to help you achieve it.*
- *You know what your company is worth and are aware of the tax ramifications of its sale.*

We turn now to the sale process itself...how it progresses, how long it takes, and your role in it. We examine in some detail the controlled auction, the most effective way to maximize your sale price in a sale to third party. Finally, we explore how owners go about breaking the news to their employees that a sale has occurred.

Sellers, start your engines.

Question 38

What are the steps in the sale process?

PHASE ONE: MAKING THE DECISION TO SELL

1. *Financial reasons*
2. *Personal reasons*

PHASE TWO: ACTING ON YOUR DECISION TO SELL

1. *Assemble an Advisory Dream Team.*
2. *Prepare Confidential Information Memorandum.*
3. *Identify, qualify, and contact buyers.*
4. *Conduct due diligence.*
5. *Negotiate Letter of Intent.*
6. *Negotiate definitive purchase agreement.*
7. *Conduct the Closing.*
8. *Celebrate.*

PHASE ONE: MAKING THE DECISION TO SELL

Basically, the sale process falls into two distinct phases: deciding to sell and acting on that decision. As discussed in Question 2, a business owner typically decides to sell when two events occur simultaneously. The "measurable" event is the point at which a business can be sold for a price that will yield its owner financial security. Generally, the transaction intermediary or an owner's CPA is in the best position to make this determination. Owners who believe they may be reaching this point are well served to secure a valuation from a reputable transaction intermediary.

Of course, a CPA is able to perform this valuation but I've found that the valuations of CPAs tend to be more conservative than those of transaction intermediaries. CPAs routinely perform valuations for estate planning, divorces, buy/sell agreements, and tax planning, in which the goal is to establish a low valuation. Because transaction intermediaries are in the market on a daily basis and actively seek information on companies similar to yours in your industry, their analyses of value tend to more closely reflect what the market will pay. If you elect to use your CPA for a valuation, simply request that he research market comparables and include them in his analysis.

The other event (the one that only an owner can gauge) is the owner's personal reasons for exiting the business. Perhaps the owner recognizes the need for a cash infusion to move the business to the next level and doesn't want to put more personal equity at risk. Perhaps the business has become so complex that no one person can run it – well – anymore. Or perhaps the owner seeks a change of pace, to slow down or to tackle a long suppressed dream. For whatever reason, the business owner simply lacks the commitment, fire, or 36-hour days to push the business to new heights. When an owner's personal motives are compelling **and** it is determined that the business can be sold for an amount that yields financial independence, many owners recognize that the time to sell has arrived.

PHASE TWO: ACTING ON YOUR DECISION TO SELL

Phase two of the sale process is actually *doing it* – moving forward with the sale. First, an owner needs to assemble a Team of Advisors. This team should consist of a CPA (usually the company's own CPA), a transaction intermediary (investment banker or business broker), a transaction attorney, a banker, and a financial planner. (Please refer to Part Four for information about how to choose these team members.) Once your team is assembled, each member will begin to perform some important tasks.

The transaction intermediary will value your business and begin to identify potential buyers. Basically, buyers fall into five categories: (1) family members; (2) employees or co-owners; (3) entrepreneurial buyers; (4) strategic buyers; and (5) financial buyers. (Owners who wish to transfer their businesses to family members can refer to Question 5. Selling to co-owners or employees is addressed in Questions 4, 21, 22, and 23.) The sale process outlined in this Question does not apply to family or employee transfers.

Sales to strategic, financial, and entrepreneurial buyers comprise the majority of privately-held business sales. As the seller, you will advise your transaction intermediary about all third parties you think may be potential buyers. Your transaction intermediary will make sure that you identify and eliminate those buyers, if any, to whom you are unwilling to sell. He will research and identify additional buyers that you may never have considered.

> "...buyers fall into five categories:
> (1) family members;
> (2) employees or
>   co-owners;
> 3) entrepreneurial
>   buyers;
> (4) strategic buyers; and
> (5) financial buyers."

Once the list of potential buyers is compiled, the transaction intermediary will gauge the interest of these parties without disclosing the identity of the seller. After making discreet inquiries, the transaction intermediary will provide to potential buyers who have shown an interest in your company the Confidential Information Memorandum. This Memorandum is a marketing piece created by the transaction intermediary. It contains critical information about your company, including: historical and limited financial information, a description of the business you are in, market conditions and your company's place in that market, sales, and product and marketing information.

Meanwhile, the seller's transaction attorney should be performing due diligence on the company. (The due diligence process is more completely described in Question 46.) Briefly, due diligence means collecting, organizing, analyzing, and reviewing all of the stock records, contracts, relationships, legal actions (threatened or pending), financial obligations, and operational practices of the company. Based on this review and analysis, the attorney will make a number of recommendations aimed at cleaning up questionable practices or murky issues before they attract the attention of a prospective buyer. It is critical that your transaction attorney conduct due diligence prior to delivering information to the buyer's attorneys.

Once the transaction intermediary has eliminated buyers who are "tire kickers" from the process, negotiations with serious buyers begin in earnest. These negotiations generally culminate in a signed Letter of Intent between buyer and seller (see Question 45). The buyer's advisors continue to conduct due diligence and to satisfy conditions precedent (see Question 48) while the attorneys open negotiations regarding the definitive purchase agreement. The closing will occur when due diligence is complete, when all conditions precedent are met, when the buyer has his financing in place, and when the definitive purchase agreement is ready to sign.

In our practice, we generally prefer that sellers sign the definitive purchase agreement and close the transaction simultaneously. Attorneys for many buyers may press sellers to sign the definitive purchase agreement as early in the process as possible, knowing that the actual closing won't occur for at least 45 days. In most cases, we object to this approach for two reasons. First, signing the definitive purchase agreement prematurely results in a more complicated document, i.e. lengthy provisions that govern how the seller will conduct the operational and financial aspects of this business during the period until closing. These provisions may also grant rights to the buyer, including requiring the seller to obtain buyer's consent before the seller can take certain specified actions. We do not want provisions that will tie our sellers' hands when it comes to the operation of their companies.

The second reason we object to a premature signing of the definitive purchase agreement is simple. Why should a seller be locked into a binding contract to sell when the buyer remains free to walk from the transaction up to the closing due to open-ended financing and due diligence contingencies?

When your transaction attorney tells you that the definitive purchase agreement is final, that all of the buyer's conditions precedent, including financing, have been satisfied and removed, you can sign it, close the deal, and begin the celebration.

Question 39

What is my role, as seller, in the sale process?

Your role will undoubtedly change several times during the ebb and flow of the transaction. Knowing in advance that your role will change and adapting to circumstances facilitates your ability to keep the process on track.

SELECTING YOUR ADVISORS

Very early in the sale process, you will need to determine if your current advisors can successfully orchestrate the sale of your business. If they do not have experience in transactions, you will need to find ones who do. Please refer to Part Four, Assembling Your Advisory Dream Team, for greater detail on what to look for in an advisor.

Making the decision to replace a longtime friend for a more experienced advisor requires courage and diplomacy. Honesty is always the best policy. If you need to replace your general practice attorney or CPA, simply explain that at this time, you need highly experienced transaction professionals who work in this area on a daily basis and who can lead the process. Existing advisors can play a valuable, albeit secondary, role by furnishing existing due diligence information, historical perspective, and insight about you and your company. Believe it or not, your professional advisors will understand and will probably be relieved that others more familiar with transactions are assuming the responsibility.

Acting As A Resource

Throughout the sale process, you will be called upon to help your advisors in a myriad of ways. You need to be available to them, to provide information, and to make your preferences known. During the legal due diligence process, your transaction attorney will need to know about every fact and document that affects your business. During the financial due diligence process, your transaction intermediary will collect, question, and organize every piece of financial data. It is important that you make sure they have every piece of the puzzle.

Acting As A Spokesman

When you meet potential buyers, you may assume the role of spokesman for your company. You will tell your story, highlight your achievements, and educate the buyer as to why he should pay a premium for your business. You, your transaction attorney, and transaction intermediary will carefully rehearse for this performance. When you meet with potential buyers you will show them your operation and answer questions you've been coached to answer. This is commonly referred to as the "Dog and Pony Show." Once the Letter of Intent is signed by a potential buyer, you will assume a less visible role until issues arise that require your input.

DETERMINING "WHO KNOWS"

Rarely is a transaction completed with only the owner knowing about the process. Every owner is sensitive to confidentiality, but each must decide who within the company should know about and can help in the process. Usually, certain key employees are told about the pending sale and are asked to assist the owner's advisors. Key employees may include: the Chief Financial Officer, Sales Manager, and Plant or Operations Manager. You do not want to cast this net any farther than necessary. Your job is to show your key employees that the sale is in their best interests as well, and that you are relying heavily on their contribution to the process and their ability to maintain strict confidentiality. (For information about confidentiality and loyalty bonuses for key employees, please see Question 9.)

STEPPING ASIDE

For many owners, stepping aside is perhaps the toughest task they are asked to perform. As an owner, it is often difficult to allow others to take control but you must allow the members of your Advisory Team to propel the process forward. Typically, you will be on the sidelines once the process is under way and you will be asked not to communicate with the buyer unless you first consult your advisors. You will need to be available, but your focus must be on running your business. It is easy to be distracted by the sale process but you must carry on with normal business activities. Ideally, you will behave as if the sale process is not happening.

We ask owners to step aside for two reasons. First, an owner who involves himself in every aspect of the sale process is not focused on running his company. An interruption in profitability during this crucial pre-closing period will wreak havoc on negotiations on sale price and terms. Second, performing at your normal level helps keep the sale confidential. If you stick to your regular business routines, your employees have no reason to suspect that all is not business as usual.

One of the owners featured in Part Eight, Bill Clymor, is a great example of how an owner can manage and facilitate the sale process. Unlike most owners, Bill had significant experience in the mergers & acquisitions world. Prior to acquiring his company, Imperial Headwear, Inc., he made acquisitions for his employer. If any seller should have been tempted to go it alone in the sale process, it was Bill. He certainly had experience and knowledge in the M&A marketplace. When it came time to sell his own company, however, Bill's instructions to his Advisory Team and key management were clear. First, he acknowledged that he had both an excellent management team and team of professional advisors. He communicated his objectives clearly to both teams. With that, he told both groups to get busy and to contact him if, and when, necessary.

Bill stuck to his game plan. When a member of his Team of Advisors needed him, he was available. He made clear decisions. When the deal hit rough spots, he maintained his cool, worked with his advisors to put the process back on track, and enjoyed an uneventful closing. Read the rest of Bill's story on page 203.

Once you have selected your transaction advisors and clearly explained to them your exit requirements, your role is to run the company, provide direction when asked, and to let them do their jobs.

Question 40

How long does the sale process take?

*F*rom the moment you engage your advisors (assuming that no buyer has approached you regarding an immediate sale), you should expect the entire process – from the legal audit through the closing – to last between nine and twelve months. If a buyer has already contacted you and you have decided to sell to this buyer rather than to test the market, the process may move more quickly.

The most frequent causes for extended delay are:

- *Issues discovered during due diligence;*
- *Obtaining third party consents; and*
- *The buyer's inability to nail down suitable financing.*

Please refer to Question 46 for a discussion of the items that will be identified, reviewed, analyzed, and examined during the due diligence process. The number of items on this list is large, as you can see if you look at Appendix B. It is not unusual for one or more items to require significant attention from your CPA or transaction attorney.

One of the items that often requires significant time and effort during the due diligence process is obtaining third party consents, i.e. landlords, franchisors, manufacturers, bankers, major contracts, etc. If your company is engaged in a business that requires a significant number of these, your transaction attorney will begin as early as possible to set up the process by which he will obtain them.

Finally, bank regulators tightly govern the loan process. A banker's desire to close quickly or be flexible in criteria may be beyond his control. Unfortunately, processing a loan can test both buyer's and seller's patience. Your best coping strategy is to be patient, to continue delivering the profits and provide the banker with needed information about your company, while your transaction attorney and transaction intermediary oversee this process.

Don't forget to suggest that your buyer contact your existing banker to obtain financing. Your banker knows you, your management team, your company, and your industry. This knowledge makes him a logical choice to review the new lending opportunity. As discussed in Question 24, your banker should be aware of your exit goal. Helping your buyer to obtain financing certainly improves the odds of closing the deal.

Question 41

What is a controlled auction?

*T*he most effective way to market a business and maximize its purchase price is through a process known as the "controlled auction." A controlled auction introduces the acquisition opportunity to a preselected list of qualified buyers and requires that they adhere to a set of bidding procedures in order to be considered as potential buyers. The controlled auction is designed to create a situation in which the buyers realize that they are competing against other qualified buyers. This process, if executed properly, should lead to a premium being paid for your company. The controlled auction should be conducted by a transaction intermediary who is financially knowledgeable and is an experienced negotiator.

My favorite example of how the controlled auction can maximize the purchase price involves a manufacturer whose CPA valued the company at $12 million. The CPA focused on how the company per-formed historically, not its future upside potential. The investment banker believed that the company would sell between $22 million and $25 million. The investment banker narrowed the qualified buyers down to four and started the controlled auction. After the third round of bidding, the offers ranged between $37 million and $40 million. Finally, the ultimate buyer couldn't bear the thought of losing this opportunity. He offered an additional $3 million to close the auction. Sold! For $43 million cash!

> "At a certain point in the controlled auction, buyers convince them-selves that they simply cannot allow the other bidders to acquire the company on the block."

Anyone who has attended an auction of any sort has seen how egos and emotions surface when bidding begins on an item that the bidders simply *must have*. The competitive envi-ronment for that special painting or trip to The Masters in Augusta, Georgia helps drive the bidding up. So it is with the controlled auction.

In addition, the "fear of loss" is part of the controlled auction process. At a certain point in the controlled auction, buyers convince themselves that they simply cannot allow the other bidders (who are probably business competitors) to acquire the company on the block. I have never seen the controlled auction fail to drive up the price when skillfully orchestrated.

During a controlled auction the transaction intermediary will not reveal to any one potential buyer the identity of the other suitors. It is better (for the seller, of course) if buyers assume that they are involved in hotly-contested auctions. In fact, I have watched skilled transaction intermediaries (without a hint of misrepresentation) negotiate a robust purchase price because the buyer assumed that the mere involvement of the transaction intermediary meant that other qualified suitors were bidding against him. In reality, the ultimate buyer was the only suitor in the parlor.

An investment banker brings you and your company instant credibility in the eyes of most buyers. Buyers know that if you have engaged an investment banker, you are sophisticated in your understanding of the sale process. The buyers further know that reputable transaction intermediaries only represent quality companies and that they will be negotiating against other pre-qualified buyers.

A controlled auction usually proceeds through the following steps:

1. *Owner selects a transaction intermediary.*

2. *The transaction intermediary performs a valuation.*

3. *The transaction intermediary researches and analyzes your industry to see who is buying and how much they are paying.*

4. *The transaction intermediary conducts a thorough due diligence of your financial history and operating procedures. Then, based upon information gained in Steps 2 and 3, the transaction intermediary prepares the Confidential Offering Memorandum about your company. This is a multi-page marketing piece that describes ownership, structure, company history, and your particular industry segment, products, and services. It also provides a financial overview of your company.*

5. *Owner and transaction intermediary work together to identify qualified potential buyers.*

6. *The transaction intermediary contacts buyers with a "teaser" about your company (e.g. "manufacturing company with strong history of earnings in Rocky Mountain region.")*

7. *Interested parties execute Confidentiality Agreements before receiving any additional information.*

8. *Upon receipt of signed Confidentiality Agreements, the transaction intermediary delivers the Confidential Information Memorandum, financial information and sale process guidelines to prospective buyers.*

   Note: *All prospective buyers receive the same information and ideally, respond within the same timeframe. The transaction intermediary does not want to give one buyer an unfair advantage over another. Similarly, from a timing standpoint, the transaction intermediary does not want one buyer out ahead of the pack pushing for a quick closing. This would disrupt the flow of the controlled auction.*

9. *Prospective buyers deliver "Expressions of Interest" to transaction intermediary. These EOIs quote a range for the purchase price and propose a deal structure. EOIs are not intended to be binding. "Bottom-feeders" are easily identified and eliminated at this stage.*

10. *The transaction intermediary narrows the field to the most serious buyers and extracts, through negotiation, their best offers. (During this Step, the transaction intermediary truly earns his success fee.)*

11. *The seller selects the buyer.*

12. *The seller and buyer sign a Letter of Intent.*

13. *Transaction attorneys use the Letter of Intent to negotiate and to draft a definitive purchase agreement and guide the transaction to closing.*

14. *Seller sips champagne at closing dinner once purchase price funds are safely deposited in his account.*

By participating in the controlled auction, the seller enjoys a distinct advantage. Bidders know (or believe) that they are competing against others and therefore submit their best prices and terms. The winning bidder continues to work toward closing, knowing that the transaction intermediary has other would-be buyers waiting on the sidelines. These buyers can and will be contacted should the winning bidder falter. These two factors, greater purchase price and greater probability of closing, almost always outweigh the single-bidder negotiating strategy.

Unlike a bidder in the controlled auction, the single bidder, in many cases, enjoys the upper hand. He negotiates knowing he is the only game in town. He is comfortable dragging the process out and wearing you down on price and terms. If selling your company is your opportunity to hit a financial grand slam, try to establish a controlled auction. If, for whatever reason, an auction is not possible, pick your buyer carefully and play to win.

Question 42

How do I tell my employees that I have sold the company?

Most owners tell their employees about a sale either immediately following the closing or the day after. At this meeting, the buyer is present when you, the former owner, deliver *your version* of the following speech:

"I am happy to announce that today I have sold my business to Mr. Buyer. From a financial standpoint, I have taken this company as far as I can. I wanted to move this company to the next level so I sought out a buyer with greater financial resources and an operating philosophy like our own. I am pleased to say that Mr. Buyer has both and can take this company forward. The future is exciting and rewarding. As a result of this sale, you will all be presented with

greater personal and financial opportunities than I was able to offer."

You then thank each employee graciously and profusely for helping you to build a company of which you can all be proud. You may wish to take this opportunity to apologize for "fibbing" when asked about selling the company. Almost without exception, employees understand the need for your white lie and are truly happy for you. Those employees who were never particularly fond of you will at least be happy that you are leaving.

If there are specific and obvious reasons for a sale, for instance failing health, you should mention those. Your audience in this speech is both the employees and the buyer so you must please both. Further, you may continue working in the company so you want both these groups to react positively to your remarks.

If the buyer of your company offers a better benefit package or stock ownership opportunities, which is typically the case, stress these advantages.

The buyer should then follow with his own remarks indicating that he was drawn to this company because of its stature, performance, and *people.*

One of the most dramatic days of my career occurred when I had to deliver a variation of this speech on behalf of a seller. On Monday, Bob (not his real name) and I had spent hours on the phone with the buyer, negotiating the final points of the purchase agreement. Bob hung up the phone feeling confident that a sale was imminent. When I arrived at the office early Tuesday morning, Bob's wife, Emma, called to tell me that while riding his exercise bike, Bob (age 57) had suffered a major heart attack and died. I was shocked. I immediately called Bob's CPA and she and I went to meet Bob's widow. Emma was an example of self-control. The three of us agreed that we needed to meet with the employees immediately. When we arrived at Bob's company, we gathered the employees in a large training room and told them not only that Bob had died but that he had just negotiated a contract to sell the company. The shock, disbelief, and sense of loss in that room were overwhelming.

The day's only bright spot was that because we had worked with Bob for over a year preparing his company for sale, he had a strong management team and working systems in place. Added to that, Bob's wife was able to lift the spirits of the employees and close the transaction. She held herself and everyone else together. It was a day that I will never forget.

Question 43

What should I expect at closing?

A closing is typically a reflection of the behavior of the parties from the time the Letter of Intent is signed to the date of closing. If both parties have been represented by teams of competent transaction professionals, have disclosed all potential issues, have been reasonable, and have negotiated with a "win-win" mentality, and if the seller has delivered to buyer a comprehensive due diligence package, the closing will be uneventful. Our typical closing has the buyer and seller sitting in different cities in their respective attorneys' offices signing documents. All major issues have been resolved in advance of this day. The sole highlight is the moment the seller hears from his bank that the purchase proceeds wire has arrived and has cleared. (See Dick Henkle's recollection of this moment on page 212.) Our goal at closing is to ensure that a bad case of writer's cramp doesn't inhibit the seller from raising a champagne glass.

On the other hand, if one of the parties has retained inexperienced counsel, has been less than forthcoming on due diligence issues, has been disorganized, or has negotiated as if this transaction were a zero sum game, an attitude of distrust and suspicion will permeate the closing – assuming there is a closing. The same bumps on the road to closing will appear at closing. There is nothing worse than attending a closing, heart in throat, hoping that the remaining "deal breakers" can be resolved favorably. This should not happen.

Your closing should be one of the happiest, most satisfying days of your life. I am confident that if you incorporate the answers in this book during the sale process, your closing will be all that and more.

PART 7 | CRITICAL LEGAL ISSUES

Please do not assume that because this section appears as near to the end of this book as it does that "Critical Legal Issues" are merely footnotes to the sale process. Discussing these issues so vital to your ability to achieve personal and financial freedom only after describing the rest of the sale process is evidence of my desire to maintain the momentum of the prior six parts. Had I written first about legal issues, I suspect that few readers would have stayed with me to Part Two.

The final twelve questions cover legal issues with which you should be familiar as you interview and hire advisors and as you work through the sale of your company. Pay close attention to covenants not to compete and to personal indemnification. These issues, along with the other topics in this Part, will have a profound effect on your financial well-being after the sale.

I urge you to familiarize yourself with all of the legal issues discussed in this Part. The answers give you enough information to ask informed questions of your advisors. Your transaction attorney should be well-versed in each of these topics.

Question 44

Are confidentiality agreements enforceable?

Simple Answer: "Yes."

N o information about your company should be disclosed without first having a signed Confidentiality Agreement. (See Appendix A for a copy of a sample Confidentiality Agreement.) This Agreement is very specific in what it proscribes and is designed to protect your confidentiality if the deal fails to close.

Like any contract, it is not absolutely bulletproof. Arguments can arise as to whether or not the information shared was actually "confidential" or already known in your industry. Having said that, a well-drafted Confidentiality Agreement is a strong deterrent and your best protection against unethical or unprofessional buyers.

> "...a well-drafted Confidentiality Agreement is a strong deterrent and your best protection against unethical or unprofessional buyers."

Confidentiality Agreements should be fairly straightforward. If, however, you are negotiating with a local competitor, there is a natural conflict between your desire to protect sensitive information and your competitor's desire to avoid legal exposure over information he already possesses. Defining "confidential" in this situation can be tricky, but your transaction attorney should be able to achieve a balance that protects both parties.

If you find yourself in extensive negotiations over the

Confidentiality Agreement, you may have cause for concern. You should ask yourself if the potential buyer is intentionally creating loop holes in the Agreement. Is he, or are his advisors, unsophisticated in the sale process? Is it his, or his advisors', style to over-negotiate and nit-pick every single item? If any of these are true in your situation, consider yourself warned. Talk with your advisors to determine if this is the type of individual (or opposing team of Team of Advisors) with whom you wish to pursue a sale.

Question 45

What is a Letter of Intent?

*I*n most transactions, buyers and sellers want to put, in writing, the basic understanding of the economic terms and conditions of their agreement before they negotiate all of the details of a full-blown purchase contract. This written expression is commonly known as a Letter of Intent (LOI) or Letter of Understanding. Please see Appendix D for a Sample LOI.

In general, an LOI identifies the parties to the sale (buyer and seller), sets a purchase price, the method of payment, (cash, promissory note, stock) states the basic structure of the transaction (stock or asset purchase or merger), and often includes certain contingencies such as financing and due diligence contingencies. The remaining issues (such as warranties and representations, conditions to closing, post-closing obligations such as employment or no competes, indemnification, etc.) are left to be negotiated in the definitive purchase agreement. Often, legal counsel or even business people want to include far more detail than is necessary in the LOI.

From the seller's perspective, I prefer that the LOI be simple and non-binding but that it include crucial business points. If a buyer insists on negotiating a detailed and complex LOI, I suggest that we skip the LOI entirely and move directly to negotiating the definitive asset or stock purchase agreement. Why endure two rounds of extensive negotiations? This is inefficient and expensive. Parties have successfully argued and courts have ruled that the intricate level of detail in an LOI as well as the actions of the parties made it a binding contract, even though the LOI explicitly stated that it was non-binding.

> "While minimizing detail is critically important, I advise my sellers to insist on an explicitly non-binding LOI."

While minimizing detail is critically important, I advise my sellers to insist on an explicitly non-binding LOI. Given that an LOI is simply an outline of the overall transaction, there are many issues that at the outset remain undecided. If negotiations break down when negotiating any of these undecided issues (en route to the final purchase contract) and the LOI is binding, your buyer could use the threat of litigation to force you to concede on a critical issue. The buyer could state, "If you don't agree to my demand, I will sue to enforce the binding LOI." This is a viable threat because the moment litigation commences, your business is off the market. No other prospective buyer will attempt to purchase a company that is involved in litigation with a former buyer. Again, keep it simple. Your transaction attorney will guide you through this delicate process.

Buyers also often want to include language in the LOI concerning post-closing employment or covenants not to compete. These and other items can be negotiated later. Don't let the process get bogged down at the LOI stage. Again, every item that you include in the LOI has a cumulative effect. Added together, they begin to resemble a contract that a judge could rule to be binding.

Once signed, the LOI is the starting point for the attorneys to draft and to negotiate the definitive purchase agreement. Simultaneously, the buyer's advisors begin the due diligence process in earnest. Prior to this point, the buyer has typically only reviewed limited financial information about the company. The LOI is always contingent upon the buyer performing due diligence and being satisfied with the results thereof. Accept the fact that this contingency constitutes a giant loophole for the buyer. This contingency allows the buyer to change his mind about purchasing your business *for any reason*. He simply informs you that he has found "something" during his due diligence that has caused him to walk away from this transaction.

This is another reason that preparing your due diligence information well in advance is so important. If there are problems that will cause the buyer heartburn, discuss these with your advisors early on in the process and defuse them. If, however, the buyer is bent on using due diligence to terminate the sale process, there isn't much you can do to stop him. (For more discussion on this issue, please see Question 47.) The best (albeit fallible) defense to this scenario is for your transaction intermediary to carefully screen all potential buyers early in the process.

Question 46

What is due diligence?

No sophisticated buyer will pay a seller one dime for a company without the opportunity to learn EVERYTHING about that company. That opportunity is commonly known as "due diligence." If you can imagine a buyer, his accountant, his lawyer, and any other professional advisors he may have, putting your company – all its contracts, practices, relationships, plans, financials, histories – under a microscope which reveals every flaw – no matter how small – you understand due diligence.

No matter how clearly or dramatically I try to explain the due diligence process to a seller, I am rarely successful in conveying its importance and intensity. Only at closing do sellers tell me, "Now that I've been through it, I understand what you tried to tell me at the outset."

> "No matter how clearly or dramatically I try to explain the due diligence process to a seller, I am rarely successful in conveying its importance and intensity. Only at closing do sellers tell me, 'Now that I've been through it, I understand what you tried to tell me at the outset.'"

Ever the optimist, let me try one more time. A buyer contemplating the purchase of a business will ask for all details on every aspect of that business. To give you an idea of the items that will likely be included, please see Appendix B.

When representing a seller, my firm does due diligence a little differently than most. We start the due diligence process as soon as an owner has decided to sell the company. The first task in the process – identifying the person in the organization to pull together all of the documents and information we will need – requires an owner's careful consideration. That person will have a new full time, albeit temporary job collecting, researching, and compiling information.

Our reasons for getting a head start on due diligence are simple. Our first goal is to remove any and all obstacles so that a buyer sees a clear path to closing. Second, delivering organized information allows the buyer's attorneys to stay focused on drafting documents and legal issues. Finally, getting a head start in preparing due diligence compresses the time between the offer and the closing.

As the seller's attorney, I want to see every piece of information before the buyer's attorney reviews it. This gives me an opportunity to take preventive measures including: updating minutes, filling in gaps in stock ownership records, and locating minority shareholders and their stock certificates. The seller may need to provide notice or obtain consents from lenders, landlords, or various vendors before any transfer can take place. There may be problems within the company that can be "fixed" before a buyer is even identified. Once everything is in place, I want to present a complete and well-organized packet of due diligence information to the opposing counsel. Why? Time kills deals. Performing due diligence properly can take months. Doing so before an offer is tendered accelerates the deal process. Significant time can be needlessly wasted in the due diligence process. If not handled properly and in advance of negotiations, due diligence can delay, if not derail, the process.

> "If not handled properly and in advance of negotiations, due diligence can delay, if not derail, the process."

I am reminded of one seller who engaged my firm to perform due diligence on his company well before he had identified a potential buyer. For three months, attorneys in my office organized, indexed, and categorized every piece of information about this company. When a buyer did tender an offer, we sent seven binders containing this information to its large New York law firm. Three days later, we received word that the information had been reviewed, there were no issues on the table, and the deal could move forward. This professional and comprehensive presentation of information not only expedited the due diligence process, but it greatly enhanced my client's credibility with the buyer. Buyers and their advisors are not accustomed to finding sellers so well prepared. Prepared sellers who establish credibility early are rewarded with smoother sailing to closing.

Getting a jump on the due diligence process also paid off for another client who owned a company that manufactured apparel. In his case, he was party to over 350 licensing agreements (colleges, universities, etc.), most of which were non-transferable to the buyer without consent. Starting early allowed us to identify not only which agreements required consent, but also the party necessary to grant the consent – not always easy when dealing with large organizations with changing personnel. Once we were ready to obtain the transfer consents, we were able to do so in a matter of days. Had we waited until we had identified a buyer, the deal would have been placed on hold for months while the work was completed. During that time, for any number of reasons, the buyer could have walked away from the deal. Completing due diligence ahead of time streamlines the sale process.

Due diligence performed in advance offers the business owner another major benefit. In Question 47, we discuss the warranties and representations that a buyer will demand from a seller. As a seller, you should not warrant and represent anything unless a thorough due diligence of your company has been performed. For example, you cannot simply warrant that there is no threatened or pending litigation without first confirming this with your management team. You may not have been aware that an employee informed your Human Resources director that she had been sexually harassed. Do you need to disclose that conversation? Probably, yes. This is the type of issue that you and your attorneys will work through during the due diligence process. If the seller, in this example, warrants that there is no threatened litigation and this employee subsequently sues the new owner (the buyer), that buyer can bring suit against the seller for a breach of warranty and will probably win.

One final thought. If, while performing his own due diligence, the buyer's attorney discovers a critical issue involving the company that was not previously disclosed, he may make these assumptions – none of which is good for the seller. He either assumes that you intentionally misrepresented the facts or that you intentionally withheld material information; or he assumes that you don't know what is going on in your own company. Perhaps he will wonder what else has not been revealed to him. This serious credibility gap can stop a deal dead in its tracks. Do your due diligence early and do it thoroughly.

Question 47

What are warranties and representations?

Warranties and representations are statements of fact that a seller makes to a buyer about aspects of his company.

A buyer has a right to know everything about your business, from its inception through the date of closing. Even a buyer's most thorough due diligence will not convince him that he has uncovered everything he needs to know to feel comfortable moving forward with the deal and assuming the financial risk involved in buying your business. Buyers, therefore, look to the seller's warranties and representations to disclose every conceivable aspect of the business, i.e. taxes, litigation, governmental compliance, contractual obligations, title, etc. (See Appendix C for a list of standard warranties and representations.)

A seller's due diligence and warranties and representations go hand-in-hand. A seller must complete its own thorough due diligence to ensure that the warranties and representations he makes are accurate and complete. A misrepresentation of facts in a warranty and representation or a failure to disclose material facts will give the buyer a cause of action for breach of contract. A seller's worst nightmare is to receive a call (at his new home in Palm Springs) from his attorney six months post-closing. His attorney tells him that the buyer is threatening litigation because he has uncovered facts that were either misrepresented or not disclosed in the warranties and representation portion of the definitive purchase agreement.

"...my firm has developed a two-step process that minimizes the possibility of our sellers being successfully sued by unhappy buyers."

If you prepare your company properly for sale, you should not be sued successfully by a buyer for breach of a warranty or of a representation. Over the years, my firm has developed a two-step process that minimizes the possibility of our sellers being successfully sued by unhappy buyers. First, this process requires the seller and his management team to produce every item that our due diligence checklist calls for. (See Appendix B.) Our attorneys, working with the owner and management, identify and clarify any issues that may exist within the company. Issues related to each warranty or representation are listed on separate schedules. For example, a litigation representation would be accompanied by a schedule disclosing the status of any pending and/or threatened lawsuits.

Once everyone on the seller's Advisory Team is convinced that all of the information called for in the Due Diligence Checklist has been assembled, we take the second step. We meet with the seller and his complete management team to go through each warranty and each representation, word by word and line by line. This step is critical.

It never ceases to amaze me, but every time we conduct this meeting we always uncover new information that has not been previously revealed. A classic example is "threatened litigation." When asked this question, the owner will say there isn't any and then one member of the management team will say, "Oh. I just remembered. Three months ago a customer told one of our service representatives that if the problem was not fixed ASAP, he was going to sue!" The owner never knew (or simply forgot) about this. This situation must be disclosed on the Litigation Schedule. Only by bringing these critical people together in one room and forcing them to listen and to think about each warranty and representation will you flush out all matters that need to be disclosed in the definitive purchase agreement.

Yes, this is a tedious process, but it is well worth the time and effort. This process is the best insurance policy a transaction attorney can provide a seller. If this process is carefully followed and after closing an undisclosed matter pops up, in most cases, the matter in question is insignificant or immaterial.

The buyer's counsel will typically draft the warranties and representations. It is your attorney's job to negotiate as much leeway for you as possible. For example, if the warranty states categorically that the company is in compliance with all federal, state, and local laws, rules, regulations, orders, etc., your counsel will insert a "knowledge" qualifier. Your new warranty will state that "To the best of Seller's knowledge, the company is in compliance with all federal, state, and local laws, rules, regulations, orders, etc." In the alternative or in addition, your attorney will seek a "materiality" qualifier. In that case, your warranty states that, "To the best of Seller's knowledge, all contracts have been performed in all material respects and conforms with all federal, state, and local laws, rules, regulations, orders, etc."

It is impossible for any seller to represent that he is in compliance with all laws, rules, etc., for obvious reasons, not the least of which is that no owner can be totally sure that he is completely compliant with the vast number of laws, regulations, and rules administered by a number of jurisdictions in all of the places where he does business. If, after closing, it is found that the company is, in fact, violating some law and the seller's attorney has succeeded in inserting a knowledge qualifier, then the buyer must prove two things in order to sustain a claim against the seller. First, that the violation indeed occurred prior to closing and second, that the owner knew that the law had been violated. Proving the latter requires exposing the seller's "state of mind" at the time the representation was made. To say the least, this task is difficult. Often, it proves impossible. For this reason, knowledge and material qualifiers are crucial in protecting a seller.

Naturally, a buyer's attorney will resist the inclusion of qualifiers in the warranties and representations. He will argue that the buyer should not be exposed to or bear the risk resulting from any actions that occurred on the seller's watch (i.e. any time prior to closing). Further, he will argue that whether the seller had knowledge or not is irrelevant and the seller should bear the risk for his activities in operating the company.

When representing a seller, a skilled transaction attorney will always ask the buyer's attorney for qualifiers, even when his experience demonstrates that in certain cases, the buyer's counsel will rarely agree. The transaction attorney makes this attempt for two reasons. First, it helps him to gauge the experience level of the adversary. If the buyer's attorney is weak or inexperienced, he may give in. If, on the other hand, he steadfastly resists the inclusion of the qualifiers, your attorney "gives up" these points and in subsequent negotiations uses these "give ups" as reasons to secure the qualifiers he really wants. If present, you would hear him say to the buyer's attorney, "I gave you what you wanted on representations X, Y and Z. I must have the qualifiers I want on representations A, B and C."

Negotiating reasonable warranties and representations is a seller's attorney's greatest challenge. If done skillfully, you benefit greatly. If they are handled poorly, you are unnecessarily exposed and the deal itself may crater.

Question 48

What are conditions precedent or contingencies?

Conditions precedent or contingencies are requirements that the buyer wants to be satisfied before the buyer closes the deal. Unless they are satisfied, the buyer can walk from the transaction. From a buyer's perspective, the more contingencies he is able to negotiate into the definitive purchase agreement, the more flexibility he has. For example, should he be unhappy or uncomfortable with anything he discovers during the due diligence process, he can probably abandon the deal. For these reasons, it is in your best interest as a seller to thoroughly understand the buyer's contingencies and decide if you are willing to move forward with this particular buyer. As a seller, fewer contingencies are better than more.

DUE DILIGENCE CONTINGENCY

Contingencies that you can expect to find in almost all transactions are due diligence and financing. Buyers always insist on a due diligence contingency – one that gives them access to all records, documents, etc. and assures them they will find the company to be in the condition it has been represented to be. The buyer has the right to learn everything there is to know about the company.

Keep in mind that the buyer is legally bound to negotiate the transaction in good faith. If, in the course of his due diligence, he finds something that was not revealed to him or which has a materially adverse effect on him or the company, he can, in good faith and based on the due diligence contingency, walk away from the deal. If, on the other hand, something outside of his due diligence (e.g. a sudden change in the economy) makes him want to abandon the deal, he should not be allowed to walk away on the pretense that he was not satisfied with an item of due diligence. If this seems like a gray area, it is. It is very difficult for a seller to prove that a buyer who abandoned the deal did so in bad faith.

At one time, my firm represented a seller facing a buyer who refused to close on the grounds that his due diligence revealed that the company's fleet of vehicles had not been maintained with due care and that the cost of necessary repair was great. In fact, the seller believed that although there were repairs that could be made, they were not major.

During negotiations of the Letter of Intent, the buyer had failed to negotiate a financing contingency. (See below for a discussion of financing contingency.) We were confident that the real reason for the buyer's refusal to close was that his lender denied his financing package. The complaint about the vehicles was just a smoke screen. We concluded that, even though we had a strong case against the buyer for breach of contract and bad faith, protracted and expensive litigation did not serve the seller well. We allowed that buyer to squirm off the hook and shortly thereafter sold to one of our backup buyers. Your best protection in these situations is to always have more than one qualified buyer waiting in the wings.

FINANCING CONTINGENCY

The financing contingency appears in many transactions. It means that the entire transaction is contingent upon the buyer securing financing acceptable to him. Again, this issue can become problematic.

Is the buyer doing his best to secure financing or is he using financing as a reason to leave the negotiating table? This can be a tough call to make. For that reason, smart sellers learn everything they can about the buyer's financial condition as early in the process as possible. Your transaction intermediary should lead this investigation and should analyze the buyer's ability to secure financing. He should know what kind of financing is currently available and should assess whether the buyer is able to secure it. Keep in mind that neither buyer nor seller has any control over lenders. We are all subject to their demands.

ADDITIONAL CONTINGENCIES

Additional contingencies may include:
- *the opportunity to talk to key employees and customers;*
- *the ability to obtain all necessary licenses and consents (governmental, landlord, licensors, etc.);*
- *the successful negotiation of employment agreements and non-competes; and*
- *the absence of material adverse changes affecting the Seller.*

Your role as seller is to provide the due diligence information in an organized package while your transaction intermediary and transaction attorney push the buyer as hard as possible to satisfy and therefore remove these contingencies as soon as possible.

Question 49

What is an earn-out?

*A*n earn-out is a post-closing performance-based formula used to bridge the valuation gap between buyers and sellers. In most transactions, both buyer and seller determine value by projecting the future cash flow and earnings of the company. Assume that you are asking $10 million and the buyer is only willing to pay $6.5 million. An earn-out can be used to bridge this gap. The buyer will agree to pay the full $10 million or more, if, over the next X years, the company achieves agreed upon earnings benchmarks.

For example, let's suppose that after closing, a company performs at a level that the seller projected but that the buyer thought was optimistic or even unlikely. According to the terms of the earn-out, the buyer then pays the seller additional money. The seller gets paid for the additional value he knew was in the company. If, on the other hand, a company fails to perform as projected by the seller, the buyer pays nothing extra to the seller.

Earn-out negotiations cover more than just value. The parties negotiate about:

- *timeframes (how long does the company have to reach certain goals?);*
- *how to measure performance;*
- *whether there is a maximum amount that will be paid;*
- *what restrictions will be placed on the seller's ability to operate the company during the earn-out process; and*
- *the allocation of overhead.*

These last two issues are critical. Sellers are generally unable to achieve earn-outs if the buyer's management style is too restrictive and/or out of sync with the seller's corporate culture. Similarly, if the buyer is operating multiple divisions in addition to the seller's company, it is normal to allocate a portion of division and corporate headquarters' overhead to seller's income statement. This will result in a hit to a seller's earnings and makes it more difficult for the seller to achieve the earn-out thresholds.

In most scenarios, we caution sellers to avoid earn-outs unless they are confident that at closing, they will receive the amount of money that satisfies their definitions of wealth and personal freedom. Any money a seller receives later via the earn-out should be considered icing on the cake.

The drafting of an earn-out provision requires a great deal of skill and understanding of legal, tax, financial, and accounting principles. Make sure your transaction attorney is experienced in this area during the initial interview process.

Question 50

What is a cap?

When choosing an attorney to represent you in a sale, ask him how he approaches the issue of caps. A cap is contained in the definitive purchase agreement and is a negotiated limit (or cap) on a seller's liability to a buyer resulting from a breach of warranties or representations.

A skilled transaction attorney should successfully negotiate, at a minimum, a cap that does not exceed the purchase price you receive. Most sellers don't realize that they can be held liable for more than the purchase price they receive. Attorneys in my firm try to negotiate for a cap lower than the purchase price and are frequently successful in doing so. The attractive seller usually obtains a lower cap.

Conceptually, buyers do not like caps. For example, if a buyer pays you $10 million for your company and later is found to be liable for $15 million on a successor liability theory (let's say an environmental claim), he would like to be able to recover his total damages ($15 million) from you. Your attorney will argue that you would rarely be held liable for the

$15 million in your personal and individual capacity as a shareholder of your company (this is one of the reasons you incorporated) and that he will not expose you to this liability now as a seller. Knowledgeable transaction attorneys usually reach a compromise on this issue quickly. Having said that, when representing buyers, I am amazed at the number of sellers' attorneys who fail to even ask for a cap.

Question 51

What is a basket?

A basket is a deductible dollar amount contained in the definitive purchase agreement that is intended to prevent a buyer from "nickel and diming" the seller every time the buyer believes he has a monetary claim against the seller. A seller's attorney will negotiate for a higher threshold dollar amount with the stipulation that once buyer's actual damages reach that threshold, the buyer will only be entitled to the excess. For example, if the basket is $50,000, the buyer's claim will not ripen until his damages are $50,001. Even then, he will only be entitled to $1. A buyer's attorney will negotiate for a lower basket with the stipulation that once the threshold dollar amount is reached, the buyer will be entitled to recover all damages from dollar one.

I am often asked if there is a standard basket amount, perhaps a percentage of the purchase price. Generally speaking, the answer is no. The greater the purchase price, however, the larger the basket. Experienced attorneys generally negotiate the basket issue fairly quickly.

Question 52

Will I have to personally indemnify the buyer?

Simple answer: "Yes."

Whether your transaction is structured as an asset or stock sale, you and other significant owners will, as individuals, have to indemnify the buyer for breaches of warranties and representations if a buyer's damages exceed the cap. This makes sense.

If your corporation sells its assets for $5 million, the purchase price will be paid to the corporation. The corporation will then distribute the purchase price to its owners, leaving the corporation without assets. Buyers like to know that they can seek to recover damages from the ultimate beneficiary of the purchase price – you, the seller. This is why it is critical that your attorney negotiate strongly for reasonable warranties and representations as well as a suitable cap and basket.

Indemnification provisions in the definitive purchase agreement can be complex and often tricky. Your transaction attorney should review these provisions very carefully to ensure that buyer's counsel, through calculated drafting, has not reinstated your personal exposure to a level greater than that which your attorney negotiated earlier in the definitive purchase agreement.

Question 53

Will I be required to sign a consulting/employment agreement?

Simple answer: "Yes."

*I*n my experience, nearly every buyer has required the seller to stay with the company post-closing for a negotiated period of time. The length of that period usually depends on a number of factors, not the least of which is the seller's preference. Some choose to leave as soon as possible; others stay with the company well through its transition.

Your flexibility in this matter positively affects both the purchase price and the probability that the deal will close. When a seller announces that he plans to leave the business immediately after closing, regardless of whether the buyer needs him or not, a buyer becomes uncomfortable. How uncomfortable depends on several factors.

First, if your company is running smoothly because there is a competent management team in place, a buyer will be more amenable to your early departure. The buyer may require that you stay only 90 days, on a part-time basis, to make the necessary introductions to key accounts, to educate the buyer about unique aspects of your business, or to complete a special project already in process. If, on the other hand, the company is short on seasoned management and you are perceived as "the business," the buyer will have serious reservations about letting you go prematurely.

Second, if the buyer of your company is a knowledgeable industry player, you will not need to spend time educating him about the industry. Consequently, he will demand less of your time than will a buyer who is not familiar with your industry. You will probably spend most of your time introducing the buyer to your key vendors and customers.

The critical question is: "What do you want to do?" Some sellers want to stay with the new company after closing because they like the work and they want to help move the company to the next level. (You will read in Part Eight about several sellers who took this approach.) Buyers typically receive this news with open arms as they are happy to see the person who made the business successful continue on with the company. This is truly a win-win situation for both buyer and seller. The seller gets to continue playing the game – with someone else's money – and typically experiences his first uninterrupted night of sleep since he got into business. In return, the buyer receives (and is usually willing to pay handsomely for): the smoothest possible transition, the benefit of the seller's experience, knowledge of the industry, relationship with the employees, and understanding of future growth opportunities.

I recall the case of a seller who was willing to stay with his company for five years after closing. He received a premium purchase price at closing as well as a generous compensation package. He lived off his compensation, leaving the purchase proceeds prudently invested and untouched for five years. After five years, he left the company, having achieved his goals while his invested purchase proceeds had almost doubled in value. This was truly a great result.

In another deal, one of the two sellers announced his post-closing plans to buy a motorcycle and relocate immediately to Florida. The other seller wanted to stay on to transform the company into a major industry player. Both sellers got exactly what they wanted. I occasionally receive postcards from sun drenched beaches from the first while the second received an extremely fair compensation package complete with stock options and warrants.

In this case, both sellers drafted their own post-closing scenarios and the buyer accepted. Why? These sellers had the leverage. Their company was in great shape, it was the largest of its kind in Colorado, and they were in an industry that hungry consolidators hotly pursued. When you enjoy that kind of advantage, no matter how valuable you are to the buyer, if it is necessary to close the deal, the buyer allows you to leave. Conversely, if you do not hold all of the cards, you will have to be flexible in your post-closing tenure, duties, and compensation.

Finally, it is not unusual to find that after "living together" for a period of time after closing, the parties agree that things are not working the way they had envisioned and that the agreement should be prematurely terminated. In this case, the seller negotiates for the buyer to "buy out" his employment agreement and the seller is on his way out the door. Negotiations also focus on the seller's existing no compete. The length of time that the seller has been out of the marketplace while working for the buyer will influence how the buyer deals with the no compete. If you are bought out of your employment agreement early, expect the no compete to remain in effect for its stated duration.

Question 54

Is a covenant not to compete enforceable?

Simple answer: "Yes."

As a seller, your company and you as an individual will have to sign a covenant not to compete. No buyer will pay you handsomely and then allow you to open for business across the street. In every state, statutes and/or case law govern the enforceability of covenants not to compete. In Colorado, covenants not to compete are enforceable when associated with the sale of a business.

In order to be enforceable in Colorado, however, the covenant not to compete must be: (1) reasonable as to length of time; (2) reasonable as to geographical proscription; and (3) reasonable as to the scope of the prohibition on competition. For example, a covenant not to compete in the same business and the same geographical area that the seller has conducted business will probably be enforceable if the timeframe is reasonable. Courts are generally comfortable with three to five years. Time periods longer than five years can be risky. Restricting a former business owner from competing with his former business anywhere in the world and until death would not be enforceable. That would be unreasonable.

> "Beware of the overzealous covenant."

Beware of the overzealous covenant. That is the one that restricts your activity in any industry that the buyer may be engaged in now or at any time in the future. Sellers negotiating with large conglomerates are most likely to see this type of covenant. In this situation, a seller should limit the covenant to the business in which he is currently engaged and then to industries in which the buyer is currently engaged that have a logical correlation to the company being acquired. Which brings us to the second important fact.

As a seller aggressively seeks to limit the terms of a covenant not to compete, a buyer may become convinced that the seller's real intent is to go back into head-to-head competition. That's why covenants not to compete are the Catch-22s of many sale transactions. The harder you resist the terms of a proposed covenant, the more restrictive your buyer's covenant may become. Therefore, if you truly never intend to go back to work in your industry, be flexible – but not stubborn.

Discuss the covenant not to compete carefully with your attorney. Be honest with him and with yourself regarding your future plans. If you are a youthful seller, with many potential years of work in your future, don't get caught up in the euphoria of the deal and capitulate too easily. Many sellers have thanked me for negotiating firmly on the short term and limited definition of "competition." These sellers surprised themselves when they discovered that they missed "being in the hunt" and could not wait to return to the fray. In one case, a 38-year-old seller opened up the exact business within three months of the expiration of his three-year no compete. He watched the national consolidator that bought his company make every mistake imaginable for three years. He was eager to start up again, picking up former employees and customers who begged him to return. The company he is currently building is outperforming his buyer and will ultimately sell for more than his first.

If you are a more "mature" seller and the sale of your company will yield more money than you will ever need, you may feel certain that nothing could lure you back into battle. If that is the case, you do not need to negotiate your covenant not to compete as vigorously.

It is not uncommon for a seller to simultaneously operate similar but distinct businesses. For example, an owner may be a manufacturer as well as a distributor of a product. In this case, the owner/seller will attempt to negotiate an exception or a "carve-out" from the no compete for that business he is not selling. Negotiating carve-outs is tricky. Buyers don't like them unless the language is clear that the seller will not be competing with the business the buyer is acquiring. If you are contemplating a carve-out, say so at the commencement of negotiations. Bringing up a carve-out later in the negotiation process will inevitably create suspicion and nervous apprehension.

One final note. If you are carrying back a promissory note, make it clear that your no compete dissolves if the buyer fails to pay off his note. You will want unfettered access to return to your company or to start up a new company.

Question 55

How can a charitable remainder trust eliminate taxes?

Creating a Charitable Remainder Trust (CRT) is a planning technique that can be used to avoid the burdensome tax consequences of a stock sale. In fact, a seller can avoid all taxation on the sale of his stock (or a significant portion of the taxes on a sale of a "C" corporation) if he is willing to donate the proceeds of the sale to charity. Here's how it works.

The business owner, anticipating the sale of his company, funds this irrevocable trust with the stock of his company. At its creation, he designates: (1) the annuity rate (or designated pay out); (2) the individuals who will receive the pay out (generally the owner and his wife); (3) the time period for which the trust will last (for example, the joint life expectancy of the owner and his wife); and (4) the charity that will be the ultimate beneficiary of the proceeds.

Prior to any sale, the owner transfers his stock to the CRT – which transfer is exempt from tax and also triggers a charitable income tax deduction. While this deduction is indeed taken in the year during which the stock is transferred to the CRT, the amount of the deduction is the remainder interest of the value that is given to charity, which in simple terms is generally determined by subtracting the present value of the intervening time period (usually the life expectancy of the creator) from the original value of the contributed stock.

> "The CRT must be established prior to signing the definitive sale contract or the CRT will be deemed invalid."

When a buyer makes an offer to purchase the stock, it is purchased from the CRT, and the CRT (now the owner and tax-exempt entity) pays no capital gains tax. It is important to emphasize the sequence of events. The CRT must be established prior to signing the definitive sale contract or the CRT will be deemed invalid.

Once the CRT receives the sale proceeds from the buyer at closing, the former business owner (now trustee) invests the proceeds with the goal of achieving the pay out designated at the trust's creation. The trust then pays a lifetime payment to the beneficiary of the CRT. When these payments are received, they are then taxed. If the trust does not achieve an interest rate sufficient to meet the pay out rate, the CRT can draw upon principal to make that pay out for the rest of the former owner's life and that of his spouse.

The CRT technique is not for everyone but it does have several distinct advantages. In addition to avoiding the capital gains taxes mentioned earlier, it increases the amount of money available for investment by as much as 50 percent. For example, if an owner sells a company for $3 million, after paying taxes he nets $2.25 million. With a CRT, that same owner will have the full $3 million to invest.

I've already mentioned the income tax deduction earned in the year the contribution of stock is made. There is also the advantage of estate tax avoidance. When the owner and his wife die, their heirs will pay no estate taxes on the sale proceeds because these proceeds belonged to the trust, not to the parents. To parents who object that in this scenario there is no money to pass to their children, I suggest that they purchase a second to die life insurance policy to be owned by an irrevocable life insurance trust. Upon the death of the second parent, the children will receive the insurance proceeds – tax-free.

Again, this technique is not a one-size-fits-all plan. There are more ways to modify and to tailor the effects of CRTs than can be mentioned here. Simply stated, a business owner should not overlook this important tool when considering his long-term financial goals. If you think that you might be interested in using a CRT, you must speak to your attorney before entering into any type of agreement – even a preliminary non-binding Letter of Intent.

PART 8 | FORMER OWNERS REFLECT ON WEALTH AND FREEDOM

I have been fortunate in my law career to have represented many wonderful business owners. These entrepreneurs have experienced the wide range of emotions that are part of starting, growing, and selling a successful business. They are hard-working visionaries who made the personal and financial sacrifices necessary to build profitable companies. They made their own luck; nothing was given to them. They built their companies and sold them for premium purchase prices. They have achieved their definition of wealth and freedom.

When I interviewed these owners about their experiences during the sale process and about how their lives had changed afterwards, they were eager to share their perspectives. They want their fellow entrepreneurs to know the relief, joy, and satisfaction they experience on a daily basis now that they have achieved financial independence. I am confident that you will relate well to their stories and I hope that you will be inspired to take the actions necessary to achieve your definition of wealth and freedom.

Dan Haney
Good Decal, Inc.

The ultimate family success story.

In 1963, Charles Haney started Good Decal, Inc., a silk screen printing business.

For the next five years, he produced decals for car dealerships on a hand press in his home. Over the next 35 years, his product line expanded to include a wide variety of silk screen pressure-sensitive and sunlight impervious decals that adhered to surfaces such as glass windows and doors, computers, PBX systems, tractors, and motorcycle helmets.

Dan Haney, Chuck's son, started working for the company when he was 16 and continued with the company until it was sold in 1998. Nine of Chuck's ten children worked in the business at one time or another. When Dan was 26, he and his father agreed that Dan would run the company full time while Chuck would handle the company's finances. The wisdom of this choice was validated as the company grew steadily over the next 10 years.

Beginning in 1975, Chuck gave stock each year to the children working in the company. Dan always received twice as much stock as his siblings with the understanding that Dan would never receive controlling interest. Dan's siblings agreed to this plan and the entire family met at Chuck's home for monthly board of directors meetings. On rare occasions when the Board was deadlocked, Dan would cast the deciding vote. Thirty-three straight years of increased revenues and profits was proof of Dan's leadership and family consensus.

At age 48, Dan reached his burn out point and knew that there were other things he wanted to do with his life. Running a family business with multiple siblings as employees was rewarding, but exhausting. With his family's consent, Dan decided the time was right to sell.

"I called Ned after reading his partner John Brown's book, *How To Run Your Business So You Can Leave It In Style.* I was very nervous at our first meeting because my entire family's interest was at stake and I was not comfortable with lawyers. Ned put me at ease while explaining the entire sale process. He introduced me to an investment banker. Shortly thereafter, Ned met the rest of my family and we put the company on the market.

"Although I had confidence in my Team of Advisors, it was still a scary process," Dan recalls. "I was especially concerned that non-family employees would discover my plans or that the sale price would not match my expectations. I realized, however, that unless I engaged in the process, I would never know how much my company was worth. On the positive side, I enjoyed my role in the 'dog and pony show' (meeting with prospective buyers to tell the story of my company). It was fun and challenging to answer the numerous questions potential buyers (and their advisors) posed. I was well prepared for these encounters."

The controlled auction process proved the ideal vehicle for the sale of Dan's company. One bidder, a large printer in the U.S. with revenues of $1.5 billion, was a strategic buyer. It competed against a financial buyer that wanted to acquire and use GDI as a platform company to consolidate the silk-screening industry. Dan ultimately selected this buyer because he liked the strategic fit and because the buyer agreed to retain all of Dan's employees. "It was important to me that my employees keep their jobs."

When the buyer made its offer, Dan instructed his investment banker to accept. The investment banker, however, believed that the best offer had not yet been made. "He asked for 24 hours to negotiate further. During that time, he convinced the buyer to significantly raise its offer. When I closed, I was glad I'd allowed my investment banker to follow his instincts, thrilled with the ultimate pay off and relieved to see the process come to a successful close."

When Dan reflects on the year he spent engaged in the sale process, he says that he performed "some of the best work of my entire working career." He also credits the "creative combination of talent" that his advisors brought to the process. "If you are going to sell your company, it is critical to have a strong investment banker and law firm on your side."

> "If you are going to sell your company, it is critical to have a strong investment banker and law firm on your side."

After the closing, Dan worked for the buyer for two years. In return, he received an excellent compensation package and did not draw on his sale proceeds. Although the buyer asked him to continue on as an employee, Dan recognized that he had "had enough" and was ready to leave the company.

The first thing Dan describes when asked about life immediately after the sale is that "the weariness created by the day-to-day challenges of running the business disappears. I felt that I was starting life all over again…this time without the pressure of running a business. I wake up every day without feeling any pressure whatsoever. The anxiety that one feels when running a business is strong but you learn to live with it. Once out from under that cloud, it is a huge relief." To this day Dan retains his enthusiasm for life without pressure. "While I sometimes miss the people I worked with, I would never go back to running a company again."

Today, Dan spends a lot of time managing his sale proceeds. "This takes a great deal of time and research but I truly enjoy doing it. I also feel great knowing that my wife doesn't have to work unless she elects to do so."

Dan offers this advice to owners contemplating a sale: "Be patient with the process so you don't leave money on the table. There were a couple of times when I grew anxious and considered stopping the process altogether. I overcame these anxieties and realized the need to be patient in order to understand all of the ramifications of the deal. Had I not had the support of my attorney and investment banker, I probably would have backed out of the deal."

> "...once you receive a valuation of your company that meets your long term financial goals and objectives, ...think very carefully about selling."

Dan believes that "deep down, most business owners truly want to sell their companies." He advises these owners that "once you receive a valuation of your company that meets your long term financial goals and objectives, you should think very carefully about selling. If I hadn't sold when I did (June 1998), I would not have been able to command the same purchase price. My timing was perfect."

Since leaving the company, Dan has enjoyed a wide variety of activities. "I was able to attend every sporting event that my son participated in during his final two years of high school." He has traveled extensively, taken cruises, bought a mountain home, and built a new house. "I paid off all of my debt and live debt-free," a lifestyle Dan fully intends to continue.

Dan derives his greatest satisfaction from the fact that through the sale, his parents and siblings also achieved financial independence and freedom. "Dad is ecstatic. This was the best thing for all of my family members. For the first time, they have the financial capability to do exactly what they want. A great result, don't you agree?"

Harry Mathews
Mark VII Equipment, Inc.

Preparation wins the race.

*I*n 1967, Harry Mathews was a salesman for the owner of a car wash. It was his job to sell car-washing equipment to oil companies that would be installed in their gas stations. In 1972, his boss retired, leaving Harry with the business but no funds. Harry obtained a line of credit and continued to sell car washing equipment.

In 1977, Harry decided that in addition to selling other companies' equipment he would sell a product that he had developed, the Bubble Brush. "This was a very hot product. It was a foaming brush that individuals could use to wash their own cars." In 1984, Harry bought a car wash manufacturing company because he recognized the ever-increasing demand for self-service car washes and high-pressure automatic car wash machines.

In 1988, Harry's newest product, Aqua-Jet, was a breakthrough in the industry. It was compact and used less

"When I learned what they thought they could sell my company for, any emotional reservations I had had about keeping the company disappeared."

water and energy than other units. Harry continued to fine tune this machine. In 1994, Harry was doing $40 million in sales and was debt free. Although he had no desire to sell, Harry attended one of my firm's seminars on the need to develop an exit strategy and became intrigued by the prospect of selling. "Based upon Ned's recommendation, I retained an investment banker to do a valuation. I wanted to know what my company might sell for on the open market. When I learned what they thought they could sell my company for, any emotional reservations I had had about keeping the company disappeared. Selling my company became purely a business proposition."

At closing, Harry received all cash. He retained 20 percent ownership of the company and all of the real estate upon which the business operated. "It was, without any doubt, a great deal for me."

During the sale process, there were times when Harry wanted to abandon the deal. One was when word got out that he was selling. "This was very frustrating for me. I didn't want anyone to know that my company was for sale. Fortunately, my transaction team knew how to handle this situation and Ned did a great job of damage control." Another was during the due diligence process – a process that drove Harry nuts. "After seeing Ned's due diligence checklist, I thought I could never sell!" Even after accepting the length and level of detail, "I was frustrated by the exacting pace of the due diligence process. I came to realize, however, that while due diligence is long and painful, it is a necessary evil. In the end, it is the due diligence that protects you from false claims that a buyer may raise after the closing." Harry warns other owners, "Don't try to hide anything. They will find it. When they do, your deal is dead."

Today Harry experiences no seller's regrets. He never looks back and wonders, What if? "The sale was great for my entire family. My wife tells me that I am much easier to get along with now that I am not dealing with 300 employees. The sale enabled me to pay off all personal debt. This meant a great deal to me. The money I received at closing more than satisfied my definition of personal financial independence."

Harry describes the first six months post-sale as "blissful." "There was nothing I had to do. We bought a house in Scottsdale, Arizona and Chris, my wife, promptly flew there to purchase all the furnishings and supplies that she had always wanted. My children benefited from the sale as well and began to pursue their dreams in earnest." Meanwhile,

Harry traveled around the country adding exotic vintage race cars to his already renowned collection. "It really was a fun time for the entire Mathews family!" (You can see his cars at www.mathewscollection.com.)

Harry continues to enjoy his international reputation as a collector of McLaren race cars. According to *The Mathews Collection*, a recent publication of Coterie Press, "With its special emphasis on the legendary McLarens, the Harry Mathews collection of racing cars is one of the best in the world." Harry, his son, and son-in-law drive these cars in vintage races held around the world. Harry houses his collection in two buildings covering 35,000 square feet.

In Harry's life after the sale, he has combined this love of cars with his entrepreneurial talents by forming a new company that sells vintage race cars to enthusiasts around the world.

On the home front, Harry has created a new routine that keeps him out of the house from 7:00 a.m. until nearly 5:00 p.m. "I enjoy being busy." Like other former owners, he has little difficulty finding activities and interests – outside of business – to stimulate his mind. He manages his commercial real estate properties and is currently contemplating the purchase of another business related to the car washing industry.

Once a driver, always a driver.

William Clymor
Imperial Headwear, Inc.

Planning for the Day After.

Unlike any seller I have ever worked with, Bill Clymor had loads of experience in the world of mergers and acquisitions. Prior to acquiring his own company, Bill had sought out and orchestrated the purchase of companies for a Chicago-based organization. In

1982, Bill decided to become an entrepreneur and acquired a Denver company, Imperial Headwear. At that time, annual revenues were approximately $1.2 million. The company applied logo patches to caps in one of four colors: tan, white, blue, and red. Its primary customers were golf and ski companies.

In 1983, Bill began to investigate embroidering directly onto the caps and sold his first order to Cherry Hills Country Club in Denver, Colorado. The concept took off at the PGA trade show and what started as a one-machine investment soon grew to 40 machines as the demand for embroidered caps exploded.

Soon after Bill pioneered the embroidery idea, he began to expand the palette of cap colors. No longer limited to just four, Imperial Headwear offered vendors a multitude of colors (including neons), as well as new cap and embroidery styles. *Golf Digest* designated Imperial Headwear's caps "Number One" in quality and style.

Bill established several exit goals when he acquired his business. "First, I wanted to retire by age 55. Second, I wanted to generate in excess of $50 million in retail sales." By 1993, Bill was 53 years old and had achieved his retail sales goal. In addition, "I realized that to move the company to the next level, I would need to invest $10 million, build a new building, acquire new equipment, and set up a new plant outside of Colorado. Being a stickler for quality control I didn't see how I could consistently apply my high standards to a plant in another location."

"After Ned and I reviewed my goals and future, I knew that my options were to sell the company, borrow millions, or take the company public. Ned and I discussed these options with my accountant and investment banker at length over the course of a year." Bill seriously investigated the possibility of taking the company public but in the end decided that he did not want to work for five more years for a new owner.

Once Bill decided to sell his company to a third party, he gave us, his team of Team of Advisors, clear instructions. He let us know how much money he wanted, when he wanted to leave, and what type of company he wanted to sell to. With that, he told us to call him if we had any questions but that he would concentrate on running his company.

Several months later, after a successful controlled auction, we met at the closing table and closed a deal that left Bill free from financial worries. Today he recalls the entire sale process as "one of the most enjoyable experiences of my life because I had a competent team managing the process." He admits that he did "collapse" after the closing "high" but has never experienced seller's remorse.

> "Some of the best advice I ever received was from a friend who told me to find a new office before selling my company."

Bill predicted that he would need a place to go – other than home – after the sale so he had located and furnished an office in an executive suite. "Some of the best advice I ever received was from a friend who told me to find a new office before selling my company. He was right. Having an office and a desk smoothed the transition to my new life." From his office, Bill manages his portfolio, plans future trips, and advises other owners as they navigate the transition from owner to former owner. Bill has held fast to his financial principle regarding his sale proceeds. "I decided I would never touch half of the principal; I would only play with or invest the other half. This discipline has worked well for me."

Since the closing, Bill has "retired" to a life complete with a new education and new hobbies. Bill has educated himself on investment management and in the world of computers. He is now competent in both. He spends four to five hours every day studying, reviewing, and tweaking his investments. In addition, Bill has purchased several homes, horses, and motorcycles. He is now able to golf at non-peak times and can concentrate on reducing his handicap. He and his wife travel at least two months of the year. Not surprisingly, Bill reports that his health at 61 is the "best ever" as is his relationship with his wife.

Bill is frequently contacted by owners contemplating a future sale and reports that the first question they all ask is "What am I going to do after the sale?" With no hesitation, Bill can answer that, "If the sale yields financial independence, worry or boredom will never be part of a former owner's 'retirement.' He believes that owners "will become busy doing all of the things they always wanted to do as well enjoying many new experiences."

Bill's experience in mergers and acquisitions certainly gave him a leg up in choosing his transaction advisors. His confidence in his team paid off as he was free to focus on running his company and to prepare for life after the sale.

Frank and Mike Barone
Barone, Inc.

Two brothers, one success story.

Frank Barone, his father, and brother, Mike, started Barone, Inc. in 1953 as equal partners. Frank's father made his sons owners at the outset because he wanted them to take on the responsibilities that accompany ownership. Their company manufactured and marketed vacuum excavating equipment used primarily to excavate around and near existing underground utilities without harming the utilities. According to Frank, their company performed "arthroscopic surgery in the dirt" in order to locate gas, fiber optic, water, sewer, power, or cable lines.

In 1960 the Barones performed contract manufacturing for other companies including VacMasters. In 1995, Frank and Mike bought out

VacMasters because they believed they could significantly grow that business. Over the next five years, Frank and Mike focused on building and selling this product line. When the Barones bought VacMasters, it had annual revenues of $1.7 million. When they sold VacMasters in 2001, the annual revenues had grown to $13.5 million and 50 percent of its revenues were attributable to the telecommunications industry.

What was it that caused the Barones to sell? First, age. In their mid-60s, they recognized that they wouldn't live forever and were growing more aware of their own mortality. They also knew that if one of them died, the other did not want to continue in the business. They anticipated that running the company solo would prove emotionally too difficult. In addition, a death of either brother would create huge estate tax issues.

Frank's biggest fear about the sale process was that an attempt to sell the business might fail. As he saw it, a failed attempt would mean that the brothers would be forced to keep the company until one of them died. At that point, the survivor would likely have to liquidate the assets. Like most sellers, both brothers had serious concerns about confidentiality. "We wanted to keep any rumors of a sale from reaching our employees."

"In an effort to maximize our chances of successfully selling our company and maintaining confidentiality, we retained Ned and his firm. Ned told me that we needed to retain an investment banker as well. We did so and eleven months passed from the time we started the sale process to closing. We engaged four potential buyers in a controlled auction that led to a purchase price that greatly exceeded our expectations."

Once Frank and Mike made the decision to sell, they did not look back. "We had thought through our options carefully." As one of their exit objectives, Frank and Mike decided that they did not want to enter into employment contracts with the buyer although they were willing to make a gentlemen's agreement that they would continue to work part-time as long as it was mutually beneficial. This unusual compromise suited the Barone brothers perfectly because it enabled them to devote substantial time to their own non-company interests.

> "The successful sale of our business validated what my entire business career had been about."

After the sale, Frank felt that "a great weight had been lifted from my shoulders. I compare the feeling – in intensity and quality – to what John Elway must have felt after winning the Super Bowl. It was a rare combination of euphoria and intense personal satisfaction. The successful sale of our business validated what my entire business career had been about." As it turned out, Frank's timing was critical. The telecom industry collapsed after the sale in May of 2001, resulting in a decrease in revenues for VacMaster.

Frank now enjoys the best of both worlds. "My financial chips are off the table and I am involved in the business for enjoyment rather than survival." He maintains an easy balance between pursuing other interests and running the company. He realizes that this formula would not suit sellers who wish to leave behind their management duties.

Frank is currently the cause of his neighbors' acute cases of "garage envy." "I am personally supervising the construction of a 1,200 square foot garage. This is something I have always wanted to do." Just as he built his company, he is building his garage brick by brick.

Frank also owns four weeks in beachfront condominiums in Cabo San Lucas, Mexico. He and his wife travel there frequently. "We especially enjoy taking our children and grandchildren with us. Spending quality time like this is simply wonderful."

Frank feels blessed, lucky, and grateful that his life has gone the way it has. "I will be 70 this year and I enjoy good health and can afford to do what I want, when I want."

Similarly, Mike derives a great deal of satisfaction from working. "I have always enjoyed the discipline, challenge and sense of accomplishment involved in building Barone, Inc. Selling the company, however, has allowed me the best of both worlds. I continue to do the satisfying work I have always loved but in a more relaxed and less demanding fashion." Mike's financial future is secure, and he relishes "taking time off when I want to. I have everything I want and nobody gives me grief. Who could ask for anything more?"

The Barones are an excellent example of a family who successfully orchestrated a very rewarding exit strategy.

Bob Quinette
Staff Administrators, Inc.
You are never too young to sell.

*I*n 1991, Bob Quinette and his partner, each with a background in human resources, formed Staff Administrators, Inc. They had some exposure to what, at that time, was a relatively new concept known as "employee leasing." An employee leasing company provides its customers with payroll services, workers' compensation insurance, and other employee benefit packages.

"I believed that businesses wanted more than just the basic menu of services," recalls Bob. "My partner and I felt that businesses wanted to insulate themselves from potential employee-related liabilities." Faced with new and constantly evolving regulations related to workplace issues (health, discrimination, and family leave), employers realized that they were exposed to liabilities in ways they had never imagined. "We believed that unless these companies could devote significant funds to maintain state of the art human resource departments, it would be difficult to stay abreast of the ever-changing world of employer/employee relationships."

It was in this niche that Bob and his partner saw great opportunities. Staff Administrators not only offered the "traditional" employee leasing services, it also provided full human resource management services, including risk management. In doing so, Bob and his partner became pioneers in a new industry called Professional Employer Organizations (PEO). As a PEO, Staff Administrators assumed total responsibility for all of their clients' employees. The employees became Staff Administrators' employees. If an employee made a claim against his employer, the claim was brought against Staff Administrators.

When Bob, at age 27 and his partner, at age 36, started the company, their goal was to build and sell the company within five years. At the five-year mark, Staff Administrators had over 3,000 employees under management and was generating $100 million per year in revenues. It was named Colorado Business of the Year and *Inc. Magazine* listed it as the 124th fastest growing company in the U.S. With this track record, Bob's partner believed that Staff Administrators was poised for a sale.

Bob was less interested in selling but was intrigued by the overtures constantly being made by large, publicly-traded companies seeking acquisition opportunities. Bob and his partner agreed to put the company on the market using a controlled auction. "The consolidators bid the price up to a point where we couldn't afford not to sell," recalls Bob.

When asked what his thoughts were at closing, Bob replies that "the money simply didn't seem to be real. The magnitude of the purchase price simply did not register." He also remembers his concern about how "his employees would react to the sale, and how much freedom" he would have to continue to run the company.

While Bob's partner had made it clear at the outset that he had no desire to work post-closing, Bob did wish to continue working to make

Staff Administrators an industry leader. Bob ran the company for 18 months after closing until he was forced to retire due to an accident and the resulting surgeries. Clearly, this was not how Bob envisioned his departure from Staff Administrators, but he realized that he was ready to leave the company and "move on with his life."

In the first few months, Bob and his family had to adjust to his presence around the house during the normal working hours. "I was concerned about what I was going to do with myself. I had never truly imagined that I would have obtained my business goals by age 33. When I was around my wife and children, I acted more like a boss than a husband or a father. In the business world, I was used to giving orders and having them carried out. I knew that I needed to change my attitude when my wife not-so-gently reminded me that she was not my employee and that our home was as much her office as it was mine."

> "I stopped worrying about what would fill my time. I quickly found myself so busy that I wondered how I had ever gotten anything done while working."

Bob's four-year-old son delivered a similarly candid message, remarking that Bob was just "too bossy." Bob quickly took the hint. He recognized that the amount of time he now had available to spend with his family presented great opportunity to develop new and deeper relationships with his wife and children.

"After those first few months," recalls Bob, "I stopped worrying about what would fill my time. I quickly found myself so busy that I wondered how I had ever gotten anything done while working." Bob's family truly loved having him at home. "I love the absolute freedom to do whatever I want to do at any time. I especially savor being a full-time dad."

Bob began to add more and more activities to his schedule. He played golf two days each week, involved himself in charitable activities, church, and continued serving as the Chairman of the Board of the Denver Metro Better Business Bureau. He constantly receives inquiries from former employees and customers asking him to start another PEO. Having been away from the fray for a while, Bob knows that he does not want to "devote the hours required to run a business my way." Bob is not willing to give up his freedom and admits that he just has "too many other fish to fry."

When asked for his advice to owners contemplating a sale, Bob relates that the best advice he received was "when Ned told me to keep focused on operating the business during the sale process. Let your advisors handle the sale. If you begin to see dollar signs too soon, it's easy to become distracted and take your eye off running your company. Cross the finish line first, and then celebrate your success." Now, at age 37, Bob has plenty of time left to celebrate.

Dick Henkle
Henkle Drilling & Supply, Inc.

Flying high and serving others: Living debt-free and loving it.

In 1938, E.W. Henkle founded Henkle & Company of Garden City, Kansas. Attracted by a vision of irrigated farmland in southwest Kansas, Henkle entered an industry in its infancy. Much of our nation's breadbasket had been cultivated as "dry land," a technique that proved disastrous in the 1930s. E.W. used this vision to inspire Kansas farmers who owned acreage suitable for irrigation. He convinced them to look to the future, forget the past, and turn their unproductive land into a producing asset for themselves, their nation, and future generations.

The opening of World War II prompted E.W. to offer his drilling expertise to the many Army Air Bases in surrounding states. Each base required a reliable water supply and each needed vast miles of security fencing. Along with the contracts for water systems for the various air bases, E.W. drilled hundreds of thousands of postholes quickly and efficiently. When not one of the postholes ever produced a drop of water, E.W. earned the nickname "Dry Hole Henkle."

After the war, E.W.'s company was well-prepared to meet the huge need for irrigation. Henkle purchased his own drilling and pump installation equipment and increased his network of small independent contractors who could add capacity when required.

This was the business in which E.W.'s two sons, Jim and Dick, grew up. Both boys swept the shop and warehouse, picked up nails in the yard and driveways, and helped the drilling crews load out for jobs. After college, Jim went on to other challenges but Dick returned to the family business. "Dad strongly suggested that I not follow his footsteps in the drilling business," recalls Dick. "I understood that he wanted me to consider very seriously the pitfalls of succession in a family business, especially one as rough and tumble and uncertain as the ground water industry. I considered the options but decided to cast my lot with what was now Henkle Drilling & Supply Co., Inc."

When Dick's father retired from active management in 1966 due to deteriorating health, Dick took over the day-to-day operation of the company. In the ensuing years he bought out his siblings' stock interests in the corporation and eventually assumed full control of the company.

In the late 1960s, revenues were less than $1 million per year. Irrigation well demand was high and Dick acquired additional drilling and support equipment to meet that demand. By the late 1970s, Dick determined that his company's continued industry leadership and future prosperity depended on expansion into the Front Range of Colorado and technical personnel.

Dick soon discovered that although Colorado's well depths were much deeper than in Kansas, the quality of construction was not as high. Henkle Drilling entered the market as a quality alternative to local drillers. "The Front Range was experiencing explosive growth," observes Henkle, "and the demand in the municipal, golf course and housing market for water supply was booming. Our revenues and net profits expanded as we introduced new drilling methods, well design and development technologies to the marketplace. By the end of the 1980s, our annual revenues exceeded $4 million."

Dick and his son, Doug, who had joined the firm in 1984 after college graduation, first started exploring the idea of selling the business in the year 2000. At that time, annual company revenues had grown to $10 million. "I had been approached by a large national ground water contracting firm seeking to expand in the Denver area. After some exchanges of documents and a face-to-face meeting, I decided that our management philosophies and business practices were not compatible." These preliminary talks did, however, open Dick's eyes to the value that the marketplace put on his company.

Dick recognized and appreciated the financial opportunities his family could enjoy due to the sale of the company. In 2000, Dick was approached by a financial buyer interested in consolidating the water well industry. This company, Hydro Resources, Inc., saw Henkle Drilling as the platform company from which additional acquisitions would be made. "When we finally sold to HRI," recalls Henkle, "our company was generating $13.5 million in revenues."

During the transaction, Dick was concerned that the deal would never close because "so many things had to come together. There is so much data and information that the buyer has to digest that I was afraid that they would either give it up or attempt to reduce the purchase price. During the sale process, our company's revenues continued to climb so I was comfortable knowing that if we did not sell to HRI, life would still be good. Of course, I would still have the pressure and strain of ownership and major decision making. Therefore, the prospect of completing the sale motivated us to work diligently to maintain positive financial results."

Dick's underlying confidence in his decision to sell remained firm. "My wife, Karin, and I never had any doubts that selling the company at this time was the right thing to do. When aspects of the transaction got rocky we held firm to our belief that we were taking the right path. Recalling the occasional sleepless nights and concern over financial decisions or personnel issues reassured us that now was the time and HRI was the proper buyer."

Dick recalls, "The transaction team that we assembled could not have been better. With Ned Minor and Dave Irvine, a CPA to whom Ned had introduced me, we were always several steps ahead of the game. The actual sale process was enlightening and very enjoyable. I was confident that our team would maximize the opportunity that this transaction presented. Ned and his partner, Tony King, devised multiple strategies to address problems as they arose. As a result, we were never taken by surprise. I remember when Ned told me at an early meeting that once the deal got started, the buyer and its team would never be left waiting for a response from us. This proved very true. Even though there were times during the transaction when I was very uncertain and concerned about some of the details, overall I found the sale process to be a pleasurable and very good experience."

While Dick's recollection of the entire process is positive, like all other owners his favorite moment occurred at closing. "I will long remember my feelings on the day of closing. At 3:12 p.m. on April 4, 2002 our bank called to inform me that the wire transfer had been received. This was the icing on the cake of a great and successful experience for Karin and me. There was a wonderful feeling of relief. A burden had been lifted from my shoulders. Sixty-plus families had depended on my every decision to be right. While I had enjoyed the experience immensely and felt privileged by the responsibility, now was the correct time to sell. In addition, becoming debt free in one instant was an exhilarating feeling. I sleep well every night and wake up each morning with a smile on my face."

> "Sixty-plus families had depended on my every decision to be right. While I had enjoyed the experience immensely and felt privileged by the responsibility, now was the correct time to sell."

After closing, Dick and his son did not close the door on their involvement with Henkle Drilling. Dick explains, "Doug and I both signed three-year contracts with HRI to work part time in a reduced role of management and also to help acquire other companies in the industry and region which are compatible with HRI's growth philosophy. Having been president of the National Ground Water Association, an industry organization of some 24,000 members, I knew numerous friends and associates who might benefit, as I had, from a sale to HRI."

Since the closing, Dick has made arrangements for the education of his 14 grandchildren. He purchased his dream aircraft, a Beechcraft C-90 King Air turboprop (which he flies himself) to replace the Cessna 340 that he sold in 2000 so he could buy another drilling rig. In the summer after the sale, Dick and Karin spent two moths touring Europe with two of their grandsons – an activity he would not have had time for before the sale.

Dick's greatest satisfaction is that he lives debt-free for the first time in many, many years. "Had I continued to own the company, I would have gone to my grave in debt. Karin and I share a warm and pleasant feeling that by selling the company at the time that we did and to the people we did, we accomplished a very good thing. We are pleased beyond measure with the team we assembled to carry out this transaction. The Lord was faithful in His care for us throughout the entire process. We intend to live out our lives in gratitude to Him."

Dick's advice to other owners is simple: Plan ahead. "I was 68 years old when we sold our company. I realize now that long range plans should have been on the table many years ago. I am free from the financial and personnel concerns that burden every business owner. Having been relieved of those burdens, I truly enjoy going to work, pursuing other interests, spending time with family, traveling, and serving others in various capacities in different parts of the world."

Having the wealth, commitment, and freedom to make our world a better place is a great beginning for the next chapter in Dick's life.

Bill and Jan Gooden
Data Entry & Informational Services Acquisition Corp. (DEIS)

Build the company or sell it? Making a choice you both can live with.

*B*ill and Jan Gooden started their company, DEIS, in 1985 when they invented a better mousetrap. For the Goodens, the mousetrap was a better way to process and file medical insurance claims.

As the CFO for Blue Cross/Blue Shield Colorado, Bill had an in-depth understanding of financial matters and personal computing. His wife, Jan (who also worked for Blue Cross) knew the ins and outs of claims processing. Although a large health insurance company had been unsuccessful in its attempt to have housewives process claims at home, Bill and Jan recognized a wide window of opportunity. Bill left Blue Cross, and he and Jan pooled their talents to develop DEIS, a new medical claim entry and processing software program.

Jan and Bill engaged "at-home" employees to complete the processing. Their workforce grew to over 1,200 employees who processed over 200,000 claims per day.

Shortly after starting their company, Jan and Bill established several guiding principles. First, they told their children that they did not plan to pass on DEIS. Second, they decided that they did not want to work forever, and third, they would remain debt-free.

In 1997, it became apparent to the Goodens that the next technological wave, image claim processing, was imminent. The capital investment required to convert to the new technology, however, was significant. Given the Goodens' desire to operate debt-free, Bill felt that this was the right time to sell. Jan had reservations about selling because "I truly enjoyed my role of designing and implementing software programs. I knew I would miss that aspect of the business but I trusted Bill's instincts and agreed to the sale."

The Goodens' objective was to sell for cash. "We knew that in order to achieve this goal, we needed the services of a strong transaction team including a transaction attorney and an investment banker. After one false start, our investment banker successfully marketed our company to five bidders in a controlled auction. We received a purchase price that exceeded our expectations and it was one hundred percent cash."

For the Goodens, there were no "what ifs?" Bill knew that his personality as a "control freak" made a lengthy transition period (during which Bill would be cashed out but required to remain in a management position) and an earn out (tying part of the purchase price to the company's future performance) non-negotiable. "I knew well in advance of the sale that I would not be comfortable working for my buyer. For that reason, I had consciously focused on developing a well-trained management team that would take my place once I sold." After closing, the Goodens left the company and turned quickly to planning the next phase of their lives.

"Neither Jan nor I have any desire to re-enter the business world," Bill explains. "Why would we? We spend several months each year in Hawaii and several months traveling." Jan adds, "We are very fortunate." Bill is under-taking charitable work and Jan has lots of time to spend with their grandchildren.

> "Owners must resist the temptation to orchestrate their own deals. The investment banker's and attorney's fees are non-issues in light of the greater purchase price they generated for us."

When asked what advice he'd give to other owners, Bill points to the role played by his transaction team. "Owners must resist the temptation to orchestrate their own deals. The investment banker's and attorney's fees are non-issues in light of the greater purchase price they generated for us."

Having sold their company on their terms, Bill and Jan summarize the results as "a dream come true." Great planning and execution lead to great results and as Bill adds, "a little bit of luck didn't hurt either!"

Bill Moore
Moore & Company

Entrepreneurs don't retire, they refocus.

*I*n 1954, fresh out of college, Bill Moore entered his father's residential real estate company as the head of the property management division. It took Bill only four months to realize that his princely salary of $250 per month could not meet his ability to spend. So, Bill left property management and joined his father's seven-man sales force.

"My father was a good mentor. Dad was smart. He was tough on me: he asked no quarter and gave none. I appreciated how he handled this situation. We had a wonderful relationship." At the end of his first year, Bill was the company's second biggest producer and loved sales.

By 1961, Bill had stopped selling residential real estate and started, from scratch, Moore & Company's commercial real estate division. This division bought and sold apartment buildings, strip centers, and new land for development. Only 9 years later, Bill's father died, leaving the entire company (3 residential offices, a commercial division, and a small mortgage company) in Bill's hands. Bill was ready to accept the challenge. Over the next 28 years, Bill grew Moore & Company to 24 offices, 500 residential sales agents, 40 commercial sales agents, and total revenues of $25 million. In 1987, Bill served as president of the National Association of Realtors, the largest trade association in the U.S. (850,000 members).

During the early 1990s, Bill and his company were part of a very prestigious, informal group called, "The Dozen." This group consisted of 24 large, non-franchise and privately-owned real estate companies located in major U.S. cities. "We met twice a year," Bill explains, "to share ideas and information to help improve our individual operations and to share client referrals." Over the years, certain members of The Dozen began to grow by acquiring other real estate companies. By the mid-1990s, large industry players such as GMAC began consolidating the real estate industry.

Consolidators did not overlook Moore & Company. Bill recalls, "I was intrigued by some of these inquiries but I first invited my daughter and son-in-law to buy into the company so that they could become the third generation of Moore family owners." For various reasons, they elected not to do so. Bill, age 66 and having "no one to pass the company on to," decided to sell.

Bill sold Moore & Co. in 1998 to NRT, a highly-motivated consolidator committed to capturing a dominant position in the Denver market. Moore & Company's strong market position enabled Bill to maximize his sale price and achieve his definition of financial independence.

When reflecting on the sale process itself, Bill recalls that he was "most surprised by the extent and the detail of the warranties and representations contained in the buyer's contract. The legal issues, documentation and due diligence were overwhelming. The process was much more complicated than I ever dreamed it would be." Bill, however, was very patient as my firm worked through the necessary details. He was an excellent negotiator when we needed him to play a role in winning certain key points. He allowed his advisors "to grind through the process" necessary to close the deal and protect his interests.

As part of the purchase agreement, Bill agreed to work for the new owner for 15 months. His task was to help build a new culture and smooth the transition for the employees of both the old and new companies. At the end of that period, Bill moved his office into his home in order to completely sever the "old ties" and start his new life.

Bill admits to feeling lost at first, not knowing exactly what to do with his time. "I knew that I needed to be productive. I needed to be doing something for the good of the cause." It did not take Bill long to find a new niche. He started taking a more active role in the management of various real estate partnerships much to the delight of his other partners. Bill, always on the look out for "raw land," intensified his search for "new deals."

Since the closing, Bill has purchased a home in Palm Springs and spends January through May there. He loves playing golf, tennis, and having time to travel with his wife. They spend a great deal of time with friends and family. "Some guys love doing nothing," observes Bill, "but I'm not one of them." Bill suggests that former owners "stay active in some endeavor that they love: business, charity, sports, travel, whatever."

I recently attended Bill's 70th birthday party with 400 other of his "close" friends. He looks great, feels great and is a vital example of the entrepreneur who has refocused without retiring.

Colman Kahn
Kahn & Company Carpet, Inc.

An industry shake-up elicits decisive response.

In 1976, Colman Kahn started his company, Kahn & Company Carpet, Inc., from scratch. Colman worked with interior designers and architects who specified carpet for commercial properties. Not satisfied with this small market niche, Colman expanded his distribution lines and services and became a full service carpet dealer for high-end commercial interiors.

As Colman's company grew, his two most competent salesmen, Fred Fisher and Lou Lanthier, became minority partners and, together, they developed a national reputation for quality and service. By 1996, Colman was fielding calls from industry consolidators. Shaw Carpet, Interface, and DuPont (the industry's largest players or "Big Three") were moving to vertically integrate the carpet industry. Colman recalls that, "They wanted to control manufacturing, distribution and installation. I initially rebuffed these offers because I simply wasn't ready to sell."

Colman changed his mind about a possible sale when Milliken, one of his primary manufacturers, decided to change Kahn & Company's status from a dealer to a franchisee. Milliken wanted Kahn to pay a franchise fee on sales of its carpet and to sell its carpet exclusively. "Milliken's action prompted me to think seriously about selling to one of the Big Three. Because one of them had already purchased a Denver company I knew that other acquisitions would follow and the window of opportunity to sell was already starting to close."

"The smartest thing I did was to hire a Team. Because they did their jobs, I did not find the sale process at all stressful."

"At that point, I contacted Ned to discuss our options and to develop a strategy. Ned helped me to analyze and prioritize my personal and financial objectives. He also introduced me to an investment banker who performed a valuation of our company. Armed with that valuation and our assessment of the demand for the company, we concluded that the timing was perfect for using a controlled auction to sell our company for a premium."

Having assembled his team of Team of Advisors and determined a well-conceived sale strategy, Colman recalls that he was "able to focus on running the company while his Team managed the sale process. The smartest thing I did was to hire a Team. Because they did their jobs, I did not find the sale process at all stressful."

Colman was extremely pleased with the results of the controlled auction involving Shaw and a financial buyer. "This process generated a price that was 50 percent higher than my expectations. We were all thrilled when the transaction closed. My financial objective was achieved. One of my personal objectives had been to sell to a buyer that I trusted and respected. Shaw met that requirement. Further, Shaw allowed me to continue to operate the company with almost total autonomy, thus fulfilling another personal objective that I set when I started the company in 1966. That objective was to continue working as long as I enjoyed doing so. I am still working and have no plans to retire."

Colman continued to operate his company as its president after the closing date. He readily admits that there was a certain amount of turmoil after the sale. "When I told my employees that I had sold the company, several left because they did not want to work for a large corporation. In addition, I lost some very talented sales people because of Shaw's policy requiring that we purchase product exclusively from Shaw. Dealing with employee issues was my greatest challenge in running the company after I sold."

Not surprisingly, sales volume dropped during this short period of re-adjustment. Looking back on that initial post-closing period, Colman notes that he "really appreciated Shaw's patience while I and my management team adjusted to working in a Corporate America environment."

Over time, Shaw asked Colman to assume greater responsibility for managing other carpet dealers that it had acquired. "Even though I hadn't planned to do this, I took on this project because I enjoyed such a good relationship with Shaw. I liked and respected their people and learned a great deal from them about how to operate a company."

As an example, Colman points out that his former company has become more corporate in its culture to the benefit of all involved. "Since closing, we have instituted many new systems that have generated absolutely great results for the bottom line. At first I was bothered by the amount of change being implemented but I soon realized how much sense these changes made."

In 2000, Colman hired a president to take over his administrative duties. "Doing so has allowed me to do what I truly love most – sales." Colman recognizes that his life, post closing, has been very different from that of the typical seller. "As the Vice President of Sales, I have the flexibility I need to work in the separate residential carpet business that I own. Shaw supports me in this effort. I continue to be a goodwill ambassador for them as well as a mentor for Shaw's sales team. This relationship of trust and respect has worked well for both of us."

Seven years into Colman's role as "former owner," he reports that he has "no desire to retire and will keep working as long as it remains fun. I was 53 when I sold the company and life has been, and continues to be very good for me." Colman characterizes his life after the sale as "marvelous."

When asked what advice he would give to business owners contemplating a sale, Colman suggests that owners select and use a competent law firm and investment banker. "Hiring experts for my Team initially cost more than hiring others less experienced in mergers and acquisitions. In the long run, however, it was worth every penny. Ned's firm prepared my company for sale well before we contacted prospective buyers. Having respected, organized and experienced advisors on my Team showed Shaw that my company had its act together. This factor definitely increased the amount they were willing to pay for my company.

"I'm convinced that careful preparation paved the way for a

smooth transaction. This was especially important to me because ill will or bad feelings generated by the process could have jeopardized my relationship with Shaw as well as our mutual desire for me to continue operating the company after the closing."

Colman's story is an excellent example of an owner who transformed a negative change in his industry into a catalyst for wealth and freedom. His story also demonstrates how owners who choose their buyers carefully maximize their chances for a long and successful relationship.

Mike Anderson
Environmental Materials, Inc.

Taking some, but not all, of your chips off the table.

In 1983, Mike Anderson was working as a CPA for an accounting firm that had been retained by Environmental Materials, Inc. to perform an audit as part of its deliberations to go public. In 1985, Mike went to work for EMI as its controller and bought a very small percentage of the company. Over the next 12 years he acquired 100 percent of the company.

EMI manufactures cultured stone products. These stone products are made of a lightweight aggregate cement poured into molds that resemble exterior stone products. They are sold for commercial, residential, and multi-family unit construction.

When Mike joined the company its annual revenues were $200,000 and the company had $1.7 million debt. When Mike sold EMI 18 years later it had annual revenues of $14 million and earnings of $4 million (EBIT).

With the sky seemingly the limit, what caused Mike to sell? "First, I realized early on that I would never transfer the business to family members. I didn't believe that they were capable of managing and operating the company." In addition, Mike wanted to sell at the top of the market and maximize his window of opportunity.

Mike chose to hire an investment banker because he knew he couldn't run the business and sell the company at the same time. He reasoned that the money spent on the investment banker's fee would be a good investment in getting the deal done.

The deal the investment banker brought to the table exceeded Mike's expectations, but it was not without bumps. At several points, the prospective buyer missed deadlines. This led Mike to believe that the buyer was looking at other options. "This was not a pleasant time for me. My advisors kept the buyer's feet to the fire and I dealt with my uncertainty by sticking to my guns. If the transaction had failed to meet all of my objectives, I was prepared to walk away from the sale."

> "My advisors kept the buyer's feet to the fire and I dealt with my uncertainty by sticking to my guns. If the transaction had failed to meet all of my objectives, I was prepared to walk away from the sale."

Two of Mike's objectives were to retain partial ownership in EMI and to continue to manage the company on a day-to-day basis. Ultimately, he sold 80 percent of the company, retained 20 percent and stayed active in the company after closing. He explains, "I believed in my buyer's expectation that my business could be replicated in key cities across the country." Mike is confident that his 20 percent stake will eventually exceed the value paid for his 80 percent. In other words, he will enjoy two incredibly great paydays.

When he sold the company, Mike wasn't sure what going to work on a daily basis would be like or how well he would get along with his new partners. His role as the leader of development meant taking the company to the next level through national expansion. Mike loves his new role because it has freed him from the details and enables him to "fly at 30,000 feet." He believes that it is truly every entrepreneur's dream to take his company to the highest possible level. This goal cannot be achieved as long as the owner is bogged down running the company and is nervous about committing the necessary financial resources. Mike now has the opportunity to achieve his entrepreneurial dream.

Two years out, Mike now realizes that at least for now, he cannot retire. He must be part of the chase. He enjoys the hunt and kill that business provides. His business is part of the fiber of his being. He absolutely must be involved. When he looks in the mirror, he sees that involvement for him is a necessity. He explains, "I know now that I can't leave the game. I need to do the things that I'm good at." In 2002, Mike won Ernst & Young's Entrepreneur of the Year for the Rocky Mountain Region for manufacturing.

The transaction that Mike negotiated enables him to fill his personal needs as well as to meet his extra-curricular needs. "I have set up a family foundation to support charitable causes and I am always looking for joint venture investments to participate in." He has deepened his involvement in Kiwanis International by becoming a Trustee. Mike plans to help his kids get started in business if they elect to do so. "I want it to be a business they want to pursue. I have no interest in controlling their lives or their businesses."

Jerry Berglund
Denpak Building Products, Inc.

"If you take care of the shop, it will take care of you."

*A*ll owners infuse their personalities into their companies. To a greater or lesser extent, every business reflects the values of its owner. In Jerry Berglund's case, he consciously integrated his values and principles into his company. Perhaps that is why his sale was emotionally more difficult than for other owners.

From the early 1940s until 1985, Berglund's father, Potts, operated and was the majority owner of Denver Wood Products. Although Jerry had been active in the company, Potts decided to sell the majority of his stock to an outside leveraged buyout company. Jerry and another employee, as minority shareholders, continued to work for the buyer after the sale.

High debt levels extracted a toll from Denver Wood Products. That and the advent of the weakest housing market in the Rocky Mountain region in 50 years contributed to the buyer's declaration of bankruptcy in 1988.

Even prior to the bankruptcy, Jerry was making plans to buy back the company. Once bankruptcy was declared, however, a simple buyout was no longer an option. Instead, he and other key employees raised the capital necessary to start a new venture – Denpak Building Products, Inc.

Denpak acquired many of Denver Wood Products' assets in liquidation. In addition, the company was able to hire many of the same employees and resurrect most of the customer and vendor relationships lost under the buyer's tenure. Jerry and a key partner also purchased real estate for a lumberyard and added a metal shop, a truss plant, and two satellite yards. As a result of these actions (and a great deal of hard work), Denpak grew to become one of the largest building materials and industrial packaging suppliers in the Rocky Mountain region. By 1995, revenues exceeded $62 million.

"From the first day Denpak's doors opened," recalls Berglund, "I knew that one day I would sell the company. But until that day arrived, I looked forward to every challenge that running a business entails." Jerry notes that "running a business requires all of your faculties. Like most business owners, I was driven by the two opposing mindsets: first, the anxiety, especially with a lot of debt, that things could go down hill quickly, and second, the belief that nothing could hold us back. The challenge is to balance and channel these opposing feelings into posi- tive change and growth."

Through the years, Jerry kept a close eye on the market cycles and, "when I perceived a dramatic upward trend in 1996, I contacted Ned. He helped me think through my decision to sell, explained the sale process and educated me about selecting an investment banker."

"My transaction team conducted a controlled auction and brought five potential buyers to the table. Once we determined which buyer and which price met my objectives, my decision to sell was made." Some of Jerry's conditions included: that the buyer have similar management philosophies and significant financial strength, and that Jerry and his partners retain ownership of all real estate used in the operations.

While many owners stay with their now-former companies to ease the transition, Berglund had other reasons for staying. "Denpak incor- porated my beliefs and principles. As my father had told me, 'If you take care of the shop, the shop will take care of you.' I lived that lesson through Denpak." Jerry stayed on for four years (two as an employee and two as a consultant) – satisfying his need to extricate himself slowly from the business that had energized him and defined him for many years.

Once Jerry's four-year stint was complete he was emotionally more at peace with his decision to sell. He was confident in his ability to carve out a new position in the business world that would engage him as completely as running a company had. He could fully enjoy the financial security he'd attained for himself and for his family as well as the freedom from the weight of personal liability that he had carried for so long. "I needed those years to truly value the benefits the sale bestowed."

Jerry was 48 when he sold the company in 1996. In early 1999, Jerry joined the board of a small but growing national television network in California. According to Jerry, "It is an active board and my duties are expanding. I've enjoyed the challenge of learning a new industry, and contributing, I hope, in a small way to the network's success."

"Selling the business certainly allowed me the opportunity to focus on non-business goals and new pursuits."

Now 54, Jerry observes, "I never wanted to retire so we retained six partnerships and leased real estate back to the buyer after the sale. Subsequently, two more properties were purchased and again, leased back to the company. I formed a family limited partnership that manages the leased properties."

In addition to his real estate work, Jerry thought it would be "fun and important to write a short history of both Denver Wood and Denpak. Since the 1940s, Denver Wood had been a Denver landmark. Hundreds of employees had worked hard and made it successful. My book pays tribute to the two companies and to their employees."

As Jerry recounts, "Selling the business certainly allowed me the opportunity to focus on non-business goals and new pursuits. I still miss the business. I knew that I would. For the first two years after the sale it was a tough mental adjustment. But I've enjoyed the new challenges. I feel very fortunate to have a loving and supportive wife and family. That makes everything worthwhile."

Since the sale of the business Jerry has had more time for charitable endeavors and for his three younger children. His two sons participate on major college athletic teams – one in tennis and the other baseball. His daughter, still in high school, also plays on three varsity athletic teams. Jerry and his wife, Marty, still attend many of the kids' events in and out of Colorado. Jerry also still enjoys playing and working with his kids in their sports activities. Above all else, Jerry and his wife are instilling the same Christian values in their kids that their parents instilled in them: honesty, hard work, humility, and integrity.

Gerry Koch
Turf Irrigation Supply, Inc.

Your first buyer may not be your last.

*I*n 1980, at age 32, Gerry Koch and a friend left good-paying sales positions in order to start their own company, Turf Irrigation Supply, Inc. Their company matured into a very large distributor of sprinkler system components. Gerry owned 70 percent and his partner owned the balance.

After five years, Gerry talked to a consultant who emphasized the need to have an exit strategy. From that point forward, he ran the company from the perspective that the company should be in a position to be sold whenever he made the decision to sell it. The last thing he wanted was to arrive at a point where he was ready to sell but his company remained unprepared. His goal was to sell the company for maximum value. For that reason, he kept the company looking good, financially and physically, in case someone dropped by to make him an offer he couldn't refuse. This focus on "readiness" is rare among business owners.

Gerry's partner was 10 years his senior. Between the years 1991 and 1996, Gerry bought him out in a friendly transition. By 1997, Gerry owned 100 percent of the company. He started to ask himself what he wanted to do with the company now that he had assumed sole control. First, he realized that he wasn't having as much fun as he had had in the past and was determined not to "die in the saddle with his boots on." Second, the competent management team that Gerry had meticulously groomed allowed him to spend a lot of time with his family. Spending time – physically and emotionally – away from the company, however, made Gerry feel guilty. This guilt provided the catalyst he needed to decide to sell. He wanted to spend guilt-free time with his wife and children.

At the time Gerry made his decision, his industry was ripe for consolidation, his company was a national leader in the industry and it was in the best possible shape to be sold. His strong management team was itching to grow so they could tackle the challenges and reap the financial rewards that growth would bring. He concluded that he had two choices. He could grow the company or he could sell and let a buyer grow it. He even considered assuming the role of consolidator until greater reflection made him realize that he had no passion for such a task. Gerry did some research on the multiples being paid for companies like his, and all things considered, decided to sell.

Gerry engaged my law firm and an investment banking firm and started the sale process. He entered into a contract (which included a financing contingency) with a consolidator. Negotiations went on for several months until Gerry and his Advisory Team concluded that the buyer was not capable of obtaining financing. The buyer sought an amount that exceeded its bank's loan capacity. The bank would have to syndicate the loan in order to get it done and in Gerry's and his team's opinion, this process would simply take too long.

At this point, spring, Gerry's busiest time of the year, had sprung. Although the investment banker had a back-up buyer lined up and ready to go, Gerry wanted a "time out" so he could steer the company through the season without the distraction of a sale. Taking his company off the market took an emotional toll on Gerry. He had psychologically committed to selling and with his first buyer, had started smelling the roses. Gerry reflects, "Not closing and walking away was a huge personal disappointment. Nevertheless, we worked hard through the spring and increased our revenues because I was committed to selling."

> "Today Gerry has no regrets about selling the company. ...he never second-guesses or wishes that he had not sold."

Approximately one year later, Gerry sold his company to another consolidator. The delay proved to be a huge benefit to Gerry. During the time between the first attempt and second transaction, Gerry's company's earnings increased and so did its purchase price. The second transaction proceeded smoothly. Hearing from the banker that the purchase proceeds had cleared provided Gerry "a great sense of joy and relief."

Today Gerry has no regrets about selling the company. From a financial standpoint, he never second-guesses or wishes that he had not sold. He achieved his definition of personal financial independence – and more. From a personal standpoint, his ego remains intact. "I don't miss any aspect of the business including being the linchpin of the operation. At first I missed the camaraderie of certain employees, vendors and customers but found that I was able to continue those relationships in different settings."

Gerry is now two years into what he calls his refocusing. "I anticipate that it could take five years to complete this transition period. I enjoy the flexibility and spontaneity of being able to do new things that I enjoy." In order to quench his thirst for travel, he has purchased a large motor home and a condo in Hawaii. He takes on new life experiences "without worry or guilt" and recognizes that he has embarked on a new life journey. To him this is a new and exciting adventure.

Like most former owners, Gerry has discovered that, "I can stop whatever I am doing to tackle whatever project excites me. I have ultimate flexibility. If I tire of my motor home, I can sell it. If I want a new challenge, I can find one." And finally, he has found new peace of mind. "When I owned the business, the risk to my family's financial security was ever-present." Those worries about finances, employees, vendors, and customers are behind him now. Gerry's story is a model for all business owners.

Conclusion

It is my most sincere hope that by reading this book, you have moved closer to your decision to sell. By now you have probably reached one of the following six conclusions.

1. You *are emotionally ready to sell and* your company *is ready for sale at a maximum price.*

2. You *are emotionally ready to sell but* your company *is not ready to be sold for a maximum price.*

3. You are not *emotionally ready to sell and* your company *is not ready to sell for a maximum value.*

4. You are not *emotionally ready to sell but* your company **is ready** *to sell for a maximum price.*

5. You *are emotionally ready to sell but a sale of* your **company will never generate financial independence.**

6. **Your company** *will always generate a salary for you but it is* **non-saleable.**

Assuming that you fall into one of the categories above, what can you do? Let's examine each scenario.

1. You *are emotionally ready to sell and* your company *is ready for sale at a maximum price.*

Assemble your Advisory Team and initiate the sale process. Wealth and freedom are knocking at your door.

2. You *are emotionally ready to sell but* your company *is not ready to be sold for a maximum price.*

Pick up the phone and call your Team of Advisors. Set a meeting to discuss Value Drivers. If they don't know what you are talking about, refer them to Question 20 in this book or to *www.exitplanning.com* to get a copy of my partner's book, *The Completely Revised How To Run Your Business So You Can Leave It In Style.* On this web site, they will learn not only what Value Drivers are but also their roles in helping you to implement them.

At your meeting, determine what improvements need to be made to your existing Value Drivers and what ones need to be installed. Assign responsibility and deadlines to each Advisor to complete each task. I suggest that you designate one advisor to spearhead this effort and to keep all the others on track.

Before this meeting ends, discuss and set a deadline for how long this process will take to achieve your goal: a value for your company that will yield your desired purchase price. Implement the necessary steps with vigor and discipline. Wealth and freedom are just around the corner.

3. You are not *emotionally ready to sell and* your company is *not ready to sell for a maximum value.*

I suggest that you follow the suggestions in the paragraph above. As you move closer to creating the value you need, review Part One of this book. Doing so will help you work through any lingering emotional issues. Wealth and freedom are waiting for you but aren't expecting you this week. As long as you remain committed to your goals and exit strategy, wealth and freedom are on your not-so-long-range calendar.

4. You are not *emotionally ready to sell but* your company is ready *to sell for a maximum price.*

Owners whose companies are ready to sell but who aren't prepared mentally for a sale run the risk that by the time they are emotionally ready, markets or other factors may have changed which affect the salability of the company. In my experience, owners whose readiness lags behind that of their companies' have a burning desire to take their companies to the next level. They are convinced that they have the drive, ideas, and skills to drive the company forward. My best advice to these owners is: Define exactly what the next level is and how long it will take to reach. Continue to reset this timeframe until you are emotionally ready to pull the trigger.

5. **You** *are emotionally ready to sell but a sale of* **your company will never generate financial independence.**

This is the classic case described in Question 2 (sell and buy another company). If you find yourself in this situation, keep "trading up" until you own a company that has the growth capacity to be sold at a price that will achieve your financial independence.

6. **Your company** *will always generate a salary for you but it is* **non-saleable.**

If you find yourself in this category, you now realize that your comfort during retirement is dictated by your ability to make and save as much money as you can while you operate your company. In my experience, however, there is usually a buyer for every business. Your search for a buyer may be difficult but not fruitless. To entice a buyer, you may have to carry back a significant portion of the purchase price. You may have to remain with the company in a more prominent role after the sale than you would have preferred. These enticements will all be worthwhile if the resulting sale proceeds are the "icing on the cake" of your existing savings. When this happens, your goals of wealth and financial freedom are achieved.

I truly hope this book has provided you the insight necessary to guide you through your own decision making process: to sell or not to sell. You now possess subjective information about what owners think, about how they make their decisions, and what they do with their lives after they sell. Similarly, you have an objective map of the sale process, the important legal issues involved, and a description of the various advisors and their roles. Armed with this, you can now orchestrate your own exit from your company with confidence.

Selling your company is not a mystery. There are advisors who have helped hundreds of owners through the sale process. Seek them out. Communicate with them clearly and let them help you to craft an exit that meets, or even exceeds, your goals of wealth and freedom.

I wish you every success.

Ned Minor

APPENDICES

APPENDIX A

This is a sample document for illustrative purposes only.
Please consult an attorney before entering into any Confidentiality Agreement.

Confidentiality Agreement

This Agreement is made and entered into effective this _____ day of
_____, 200___, by _____, a
_____ corporation ("Seller"), and
_____, a _____ ("Interested Party").

Recitals

A. Interested Party is interested in acquiring the stock or assets of Seller by way of, purchase, merger, consolidation or otherwise (the "Proposed Transaction").

B. In order for Seller and Interested Party to continue their negotiations regarding the Proposed Transaction, it will be necessary for each party to disclose to the other certain valuable proprietary information.

C. Each party agrees and acknowledges that any proprietary information which it receives from the other party must be maintained in the strictest confidence and used solely and only for the purpose of evaluating the desirability of proceeding with the Proposed Transaction.

NOW, THEREFORE, in consideration of the mutual covenants herein contained and other good and valuable consideration, the sufficiency and receipt of which is hereby acknowledged, the parties agree as follows:

Agreement

1. Definitions. For purposes of this Agreement the following terms shall carry the meaning set forth below:

A. The term "documents" shall be in any form of or medium provided, including, but not be limited to, writings, drawings, graphs, charts, photographs, phonographic records, tape recordings, discs and data compilations in whatever form recorded or stored from which information can be obtained and/or translated, if necessary, into reasonably usable form and any reproductions thereof.

B. The term "Confidential Information" means all information, tangible or intangible, in whatever form or medium provided or obtained by a party or its representative, directly or indirectly, including all information generated by a party or its representative that contains, reflects or is derived from such information, whether orally, in documents, through and by observation or otherwise, in any way relating to the Proposed Transaction including, but not limited to, the fact of the Proposed Transaction, that Seller is contemplating a potential sale of its business, information about existing or contemplated products, services, client lists, marketing techniques, pricing policies, financial information, sales processes, bidding processes, costs, profits, sales, markets and all other data. In addition, Confidential Information shall include the fact that this Agreement exists as well as the fact that discussions between the parties concerning a Proposed Transaction are taking place.

2. Confidentiality. Each party agrees that it will not, directly or indirectly, use, disseminate or disclose, and will use its best efforts to prevent the use, dissemination or disclosure of, the Confidential Information to any person or entity for any purpose or at any time, except for purposes of evaluating the desirability of proceeding with the Proposed Transaction and as otherwise expressly authorized herein or in writing by the other party. Each party may disclose Confidential Information to its officers, directors, full time employees responsible for the Proposed Transaction, professional advisors and agents all with a need to know in connection with its evaluation of the desirability of proceeding with the Proposed Transaction; provided, however, any unauthorized disclosure or use by any such persons shall be deemed to be an unauthorized disclosure or use by the disclosing party to this Agreement.

At the request of Seller, Interested Party shall provide Seller with (i) a list of all such individuals who have been provided Confidential

Information along with a written acknowledgment from each such party agreeing to comply with the terms of this Agreement, and (ii) a list of all copies made of Confidential Information. This obligation of confidentiality shall continue for so long as the information described in Paragraph 1.B. is not in the public domain and not generally known or used in the industry in which any party to this agreement does business.

Finally, each party agrees that, until and unless the Proposed Transaction is completed, it will not, directly or indirectly, disclose, and will use its best efforts to prevent the disclosure of, the Confidential Information and the fact that the parties are discussing a Proposed Transaction and that the parties are disclosing Confidential Information for purposes of evaluating the desirability of proceeding with the Proposed Transaction.

In the event any party or anyone to whom it transmits the Confidential Information pursuant to this Agreement become legally compelled to disclose any of the Confidential Information, such party will provide the other party with prompt notice thereof so that the other party may seek a protective order or other appropriate remedy and/or waive compliance with the provisions of this Agreement. The party compelled to disclose will furnish only the portion of the Confidential Information which is legally required and will exercise its best efforts to obtain a protective order or other reliable assurance that confidential treatment will be accorded the Confidential Information.

3. No License. The receiving party agrees that no license under copyright or intellectual property right by implication or otherwise is granted to the receiving party either by delivery or providing any of the Confidential Information or otherwise.

4. Reproduction and Return of Documents. A party shall only reproduce documents containing Confidential Information of the other party as necessary to evaluate the Proposed Transaction and the party reproducing such Confidential Information shall maintain a written list of all such copies. All documents containing Confidential Information of a party, including but not limited to copies, analyses and derivations of the Confidential Information, shall be delivered to the disclosing party promptly upon receipt of a written request therefore.

5. Non-Solicitation. Without the prior written consent of Seller, if the Proposed Transaction is not consummated between Interested Party and Seller, Interested Party shall not for a period of one-year from the date of this Agreement, hire, solicit or cause to be hired or solicited any employee, independent contractor, or consultant of Seller.

6. Remedies. In the event of the actual or threatened breach of any provision of this Agreement by a party, the other party shall have the right to obtain injunctive relief and/or specific performance and to seek any other remedy available to it.

7. Law, Venue, Jurisdiction. This Agreement and all matters and issues collateral thereto shall be governed by the laws of the State of Colorado. The parties agree that any and all controversies or claims arising out of or relating to this Agreement, or breach thereof, shall be decided in the District Court of the City and County of _____, State of Colorado, and that such court shall have exclusive jurisdiction, including *in personam* jurisdiction and shall be the exclusive venue for any and all such controversies and claims except as otherwise unanimously agreed by the parties. Each party understands that each has a constitutional right of due process which guarantees that each party must have minimum contacts with the State of Colorado prior to the exercise by a Colorado court of *in personam* jurisdiction over any party and said constitutional right is hereby expressly waived by each party.

8. Severability. If any provision of this Agreement becomes or is found to be illegal or unenforceable for any reason, such clause or provision must first be modified to the extent necessary to make this Agreement legal and enforceable and then if necessary, second, severed from the remainder of the Agreement to allow the remainder of the Agreement to remain in full force and effect.

9. Counterparts; Facsimile. This Agreement may be executed in several counterparts, and all of such counterparts taken together shall be deemed to be one Agreement. Facsimile notice and signatures hereunder shall be deemed to be originals.

10. Attorneys' Fees. If either party shall commence any action or proceeding against the other in order to enforce the provisions hereof, or to recover damages resulting from the alleged breach of any of the provisions hereof, the prevailing party therein shall be entitled to recover all reasonable costs incurred in connection therewith, including, but not limited to, reasonable attorneys' fees.

11. Waiver of Breach. The waiver by any party of a breach of any provision of this Agreement shall not operate or be construed as a waiver of any subsequent breach by any party.

12. Gender and Number. As used herein, the masculine gender shall include the feminine and neuter genders, and the singular shall include the plural, and vice versa, where the context requires.

13. Survival. The terms and conditions of this Agreement shall survive any termination hereof.

IN WITNESS WHEREOF, the parties execute this Agreement as of the date set forth below.

SELLER	INTERESTED PARTY
By: _____	By: _____
Name:_____	Name: _____
Its: _____	Its: _____
Date:_____	Date: _____

APPENDIX B

This is a sample document for illustrative purposes only.

Due Diligence Information Request List

Please provide copies of all items listed or indicate "N/A" for those that are **not** applicable. Please compile and deliver to me copies of all documents which are requested or which respond to the items below. It is very important that entire documents (front and back) be copied. Please call if you do not understand the request or have any concerns.

RESPONSIBLE PARTY　　　　DUE DILIGENCE ITEM　　　　COMPLETED

1. Corporate/Operational Matters

(A) Articles of Incorporation together with all amendments

(B) Bylaws as amended and currently in effect

(C) Stock Certificates and Stock Book (including copies of the front and back of all stock certificates including cancelled certificates), stock transfer records and all documents relating to stock ownership including a list of all outstanding options, warrants or other rights relating to the stock

(D) Minutes of Board of Directors Meetings and any committees thereof (or written consents in lieu thereof)

(E) Minutes of Shareholder's Meetings (or written consents in lieu thereof)

(F) Shareholder's Agreements, including Buy-Sell or Stock Redemption Agreements; stock options or conversion rights

(G) Voting Agreements, proxies, powers of attorney

(H) All agreements, arrangements or understandings by Company or its shareholders
to issue, purchase or sell any securities of
the Company

(I) List of Shareholders, including number of
shares and percent of ownership

(J) List of current Board of Directors

(K) List of current Officers

(L) All licenses, permits and certificates from
regulatory authorities

(M) List of all jurisdictions outside home state
where Company has facilities or authority
to transact business. Has company "qualified" to do business in each state?

(N) List of all locations where the Company
maintains offices (owned or leased), facilities or employees, pays any kind of taxes
on a recurring basis to solicit or perform
business, identifying the nature and function of each location including the street
address of each

(O) Good Standing certificates for the state of
incorporation and business qualification
certificates for each foreign jurisdiction in
which the Company is qualified

(P) List of any subsidiaries or related companies in which officers, directors or shareholders or their families have an interest,
including name, state of incorporation and
capitalization

(Q) List of all partnerships, joint ventures or

affiliates

(R) List of professional advisors and consultants including attorneys, accountants,
marketing and advertising firms

(S) List of ten largest customer and suppliers
and related contracts

(T) All business plans prepared by or for the
Company in the last two years

(U) All projections, forecasts and budgets
(including capital budgets) prepared by or
for the Company in the last two years,
including all assumptions integral thereto

(V) All studies, reports, analyses, summaries
or memoranda prepared by or for the
Company in the last two years (for any
purpose) relating to the Company's business operations, prospects or financing

(W) Independent valuation or appraisals of the
Company's capital stock and/or its assets

(X) List of any related party activities, i.e.,
related party contracts agreements, leases

2. EMPLOYEE MATTERS

(A) List of all employees by:

- Position/title

- Compensation/annual

- Commission/commission plan

- Full or part-time status

- Date of hire

- Accrued vacation, sick time, etc.

- Other eligible benefits, i.e., automobile, cell phone, pager, cafeteria plan

(B) Organization chart with reporting responsibilities

(C) Employment, consulting, commission and independent contractor agreements

(D) Confidentiality, non-compete, and trade secret agreements with present and former employees

(E) Employee Handbooks and employment and personnel policies and procedures (both written and informal policies), including Separation pay (severance)

(F) Union or collective bargaining agreements

(G) Unfair labor practice or labor law violations

(H) Subcontractor Labor Agreements or Outsourcing Service Agreements

(I) Pension, profit-sharing 401(k) Plan:

- Plan Document

- Summary Plan Description

- Summary of Material Modifications

- Related Trust Agreement

- Group Annuity Contract

- IRS Form 5500 and Schedules for the last three years

- Most recent actuarial report

- IRS Determination Letter

- ADP/ACP Testing Reports for the last three years

(J) Deferred compensation plans and salary continuation plans

(K) Stock option plans, including a list of each employee who has been granted options and the number of shares subject to the option

(L) Bonus plans or arrangements

(M) Incentive compensation plans and phantom stock plans

(N) Severance agreements, arrangements or policies

(O) List of all employees entitled to or receiving COBRA benefits

(P) Other Employee Benefits:

- Medical, dental, vision
- Life, disability insurance
- Retirement benefits
- Medical reimbursement
- "Cafeteria"
- Tuition Reimbursement
- Savings Programs
- Automobiles or automobile allowances
- Club membership
- Telephone/pager services
- Computers
- Other incentives

3. Contracts, Agreements and Arrangements

(A) Contracts and agreements with manufacturers, distributors, customers, vendors, suppliers, i.e., preferred vendor or supplier contracts

(B) Sales, supply, service, maintenance, or requirements agreements (including long-term agreements)

(C) Government contracts, Minority Entitlement Contracts

(D) Any forms of express warranties and disclaimers of warranty made by the Company during the past five years and a summary of any breach of representation claims against the Company during the past five years

(E) Joint venture/partnership agreements

(F) Agreements with advertising/public relations agencies

(G) Performance or customs bonds

(H) Powers of attorney

(I) Research and development contracts

(J) Agreements with investment bankers, brokers and finders

(K) Agreements restricting the conduct of the company or its business

(L) Letters of intent

(M) Personal property leases (i.e. equipment and computer leases, maintenance leases, telephone leases, leases of photocopy machines, postage meters, and automobiles)

(N) Other contracts, agreements and arrangements, including descriptions of all the foregoing that are oral

(O) Standard company business forms, i.e. purchase orders, and invoices

(P) All indemnification agreements

4. Personal Property

   (A) Any and all bills of sale, leases and other agreements to purchase or lease personal property (together with financing and security arrangements)

   (B) Schedule of all tangible personal property such as machinery, equipment, vehicles, furniture and fixture, including but not limited to the following:

- Owned or leased status

- Financing agreement or lease contracts

- Date acquired

- Summary of insurance in force

5. Real Property

   (A) Owned real property - Provide the following information for each parcel of owned real property:

- Transfer Deed

- Location/Address, including the county

- Name of record owner

- Deeds of Trusts/other encumbrances, i.e., purchase option agreements

- Encroachments or boundary disputes

- Title insurance policy

- Any "Phase I" or other environmental assessment, audit, or other study

- Zoning letters

- Building code restrictions

- Inspection reports

- Appraisals

- Surveys

- Copies of leases between the company, as lessor, and the third parties for land not used by the company

(B) Leased real property - all lease documents, including:

- Location/Address, including the county

- Name, address and phone number of lessor and/or property manager

- Lease Agreement with all amendments

- Any subleases or assignments of leases

- Deeds of Trust and other encumbrances or liens

- Was it originally owned by you, then sold and leased back?

- Purchase options or rights of first refusal

6. INTELLECTUAL PROPERTY

(A) List of all patents, trademarks, service marks or copyrights issued or applied for, including the name of the record owners and the registration/application number

(B) List of all trade names used by the company and registered jurisdiction, if any (current and discontinued)

(C) Patent/trademark/copyright licensing agreements (company as licensee or licensor; royalties paid out or received)

(D) Infringement actions or challenges to ownership (pending or threatened)

(E) Inventory of computer systems (hardware and software), including copies of all leases and licenses

(F) Other agreements respecting trade secrets or confidential designs or information

7. INDEBTEDNESS

(A) List of all banking and credit activities and relationships by bank name, account number, account type and/or purpose, authorized signer

(B) All agreements related to indebtedness for borrowed money or trade credit:

- Loan and Credit Agreements

- Promissory Notes

- Financing Statements

- Security Agreements

- Pledge Agreements

- Subordination Agreements

- Deeds of Trust

(C) List of all guarantees or indemnity contracts in connection with obligations of the company, including personal guarantees

(D) Letters of Credit

(E) Revolving credit agreements/line of credit

(F) Lease-purchase agreements

- Automobiles

- Equipment

(G) Equity purchase agreements/arrangements

8. LITIGATION

(A) List of all pending or threatened legal proceedings and all files related thereto; investigations, grievance proceedings, arbitration or mediation

(B) All settlement agreements, court orders or judgements or threatened litigation or asserted claims

(C) List of all potential claims (asserted or unasserted, liquidated or contingent), i.e., discrimination, products liability

(D) Summary of all administrative proceedings, claims or investigations by or before federal, state or local governmental bodies (i.e., OSHA, EPA)

9. INSURANCE

(A) All insurance certificates and schedule of insurance policies, coverage, expiration dates, rate and summary of claims history:

- Health

- Vehicles

- Property

- Liability

- Business interruption and discontinuance

- Key Man

- Other

(B) List of any pending uninsured claims indicating whether and to what extent any reserves have been established in the financial statements of the Company

(C) All outstanding workers' compensation claims

(D) Insurance claims loss runs for the last five years, including:

- General commercial liability

- Workers' compensation

10. Governmental Compliance

(A) Describe the Company's compliance or noncompliance with applicable governmental regulations. Possible regulated areas of the Company's business include:

- Health, safety, labeling of products

- Health and safety in Company's plants and facilities

- Equal Employment Opportunity

- Wages and hours of employment

- Environmental protection and pollution controls (including hazardous waste disposal)

- Pricing, sale and distribution of products

- Import/export permits or licenses

- Interstate Commerce Commission requirements

- Unclaimed property, including customer deposits

(B) List any governmental or non-governmental agencies (such as Underwriter's Laboratories) which regulate or affect the Company's business

(C) Federal, state and local permits, authorizations, registrations, licenses or qualifications necessary for the conduct of the Company's business. List the name of the government agency, type of license, expiration date and whether it is assignable or transferable

(D) Any violations cited in inspections by Federal, State or local regulatory agencies (e.g. EPA, OSHA, FDA, USDA, etc.) in the last year

11. TAX

    (A) Income tax returns for the last five years:

        • Federal

        • State

        • Local

    (B) Sales and use tax returns for the last three years (grouped by jurisdiction)

    (C) Payroll and unemployment tax returns for the last three years:

        • Federal

        • State

    (D) List of all states where the Company is registered to collect sales and use taxes

    (E) List of all out-of-state customers for whom sales and use taxes are withheld

    (F) All correspondence from IRS or Department of Revenue as to audits or disputes

12. FINANCIAL INFORMATION

    (A) Historical financial statements together with accountants opinions (audit, review or compilation) for last three years

    (B) Monthly financial statements for each month of current fiscal year

    (C) Year-to-date financial statements for the current fiscal year

    (D) Detailed accounts receivable aging and reconciliation to general ledger

    (E) Credit issues and analysis of bad debt expense and write-offs for the last three years

(F) Detailed inventory list by department and by item (units and value) and reconciliation to general ledger

(G) Analysis of inventory write-offs/obsolescence (including write-downs for last three years)

(H) Detailed accounts payable aging and reconciliation to general ledger

(I) Detail of accrued liabilities and reconciliation to general ledger

(J) Schedule of notes and loans receivable

(K) Schedule of notes and loans payable (with copies of all notes and agreements) for the three most recent fiscal years, and the most recent period including copies of the following:

- Any of all outstanding bonds, notes, debentures, trust indentures, loan agreements, bank credit lines (whether or not drawn upon), guarantees, or other indebtedness, and all amendments, consents, and waivers related thereto, as well as a list of all lenders or holders and certificates to the lenders or the holders during the past three years

- Any and all documents and agreements, evidencing other material financing arrangements, such as sale and leaseback arrangements, capitalized leases and installment purchases

- Any and all bad debts and any agreements which might reasonably be expected to result in a loss

- All warranties, guarantees, and other obligations given or incurred by the Company or any of its subsidiaries

(L) Schedule of prepaid expenses

(M) Schedule of all bank accounts (operating, savings or investment), certificates of deposit and safe deposit boxes, including the following information:

- Name and address of institution

- Account number

- Purpose of account

- Authorized signer

- Current month-end balance

(N) General ledger, sales journals, and cash receipts journals for last fiscal year

(O) A breakdown of the officer's and other salary component of general and administrative expenses for fiscal the last three fiscal years and for the most recent subsequent period

(P) Description of accounting policies, estimates and methods used and any changes to these

(Q) Written documentation of the Company's accounting system/procedures/controls relating to:

- Cash receipts

- Cash disbursements

- Payroll

- Credit, billings and collections

- Purchasing procedures

- Production (including quality control)

- Distribution
- Sales
- Budgeting process
- Financial reporting
- Management Information Systems

(R) Detail fixed asset schedule (furniture, fixtures, equipment, automobiles) with historical cost, accumulated depreciation, including recent appraisals of assets, if any, and reconciliation to general ledger

(S) Management letters (internal control letters from auditors; copies of attorneys' audit letters)

(T) Recent projections including forecasted balance sheets, income and cash flow statements and assumptions upon which the forecasts are based

(U) List and description of any other liabilities or obligations (including contingent ones) not reflected in the interim financial statements or incurred in the ordinary course of business since the date of the last financial statements.

APPENDIX C

This is a sample document for illustrative purposes only. Please consult an attorney before making any warranties or representations about your company.

The following warranties and representations are pro-buyer. They do not reflect any changes that a seller's attorney may negotiate.

WARRANTIES AND REPRESENTATIONS OF THE SELLER

ARTICLE 3

Each of the Sellers, jointly and severally, hereby represents and warrants to the Buyer, as follows:

3.1 Ownership of Shares. Each Seller owns of record and beneficially the number of Shares set forth opposite such Seller's name on Exhibit A hereto. Each Seller has, and will have at the time of the Closing, good and valid title to the Shares to be sold by such Seller hereunder, free and clear of all Encumbrances.

3.2 The Sellers' Power and Authority; Consents and Approvals.

(a) Each Seller has full capacity, right, power and authority to execute and deliver this Agreement and the other agreements, documents and instruments to be executed and delivered by such Seller in connection herewith, to consummate the transactions contemplated hereby and thereby and to perform its obligations hereunder and thereunder.

(b) Except as set forth on Schedule 3.2(b) hereto, no authorization, approval or consent of, or notice to or filing or registration with, any governmental agency or body, or any other third party, is required in connection with the execution and delivery by each Seller of this Agreement and the other agreements, documents and instruments to be executed and delivered by each Seller in connection herewith, the consummation of the transactions contemplated hereby and thereby and the performance by each Seller of his or her obligations hereunder and thereunder.

3.3 Execution and Enforceability. This Agreement and the other agreements, documents and instruments to be executed by the Sellers in connection herewith, and the consummation by each Seller of the transactions contemplated hereby and thereby, have been duly authorized, executed and delivered by each Seller and constitute, and the other agreements, documents and instruments contemplated hereby, when executed and delivered by each Seller, shall constitute, the legal, valid and binding obligations of each Seller, enforceable against each such Seller in accordance with their respective terms, except to the extent that enforceability may be limited by bankruptcy, insolvency and other similar laws affecting the enforcement of creditor's rights generally and general equity principles.

3.4 Litigation Regarding the Sellers. There are no actions, suits, claims, investigations or legal, administrative or arbitration proceedings pending or, to each of the Sellers' knowledge, threatened or probable of assertion, against such Seller relating to the Shares, this Agreement or the transactions contemplated hereby before any court, governmental or administrative agency or other body. None of the Sellers knows of any basis for the institution of any such suit or proceeding. No judgment, order, writ, injunction, decree or other similar command of any court or governmental or administrative agency or other body has been entered against or served upon any Seller relating to the Shares, this Agreement or the transactions contemplated hereby.

3.5 Interest in Competitors and Related Entities; Certain Transactions.

(a) Except as set forth on Schedule 3.5 hereto, neither any Seller nor any Affiliate of any Seller (i) has any direct or indirect interest in any person or entity engaged or involved in any business which is included in the definition of the "Buyer's Business" as defined in the Non-Competition Agreement, (ii) has any direct or indirect interest in any person or entity which is a lessor of assets or properties to, material supplier of, or provider of services to, the Company, or (iii) has a beneficial interest in any contract or agreement to which the Company is a party; provided, however, that the foregoing representation and warranty shall not apply to any person or entity, or any interest or agreement with any person or entity, which is a publicly held corporation in which such Seller individually owns less than _____% of the issued and outstanding voting stock. For purposes of this Agreement, the term "Affiliate" shall mean any entity directly or indirectly controlling, controlled by or under common control with the specified person, whether by stock ownership, agreement or otherwise, or any parent, child or sibling of such specified person and the concept of "control" means the possession, direct or indirect, of the power to direct or cause the direction of the management and policies of such person or entity, whether through the ownership of voting securities, by contract or otherwise.

(b) Except as set forth in Schedule 3.5 hereto, there are no transactions between the Company and any of the Sellers (including the Sellers' Affiliates), or any of the directors, officers or salaried employees of the Company, or the family members or Affiliates of any of the above (other than for services as employees, officers and directors), including, without limitation, any contract, agreement or other arrangement providing for the furnishing of services to or by, providing for rental of real or personal property to or from, or otherwise requiring payments to or from, any of the Sellers, or any such officer, director or salaried employee, family member, or Affiliate or any corporation, partnership, trust or other entity in which such family member, Affiliate, officer, director or employee has a substantial interest or is a shareholder, officer, director, trustee or partner.

3.6 The Sellers Not Foreign Persons. Each Seller is a "United States person" as that term is defined in Section 7701(a)(30) of the Internal Revenue Code of 1986, as amended (the "Code"), and the regulations promulgated thereunder.

3.7 Organization; Good Standing, Etc.

(a) The Company is a corporation duly organized, validly existing and in good standing under the laws of the State of Colorado and has all requisite power and authority to own, lease and operate its properties and to carry on its business as now being conducted. The Company is not qualified, and the nature of its business does not require it to be qualified, to do business as a foreign corporation in any other jurisdictions.

(b) The Holding Company is a corporation duly organized, validly existing and in good standing under the laws of the State of Colorado and has all requisite power and authority to own, lease and operate its properties and to carry on its businesses as now being conducted. The Holding Company is not qualified, and the nature of its business does not require it to be qualified, to do business as a foreign corporation in any other jurisdictions.

3.8 Capitalization. The authorized capital stock of the Holding Company consists of _____ shares of [common] stock, par value $_____ per share, of which _____shares are issued and outstanding and constitute all of the Shares. All of the Shares are duly authorized, validly issued, fully paid and non-assessable and are held by the Sellers in the amounts indicated on Exhibit A hereto. The authorized capital stock of the Company consists of _____ shares of [common] stock, par value $_____ per share of which _____ shares are issued and outstanding and held by the Holding Company. Except as set forth on Schedule 3.8 hereto, there are no preemptive rights, whether at law or otherwise, to purchase any of the securities of the Holding Company or the Company, and there are no outstanding options, warrants, "phantom" stock plans, subscriptions, agreements, plans or other commitments pursuant to which the Holding Company or the Company is or may become obligated to sell or issue any shares of its capital stock or any other debt or equity security, and there are no outstanding securities convertible or exchangeable into shares of such capital stock or any other debt or equity security. There are no voting trusts, shareholder agreements or other agreements, instruments or rights of any kind or nature outstanding or in effect with respect to shares of capital stock of Holding Company or the Company.

3.9 Subsidiaries and Investments. Except for the Holding Company's interests in the Other Dealerships, as described in Schedule 3.9 hereto, neither the Holding Company nor the Company owns or maintains, directly or indirectly, any capital stock of or other equity or ownership or proprietary interest in any other corporation, partnership, limited liability company, association, trust, joint venture or other entity and does not have any commitment to contribute to the capital of, make loans to, or share in the losses of, any such entity.

3.10 No Violation; Conflicts. Except as set forth on Schedule 3.10 hereto, the execution and delivery by the Sellers of this Agreement and the other agreements, documents and instruments to be executed and delivered by the Sellers in connection herewith, the consummation by the Sellers of the transactions contemplated hereby and thereby and the performance by the Sellers of their respective obligations hereunder and thereunder do not and will not (a) conflict with or violate any of the terms of the Articles of Incorporation or By-Laws of the Holding Company or the Company, (b) violate or conflict with any law, ordinance, rule or regulation, or any judgment, order, writ, injunction, decree or similar command of any court, administrative or governmental agency or other body, applicable to the Holding Company or the Company, (c) violate or conflict with the terms of, or result in the acceleration of, any indebtedness or obligation of the Holding Company or the Company under, or violate or conflict with or result in a breach of, or constitute a default under, any indenture, mortgage, deed of trust, agreement or instrument to which the Holding Company or the Company is a party or by which the Holding Company or the Company or any of its assets or properties is bound or affected, (d) result in the creation or imposition of any Encumbrance of any nature upon any of the assets or properties of the Holding Company or the Company, (e) constitute an event permitting termination of any material agreement, license or other right of the Holding Company or the Company, or (f) require any authorization, approval or consent of, or any notice to or filing or registration with, any governmental agency or body, or any other third party, applicable to the Holding Company or the Company or any of its properties or assets.

3.11 Title to Assets; Related Matters.

(a) The Company has good and valid title to all assets, rights, interests and other properties, real, personal and mixed, tangible and intangible, owned by it, other than the Distributed Assets (collectively, the "Assets"), free and clear of all Encumbrances, except those specified on Schedule 3.11 and liens for Taxes not yet due and payable. The Assets (a) include all properties and assets (real, personal and mixed, tangible and intangible) owned by the Company and used or held for use in the conduct of its business; and (b) do not include (i) any contracts for future services, prepaid items or deferred assets or charges the full value or benefit of which will not be transferable to and usable by the Buyer, or (ii) any goodwill, organizational expense or other similar intangible asset.

(b) As of the Closing, the Holding Company will have no assets other than (i) its stock ownership interest in the Company, and (ii) the cash or marketable securities included in the Holding Company Net Assets Value. Such cash and marketable securities will be free and clear of all Encumbrances.

3.12 Possession. The tangible assets included within the Assets are physically identifiable and are in the possession or control of the Company and no other person or entity has a right to possession or claims possession of all or any part of such Assets, except the rights of lessors of Leased Equipment and Leased Premises (each as defined in Section 3.16 hereof) under their respective contracts and leases.

3.13 Financial Statements.

(a) The Sellers have delivered to the Buyer prior to the date hereof:

(i) the [unaudited] balance sheet of the Company and the related unaudited statements of income, stockholders' equity and changes in cash flows for the last two fiscal years of the Company (including the notes thereto and any other information included therein) (collectively, the "Annual Financial Statements"); and

(ii) the monthly year-to-date unaudited balance sheet of the Company and the related unaudited statements of income, stockholders' equity and changes in cash flow, as certified by the Company's President (collectively, the "Interim Financial Statements"; the Annual Financial Statements and the Interim Financial Statements are hereinafter collectively referred to as the "Financial Statements").

(b) The Financial Statements (i) are in accordance with the books and records of the Company, which books and records are true, correct and complete, (ii) fully and fairly present the financial condition of the Company as of the dates indicated and the results of operations, changes in stockholders' equity and cash flow of the Company for the periods indicated, and (iii) except as set forth in Schedule 3.13, have been prepared in accordance with GAAP consistently applied.

3.14 Accounts Receivable. All accounts receivable of the Company are collectible at the aggregate recorded amounts thereof, subject to the reserve for doubtful accounts maintained by the Company in the ordinary course of business, and are not subject to any known counterclaims or setoffs. An adequate reserve for doubtful accounts for the Company has been established and such reserve is consistent with the operation of the Company in both the ordinary course of business and past practice.

3.15 Inventories. All inventories of the Company consist of items of a quality and quantity usable and saleable in the ordinary course of business of the Company, and the levels of inventories are consistent with the levels maintained by the Company in the ordinary course consistent with past practice and the Company's obligations under its agreements with the

Manufacturer and all applicable distributors. The values at which such
inventories are carried are based on the FIFO method and are stated in
accordance with GAAP by the Sellers at the lower of historic cost or
market. An adequate reserve has been established by the Company for
damaged, spoiled, obsolete, defective, or slow-moving goods and such
reserve is consistent with both the operation of the Company in the ordinary course of business and past practice.

3.16 Real Property; Machinery and Equipment.

(a) Schedule 3.16(a) hereto contains a complete list and brief description of all real property, if any, owned by the Company, and a
summary description of the improvements (including buildings
and other structures) located thereon (collectively, the "Owned
Real Property"). True and correct copies of the deeds with respect
to the Owned Real Property have been delivered to the Buyer. The
Company is the sole owner of the Owned Real Property and holds
the Owned Real Property in fee simple or its equivalent under
local law, free and clear of all building use restrictions, exceptions,
variances, limitations or other title defects of any nature whatsoever, except those set forth in Schedule 3.16(a) hereto (the
"Permitted Encumbrances"). There are no leases, written or oral,
affecting all or any part of the Owned Real Property. The only real
property (other than the Leased Premises) used by the Company
in connection with the Company's business is the Owned Real
Property. The Owned Real Property (including, without limitation,
the roof, the walls and all plumbing, wiring, electrical, heating, air
conditioning, fire protection and other systems, as well as all
paved areas, included therein or located threat) is in good
working order, condition and repair and is not in need of maintenance or repairs except for maintenance and repairs which are
routine, ordinary and not material in nature or cost.

(b) Schedule 3.16(b) hereto contains a complete list and description
(including buildings and other structures thereon and the name of

the owner thereof) of all real property of which the Company is a tenant (herein collectively referred to as the "Leased Premises," and, together with the Owned Real Property, sometimes collectively referred to as the "Real Property"). True, correct and complete copies of all leases, including, without limitation, the Existing Lease, of all Leased Premises (the "Leases") have been delivered to the Buyer. The Leased Premises (including, without limitation, the roof, the walls and all plumbing, wiring, electrical, heating, air conditioning, fire protection and other systems, as well as all paved areas, included therein or located thereat) are in good working order, condition and repair and are not in need of maintenance or repairs except for maintenance and repairs which are routine, ordinary and not material in nature or cost. With respect to each Lease, no event or condition currently exists which would give rise to a material repair or restoration obligation if such Lease were to terminate. The Sellers have no knowledge of any event or condition which currently exists which would create a legal or other impediment to the use of the Leased Premises as currently used, or would increase the additional charges or other sums payable by the tenant under any of the Leases (including, without limitation, any pending Tax reassessment or other special assessment affecting the Leased Premises).

(c) There has been no work performed, services rendered or materials furnished in connection with repairs, improvements, construction, alteration, demolition or similar activities with respect to the Real Property for at least ninety (90) days before the date hereof; there are no outstanding claims or persons entitled to any claim or right to a claim for a mechanics' or material man's lien against the Real Property; and there is no person or entity other than the Company in or entitled to possession of the Real Property.

(d) The Company has all easements and rights, including, but not limited to, easements for power lines, water lines, sewers, roadways and other means of ingress and egress, necessary to conduct the business the Company now conducts, all such easements and rights are perpetual, unconditional appurtenant rights to the Real Property, and none of such easements or rights are subject to any forfeiture or divestiture rights. Insofar as the representations and warranties in this Subsection are made with respect to the Leased Premises, they are made to the Sellers' knowledge.

(e) Neither the whole nor any portion of any of the Real Property has been condemned, expropriated, ordered to be sold or otherwise taken by any public authority, with or without payment or compensation therefor, and the Sellers do not know of any such condemnation, expropriation, sale or taking, or have any grounds to anticipate that any such condemnation, expropriation, sale or taking is threatened or contemplated. The Sellers have no knowledge of any pending assessments which would affect the Real Property.

(f) None of the Real Property is in violation of any public or private restriction or any law or any building, zoning, health, safety, fire or other law, ordinance, code or regulation, and no notice from any governmental body has been served upon the Company or upon any of the Real Property claiming any violation of any such law, ordinance, code or regulation or requiring or calling to the attention of the Company the need for any work, repair, construction, alterations or installation on or in connection with said properties which has not been complied with. All improvements which comprise a part of the Real Property are located within the record lines of the Real Property and none of the improvements located on the Real Property encroach upon any adjoining property or any easements or rights of way and no improvements located on any adjoining property encroach upon any of the Real Property or any easements or rights of way servicing the Real Property.

(g) Schedule 3.16(g) hereto sets forth a list of all material machinery, equipment, motor vehicles, furniture and fixtures owned by the Company (collectively, the "Owned Equipment").

(h) Schedule 3.16(h) hereto contains a list of all leases or other agreements, whether written or oral, under which the Company is lessee of or holds or operates any items of machinery, equipment, motor vehicles, furniture and fixtures or other property (other than real property) owned by any third party (collectively, the "Leased Equipment").

(i) The Owned Equipment and the Leased Equipment are in good operating condition, maintenance and repair in accordance with industry standards taking into account the age thereof.

3.17 Patents; Trademarks; Tradenames; Service Marks; Copyrights; Licenses, Etc.

(a) Except as set forth on Schedule 3.17 hereto, there are no patents, trademarks, trade names, service marks, service names, domain names, or copyrights, and there are no applications therefor or licenses thereof, inventions, trade secrets, computer software, logos, slogans, proprietary processes and formulae or other proprietary information, know-how and intellectual property rights, whether patentable or unpatentable, that are owned or leased by the Company or used in the conduct of the Company's business. The Company is not a party to, and the Company pays no royalty to anyone under, any license or similar agreement. There is no existing claim, or, to the knowledge of the Sellers, any basis for any claim, against the Company that any of its operations, activities or products infringe the patents, trademarks, trade names, copyrights or other property rights of others or that the Company is otherwise wrongfully using the property rights of others. There is no existing claim or, to the knowledge of the Sellers, any basis for any claim by the Company against any third party that the operations, activities or products of such third party infringe the patents, trademarks, trade names, service marks, service names, copyrights or other property rights of the Company or that such third party is otherwise wrongfully using the property rights of the Company.

(b) The Company has the right to use in the State of Colorado the names, tradenames and service marks [_____] and [INSERT ANY OTHER NAMES USED, INCLUDING FAMILY NAME(S) IF APPLICABLE], as well as the names, tradenames and service marks listed on Schedule 3.17 hereto, and to the knowledge of the Sellers, no person uses, or has the right to use, such names, tradenames or service marks or any derivation thereof in connection with the manufacture, sale, marketing or distribution of products or services commonly associated with an the Company's business automobile dealership.

3.18 Certain Liabilities.

(a) All accounts payable by the Company to third parties as of the date hereof arose in the ordinary course of business and none are delinquent or past-due.

(b) Schedule 3.18 hereto sets forth a list of all indebtedness of the Company, other than accounts payable, as of the close of business on the day preceding the date hereof, including, without limitation, money borrowed, indebtedness of the Company owed to stockholders and former stockholders, the deferred purchase price of assets, letters of credit and capitalized leases, indicating, in each case, the name or names of the lender, the date of maturity, the rate of interest, any prepayment penalties or premiums and the unpaid principal amount of such indebtedness as of such date.

Except as set forth on Schedule 3.18, the Company has not guaranteed, or in any way agreed to pay, discharge or otherwise be responsible, directly or indirectly, for, any indebtedness or other obligation of any person or entity including, without limitation, an Affiliate of the Company of the Sellers (collectively, "Company Guaranty Obligations"). The amount of any Company Guaranty Obligations not fully satisfied and discharged at or prior to the Closing, or not fully and unconditionally released by the holders thereof at or prior to the Closing, shall be included as liabilities on the Closing Balance Sheet.

(d) As of the Closing, the Holding Company will have no liabilities or obligations of any nature, known or unknown, fixed or contingent, matured or unmatured (including, without limitation, any of the foregoing which may be owed to the Sellers or any of their Affiliates), other than the accruals for Tax liabilities included in the Holding Company Net Assets Value.

3.19 No Undisclosed Liabilities. The Company has no material liabilities or obligations of any nature, known or unknown, fixed or contingent, matured or unmatured (including, without limitation, any of the foregoing which may be owed to the Sellers or any of their Affiliates), other than those (a) reflected in the Financial Statements, (b) incurred in the ordinary course of business since the date of the Financial Statements and of the type and kind reflected in the Financial Statements, or (c) disclosed specifically on Schedule 3.19 hereto or otherwise reasonably disclosed in this Agreement or the other schedules hereto.

3.20 Absence of Changes. Since December 31, [INSERT DATE OF MOST RECENT BALANCE SHEET INCLUDED IN THE ANNUAL FINANCIAL STATEMENTS], the business of the Company has been operated in the ordinary course, consistent with past practices and, except as set forth on Schedule 3.20 hereto, there has not been incurred, nor has there occurred, except as contemplated in Section 1.5 hereof: (a) any damage, destruction or loss (whether or not covered by insurance), adversely affecting the business or assets of the Company in excess of $_____; (b) any strikes, work stoppages or other labor disputes involving the employees of the Company; (c) any sale, transfer, pledge or other disposition of any of the assets of the Company having an aggregate book value of $_____ or more (except sales of vehicles and parts inventory in the ordinary course of business); (d) any declaration or payment of any dividend or other distribution in respect of its capital stock or any redemption, repurchase or other acquisition of its capital stock; (e) any amendment, termination, waiver or cancellation of any Material Agreement (as defined in Section 3.29 hereof) or any termination, amendment, waiver or cancellation of any material right or claim of the Company under any Material Agreement (except in each case in the ordinary course of business and consistent with past practice); (f) any (i) general uniform increase in the compensation of the employees of the Company (including, without limitation, any increase pursuant to any bonus, pension, profit-sharing, deferred compensation or other plan or commitment), other than in the ordinary course of business, (ii) increase in any such compensation payable to any individual officer, director, consultant or agent thereof, other than in the ordinary course of business, or (iii) loan or commitment therefor made by the Company to any officer, director, stockholder, employee, consultant or agent of the Company; (g) any change in the accounting methods, procedures or practices followed by the Company or any change in depreciation or amortization policies or rates theretofore adopted by the Company; (h) any material change in policies, operations or practices of the Company with respect to business operations followed by the Company, including, without limitation, with respect to selling methods, returns, discounts or other terms of sale, or with respect to the policies, operations or practices of the Company concerning the employees of the Company; (i) any capital appropriation or expenditure or commitment therefor on behalf of the Company in excess of $_____ individually or $_____ in the aggregate; (j) any write-down or write-up of the value of any inventory or equipment of the Company or any increase in inventory levels in excess of historical levels for comparable periods; (k) any account receivable in excess of $_____ or note receivable in excess of $_____ owing to the Company which (1) has been written off as uncollectible, in whole or in part, (2) has had asserted against it any claim, refusal or right of setoff, or (3) the account or note debtor has refused to, or threatened not to, pay for any reason, or such account or note debtor has become insolvent or bankrupt; (l) any other change in the condition (financial or otherwise), business operations, assets, earnings, business or prospects of the Company which has, or could reasonably be expected to have, a material adverse effect on the assets, business or operations of the Company; or (m) any agreement, whether in writing or otherwise, for the Company to take any of the actions enumerated in this Section 3.20.

3.21 Tax Matters.

(a) All federal, state and local income, profits, franchise, sales, use, occupation, property, excise, payroll, withholding, employment, estimated and other taxes of any nature, including interest, penalties and other additions to such taxes ("Taxes"), payable by, or due from, the Company for all periods prior to the date hereof have been fully paid or adequately reserved for by the Company or, with respect to Taxes required to be accrued, the Company has properly accrued or will properly accrue such Taxes in the ordinary course of business consistent with past practice of the Company. References herein to "Tax" are references to one or more Taxes.

(b) All federal, state and local Tax returns and Tax reports required as of the date hereof to be filed by the Company for taxable periods ending prior to the date hereof have been duly and timely filed prior to the due date thereof (as such due date may have been lawfully extended) by the Company with the appropriate governmental agencies, and all such returns and reports are true, correct and complete.

(c) The federal and state income Tax returns of the Company have been audited by the Internal Revenue Service ("IRS") or are closed by the applicable statutes of limitations for all taxable years through [INSERT DATE]. Except as set forth on Schedule 3.21 hereto, the Company has not received any notice of any assessed or proposed claim or deficiency against it in respect of, or of any present dispute between it and any governmental agency concerning, any Taxes. Except as set forth on Schedule 3.21 hereto, no examination or audit of any Tax return or report of the Company by any applicable Taxing authority is currently in progress and there are no outstanding agreements or waivers extending the statutory period of limitation applicable to any Tax return or report of the Company. Copies of all federal, state and local Tax returns and reports required to be filed by the Company for the years ended 2003, 2002, 2001, and 2000, together with all schedules and attachments thereto, have been delivered by the Sellers to the Buyer.

(d) The Company is not now, nor has it ever been, a member of a consolidated group for federal income Tax purposes or a consolidated, combined or similar group for state Tax purposes. No consent under Code Section 341 has been made affecting the Company. The Company is not a party to any agreement or arrangement that would result in the payment of any "excess parachute payments" under Code Section 280G. The Company is not required to make any adjustment under Code Section 481(a). No power of attorney relating to Taxes is currently in effect affecting the Company.

3.22 Compliance with Laws, Etc. The Company has conducted its operations and business in compliance with, and all of the Assets (including all of the Real Property and Leased Equipment) comply with, (a) all applicable laws, rules, regulations and codes (including, without limitation, any laws, rules, regulations and codes relating to anti-competitive practices, contracts, discrimination, employee benefits, employment, health, safety, fire, building and zoning, but excluding Environmental Laws which are the subject of Section 3.36 hereof) and (b) all applicable orders, rules, writs, judgments, injunctions, decrees and ordinances. The Company has not received any notification of any asserted present or past failure by it to comply with such laws, rules or regulations, or such orders, writs, judgments, injunctions, decrees or ordinances. Set forth on Schedule 3.22 hereto are all orders, writs, judgments, injunctions, decrees and other awards of any court or governmental agency applicable to the Company and/or its business or operations. The Sellers have delivered to the Buyer copies of all reports, if any, of the Company required to be submitted under the Federal Occupational Safety and Health Act of 1970, as amended, and under all other applicable health and safety laws and regulations. The deficiencies, if any, noted on such reports have been corrected by the Company and any deficiencies noted by inspection through the Closing Date will have been corrected by the Company by the Closing Date.

3.23 Litigation Regarding the Company. Except as set forth on Schedule 3.23 hereto, there are no actions, suits, claims, investigations or legal, administrative or arbitration proceedings pending, or, to the Sellers' knowledge, threatened or probable of assertion, against the Company or relating to any of its assets, business or operations or the transactions contemplated by this Agreement, and the Sellers do not know of any basis for the institution of any such suit or proceeding. Except as set forth on Schedule 3.23, all actions, suits or proceedings pending or, to the knowledge of the Sellers, threatened against or affecting the Company are covered in full by insurance, without any reservations of rights, subject only to the payment of applicable deductibles. No order, writ, judgment, injunction, decree or similar command of any court or any governmental or administrative agency or other body has been entered against or served upon the Company relating to the Company or any of its assets, business or operations.

3.24 Permits, Etc. Set forth on Schedule 3.24 hereto is a list of all governmental licenses, permits, approvals, certificates of inspection and other authorizations, filings and registrations that are necessary for the Company to own and operate its business as presently conducted (collectively, the "Permits"). All such Permits have been duly and lawfully secured or made by the Company and are in full force and effect. There is no proceeding pending, or, to the Sellers' knowledge, threatened or probable of assertion, to revoke or limit any such Permit. Except as set forth on Schedule 3.24 hereto, none of the transactions contemplated by this Agreement will terminate, violate or limit the effectiveness of any such Permit.

3.25 Employees; Labor Relations. As of the date hereof, the Company employs a total of approximately _____employees. As of the date hereof: (a) the Company is not delinquent in the payment (i) to or on behalf of its past or present employees of any wages, salaries, commissions, bonuses, benefit plan contributions or other compensation for all periods prior to the date hereof, or (ii) of any amount which is due and payable to any state or state fund pursuant to any workers' compensation statute, rule or regulation or any amount which is due and payable to any workers' compensation claimant; (b) there are no collective bargaining agreements currently in effect between the Company and labor unions or organizations representing any employees of the Company; (c) no collective bargaining agreement is currently being negotiated by the Company; (d) to the knowledge of the Sellers, there are no union organizational drives in progress and there has been no formal or informal request to the Company for collective bargaining or for an employee election from any union or from the National Labor Relations Board; and (e) no dispute exists between the Company and any of its sales representatives or, to the knowledge of the Sellers, between any such sales representatives with respect to territory, commissions, products or any other terms of their representation. No employees of the Company will be entitled to any severance or other payment in connection with the execution and delivery of this Agreement or the consummation of the transactions contemplated hereby.

3.26 Compensation. Schedule 3.26 contains a schedule of all employees (including sales representatives) and consultants of the Company (a) whose individual cash compensation for the year ended December 31, 200___ is in excess of $_____, or (b) whose individual cash compensation is expected to exceed $_____ in the current calendar year, together with the amount of total compensation paid to each such person for the twelve month period ended December 31, 200___ and the current aggregate base salary or hourly rate (including any bonus or commission) for each such person.

3.27 Employee Benefits.

(a) The Sellers have listed on Schedule 3.27 and have delivered to the Buyer true and complete copies of all Employee Plans (as defined below) and related documents, established, maintained or contributed to by the Company (which shall include for this purpose and for the purpose of all of the representations in this Section 3.27, the Sellers and all employers, whether or not incorporated, that are treated together with the Company as a single employer within the meaning of Section 414 of the Code). The term "Employee Plan" shall include all plans described in Section 3(3) of the Employee Retirement Income Security Act of 1974, as amended ("ERISA") and also shall include, without limitation, any deferred compensation, stock, employee or retiree pension benefit, welfare benefit or other similar fringe or employee benefit plan, program, policy, contract or arrangement, written or oral, qualified or nonqualified, funded or unfunded, foreign or domestic, covering employees or former employees of the Company and maintained (whether as a plan sponsor, participating employer or otherwise) or contributed to by the Company.

(b) Where applicable, each Employee Plan (i) has been administered in material compliance with the terms of such Employee Plan and the requirements of ERISA, the Code and all other applicable laws; and (ii) is in material compliance with the reporting and disclosure requirements of ERISA and the Code. The Company neither maintains nor contributes to, and has never maintained or contributed to, an Employee Plan that is either (i) subject to Title IV of ERISA, or (ii) a "multi-employer plan" or (iii) subject to the minimum funding standards of Section 412 of the Code or Section 302 of ERISA. There are no facts relating to any Employee Plan that (i) have resulted in a "prohibited transaction" of a material nature or have resulted or are reasonably likely to result in the imposition of a material excise tax, penalty or liability pursuant to Section 4975 of the Code, (ii) have resulted in a material breach of fiduciary duty or violation of Part 4 of Title I of ERISA, or (iii) have resulted or are reasonably likely to result in any material liability (whether or not asserted as of the date hereof) of the Company or any ERISA affiliate pursuant to Section 412 of the Code arising under or related to any event, act or omission occurring on or prior to the date hereof. Each Employee Plan that is intended to qualify under Section 401(a) or to be exempt under Section 501(c) of the Code is so qualified or exempt as of the date hereof in each case as such Employee Plan has received favorable determination letters from the Internal Revenue Service with respect thereto. To the knowledge of the Sellers, the amendments to and operation of any Employee Plan subsequent to the issuance of such determination letters do not adversely affect the qualified status of any such Employee Plan. No Employee Plan has an "accumulated funding deficiency" as of the date hereof, whether or not waived, and no waiver has been applied for. The Company has not made any promises or incurred any liability under any Employee Plan or otherwise to provide health or other welfare benefits to current or future retirees or other former employees of the Company (or to their spouses or dependents), except as specifically required by law. There are no pending or, to the best knowledge of the Sellers, threatened, claims (other than routine claims for benefit) or lawsuits with respect to the Company's Employee Plans. No termination, "back-end" load or other similar fee or expense is payable in connection with the termination and winding up of any of the Employee Plans in accordance with Section 5.15 below. As used in this Section 3.27, all technical terms enclosed in quotation marks shall have the meaning set forth in ERISA or the Code, as the case may be.

3.28 Powers of Attorney. There are no persons, firms, associations, corporations or business organizations or entities holding general or special powers of attorney from the Company.

3.29 Material Agreements.

(a) Set forth on Schedule 3.29(a) hereto is a list or, where indicated, a brief description of all leases and all other contracts, agreements, documents, instruments, guarantees, plans, understandings or arrangements, written or oral, which are material to the Company or its business or assets (collectively, the "Material Agreements"). True copies of all written Material Agreements and written summaries of all oral Material Agreements described or required to be described on Schedule 3.29(a) have been furnished to the Buyer.

(b) The Company has in all material respects performed all of its obligations required to be performed by it to the date hereof, and is not in default or alleged to be in default in any material respect, under any Material Agreement, and there exists no event, condition or occurrence which, after notice or lapse of time or both, would constitute such a default. To the knowledge of the Sellers, no other party to any Material Agreement is in default in any material respect of any of its obligations thereunder. Each of the Material Agreements is valid and in full force and effect and enforceable against the parties thereto in accordance with their respective terms, and, except as set forth in Schedule 3.29(b) hereto, the consummation of the transactions contemplated by this Agreement will not (i) require the consent of any party thereto or (ii) constitute an event permitting termination thereof.

3.30 Brokers' or Finders' Fees, Etc. No agent, broker, investment banker, person or firm acting on behalf of the Company or any of the Sellers or any person, firm or corporation affiliated with any of the Sellers or under their authority is or will be entitled to any brokers' or finders' fee or any other commission or similar fee directly or indirectly from any of the parties hereto in connection with the sale of the Shares contemplated hereby, other than any such fee or commission the entire cost of which will be borne by the Sellers.

3.31 Bank Accounts, Credit Cards, Safe Deposit Boxes and Cellular Telephones. Schedule 3.31 hereto lists all bank accounts, credit cards and safe deposit boxes in the name of, or controlled by, the Company, and all cellular telephones provided and/or paid for by the Company, and details about the persons having access to or authority over such accounts, credit cards, safe deposit boxes and cellular telephones.

3.32 Insurance.

(a) Schedule 3.32(a) hereto contains a list of all policies of liability, theft, fidelity, life, fire, product liability, workers' compensation, health and any other insurance and bonds maintained by, or on behalf of, the Company on their respective properties, operations, inventories, assets, business or personnel (specifying the insurer, amount of coverage, type of insurance, policy number and any pending claims in excess of $5,000 thereunder). Each such insurance policy identified therein is and shall remain in full force and effect on and as of the Closing Date and the Company is not in default with respect to any provision contained in any such insurance policy and has not failed to give any notice or present any material claim under any such insurance policy in a due and timely fashion. The insurance maintained by, or on behalf of, the Company is adequate in accordance with the standards of business of comparable size in the location and industry in which the Company operates and no notice of cancellation or termination has been received with respect to any such policy. The Company has not, during the last three (3) fiscal years, been denied or had revoked or rescinded any policy of insurance.

(b) Set forth on Schedule 3.32(b) hereto is a summary of information pertaining to material property damage and personal injury claims in excess of $_____ against the Company during the past five (5) years, all of which are fully satisfied or are being defended by the insurance carrier and involve no exposure to the Company.

3.33 Warranties. Set forth on Schedule 3.33 hereto are descriptions or copies of the forms of all express warranties and disclaimers of warranty made by the Company (separate and distinct from any applicable manufacturers,' suppliers' or other third-parties' warranties or disclaimers of warranties) during the past five (5) years to customers or users of the vehicles, parts, products or services of the Company. There have been no breach of warranty or breach of representation claims against the Company during the past five (5) years which have resulted in any cost, expenditure or exposure to the Company of more than $_____ individually or in the aggregate.

3.34 Directors and Officers. Set forth on Schedule 3.34 hereto is a true and correct list of the names and titles of each director and officer of the Company.

3.35 Suppliers and Customers. The Company is not required to provide bonding or any other security arrangements in connection with any transactions with any of its respective customers and suppliers. To the knowledge of the Sellers, no such supplier, customer or creditor intends or has threatened, or reasonably could be expected, to terminate or modify any of its relationships with the Company.

3.36 Environmental Matters.

(a) For purposes of this Section 3.36, the following terms shall have the following meaning: (i) "Environmental Law" means all applicable federal, state and local laws, statutes, regulations, rules, ordinances and common law, and all judgments, decrees, orders, agreements, or permits, issued, promulgated, approved or entered thereunder by any government authority relating to pollution, Hazardous Materials, worker safety or protection of human health or the environment; (ii) "Hazardous Materials" means any waste, pollutant, chemical, hazardous material, hazardous substance, toxic substance, hazardous waste, special waste, solid waste, asbestos, radioactive materials, polychlorinated biphenyls, petroleum or petroleum-derived substance or waste (regardless of specific gravity), or any constituent or decomposition product of any such pollutant, material, substance or waste, including, but not limited to, any hazardous substance or constituent contained within any waste and any other pollutant, material, substance or waste regulated under or as defined by any Environmental Law.

(b) The Company has obtained all permits, licenses and other authorizations or approvals required under Environmental Laws for the conduct and operation of the Assets and the business of the Company ("Environmental Permits"). All such Environmental Permits are in good standing, the Company is and has been in compliance in all material respects with the terms and conditions of all such Environmental Permits, and no appeal or any other action is pending or threatened to revoke any such Environmental Permit.

(c) The Company and its business, operations and assets are and have been in compliance in all material respects with all Environmental Laws.

(d) Neither the Company nor any of the Sellers has received any written or oral order, notice, complaint, request for information, claim, demand or other communication from any government authority or other person, whether based in contract, tort, implied or express warranty, strict liability, or any other common law theory, or any criminal or civil statute, arising from or with respect to (i) the presence, release or threatened release of any Hazardous Material or any other environmental condition on, in or under the Real Property or any other property formerly owned, used or leased by the Company, (ii) any other circumstances forming the basis of any actual or alleged violation by the Company or the Sellers of any Environmental Law or any liability of the Company or the Sellers under any Environmental Law, (iii) any remedial or removal action required to be taken by the Company or the Sellers under any Environmental Law, or (iv) any harm, injury or damage to real or personal property, natural resources, the environment or any person alleged to have resulted from the foregoing, nor are the Sellers aware of any facts which might reasonably give rise to such notice or communication. Neither the Company nor any of the Sellers has entered into any agreements concerning any removal or remediation of Hazardous Materials.

(e) No lawsuits, claims, civil actions, criminal actions, administrative proceedings, investigations or enforcement or other actions are pending or threatened under any Environmental Law with respect to the Company, the Sellers or the Real Property.

(f) No Hazardous Materials are or have been released, discharged, spilled or disposed of or have migrated onto, the Real Property or any other property previously owned, operated or leased by the Company, and no environmental condition exists (including, without limitation, the presence, release, threatened release or disposal of Hazardous Materials) related to the Real Property, to any property previously owned, operated or leased by the Company, or to the Company's past or present operations, which would constitute a violation of any Environmental Law or otherwise give rise to costs, liabilities or obligations under any Environmental Law.

(g) Neither the Company or the Sellers, nor, to the knowledge of the Sellers, any of their respective predecessors in interest, has transported or disposed of, or arranged for the transportation or disposal of, any Hazardous Materials to any location (i) which is listed on the National Priorities List, the CERCLIS list under the Comprehensive Environmental Response, Compensation and Liability Act of 1980, as amended, or any similar federal, state or local list, (ii) which is the subject of any federal, state or local enforcement action or other investigation, or (iii) about which the Company or the Sellers has received or has reason to expect to receive a potentially responsible party notice or other notice under any Environmental Law.

(h) No environmental lien has attached or is threatened to be attached to the Real Property.

(i) No employee of the Company in the course of his or her employment with the Company has been exposed to any Hazardous Materials or other substance, generated, produced or used by the Company which could give rise to any claim (whether or not such claim has been asserted) against the Company.

(j) Except as set forth on Schedule 3.36 hereto, the Real Property does not contain any: (i) septic tanks into which process wastewater or any Hazardous Materials have been disposed; (ii) asbestos; (iii) polychlorinated biphenyls (PCBs); (iv) underground injection or monitoring wells; or (v) underground storage tanks.

(k) Except as set forth on Schedule 3.36, there have been no environmental studies or reports made relating to the Real Property or any other property or facility previously owned, operated or leased by the Company.

(l) The Company has not agreed to assume, defend, undertake, guarantee, or provide indemnification for, any liability, including, without limitation, any obligation for corrective or remedial action, of any other person or entity under any Environmental Law for environmental matters or conditions.

3.37 Business Generally. None of the Sellers is aware of the existence of any conditions, including, without limitation, any actual or potential competitive factors in the markets in which the Company participates, which have not been disclosed in writing to the Buyer and which could reasonably be expected to have a material adverse effect on the business and operations of the Company, other than general business and economic conditions generally affecting the industry and markets in which the Company participates.

3.38 Manufacturer Communications. Except as set forth on Schedule 3.38, the Manufacturer has not (a) notified any of the Sellers of any deficiency in dealership operations, including, but not limited to, the following areas: (i) brand imaging, (ii) facility conditions, (iii) sales efficiency, (iv) customer satisfaction, (v) warranty work and reimbursement, or (vi) sales incentives; (b) otherwise advised any of the Sellers of a present or future need for facility improvements or upgrades in connection with the Company's business; or (c) notified any of the Sellers of the awarding or possible awarding of its franchise to an entity or entities other than the

Company in the Metropolitan Statistical Area in which the Company operates.

3.39 Misstatements and Omissions. No representation and warranty by the Sellers contained in this Agreement, and no statement contained in any certificate or Schedule furnished or to be furnished by the Sellers to the Buyer in connection with this Agreement, contains or will contain any untrue statement of a material fact or omits or will omit to state a material fact necessary in order to make such representation and warranty or such statement not misleading.

ARTICLE 4

A Buyer's warranties and representations are fairly standard. They typically do not require extensive negotiation.

WARRANTIES AND REPRESENTATIONS OF THE BUYER

The Buyer hereby represents and warrants to the Sellers as follows:

4.1 Organization and Good Standing. The Buyer is a corporation duly organized and validly existing and in good standing under the laws of the State of _____.

4.2 Buyer's Power and Authority; Consents and Approvals.

(a) The Buyer has, or will have prior to Closing, all requisite corporate power and authority to execute and deliver this Agreement and the other agreements, documents and instruments to be executed and delivered by the Buyer in connection herewith, to consummate the transactions contemplated hereby and thereby and to perform its obligations hereunder and thereunder.

(b) Except as set forth in Schedule 4.2(b) hereto, no authorization, approval or consent of, or notice to or filing or registration with, any governmental agency or body, or any other third party, is required in connection with the execution and delivery by the Buyer of this Agreement and the other agreements, documents and instruments to be executed by the Buyer in connection herewith, the consummation by the Buyer of the transactions contemplated hereby or thereby or the performance by the Buyer of its obligations hereunder and thereunder.

4.3 Execution and Enforceability. This Agreement and the other agreements, documents and instruments to be executed and delivered by the Buyer in connection herewith, and the consummation by the Buyer of the transactions contemplated hereby and thereby, have been, or will be prior to Closing, duly and validly authorized, executed and delivered by all necessary corporate action on the part of the Buyer and this Agreement constitutes, and the other agreements, documents and instruments to be executed and delivered by the Buyer in connection herewith, when executed and delivered by the Buyer, shall constitute the legal, valid and binding obligations of the Buyer, enforceable against the Buyer in accordance with their respective terms, except to the extent that enforceability may be limited by bankruptcy, insolvency and other similar laws affecting the enforcement of creditor's rights generally and general equity principles.

4.4 Litigation Regarding Buyer. There are no actions, suits, claims, investigations or legal, administrative or arbitration proceedings pending or, to the Buyer's knowledge, threatened or probable of assertion against the Buyer relating to this Agreement or the transactions contemplated hereby before any court, governmental or administrative agency or other body, and no judgment, order, writ, injunction, decree or other similar command of any court or governmental or administrative agency or other body has been entered against or served upon the Buyer relating to this Agreement or the transactions contemplated hereby.

4.5 No Violation; Conflicts. The execution and delivery by the Buyer of this Agreement and the other agreements, documents and instruments to be executed and delivered by the Buyer in connection herewith, the consummation by the Buyer of the transactions contemplated hereby and thereby and the performance by the Buyer of its obligations hereunder and thereunder do not and will not (a) conflict with or violate any of the terms of the Certificate of Incorporation or By-Laws of the Buyer, or (b) violate or conflict with any domestic law, ordinance, rule or regulation, or any judgment, order, writ, injunction or decree of any court, administrative or governmental agency or other body, material to the Buyer.

4.6 Brokers' or Finders' Fees, Etc. No agent, broker, investment banker, person or firm acting on behalf of the Buyer or any person, firm or corporation affiliated with the Buyer or under its authority is or will be entitled to any brokers' or finders' fee or any other commission or similar fee directly or indirectly from any of the parties hereto in connection with the sale of the Shares contemplated hereby.

4.7 Misstatements and Omissions. No representation and warranty by the Buyer contained in this Agreement, and no statement contained in any certificate or Schedule furnished or to be furnished by the Buyer to the Sellers in connection with this Agreement, contains or will contain any untrue statement of a material fact or omits or will omit to state a material fact necessary in order to make such representation and warranty or such statement not misleading.

APPENDIX D

This is a sample document for illustrative purposes only. Please consult an attorney before entering into any Letter of Intent.

SAMPLE LETTER OF INTENT

AND

ACCOMPANYING TERM SHEET

PRIVATE & CONFIDENTIAL

Seller's Name

Company Name

Denver, Colorado

Re: Non-Binding Letter of Intent

Dear Mr. Seller:

This letter (this "Letter") sets forth the mutual understanding between BUYER'S COMPANY, an Illinois corporation ("Buyer") and SELLER'S COMPANY, a Colorado corporation (Seller"), with respect to a proposed acquisition of the business of the Seller in accordance with the terms and conditions of the non-binding term sheet attached hereto as Exhibit A (the "Proposed Acquisition"). This Letter will establish a general basis of negotiations which, if negotiations are successful, will result in terms and conditions set forth in the Definitive Agreements (as defined below). Neither Buyer nor Seller considers this Letter to be legally binding or enforceable against either party, except as otherwise specifically provided in the section entitled Binding Provisions.

NONBINDING PROVISION

> **Basic Terms of the Proposed Acquisition.** The parties hereto will collectively promptly proceed with the negotiation, preparation and execution of a definitive acquisition agreement (together with all related agreements, documents and instru-

ments, the "Definitive Agreements") containing among other things, the terms and conditions set forth in the non-binding term sheet attached hereto as Exhibit A. Buyer's counsel will be responsible for the drafting of the Definitive Agreements.

BINDING PROVISIONS

1. Access to Information. From the date hereof, Seller shall afford the Buyer, its attorneys, accountants and other representatives and agents full access to all of the facilities, management, employees and other personnel, customers, vendors, suppliers, and outside advisors, and to all books and records, accountant's work papers, if available, documents, financial information and data pertaining to Seller's business, its operations, assets and liabilities (the "Due Diligence"). In addition, Seller shall fully cooperate with Buyer in the discovery and identification of Due Diligence. Buyer shall have the full opportunity to conduct its Due Diligence review of Seller's business, operations, assets, liabilities, books and records and obtain all information requested by Buyer as to the business of Seller and the principals of Seller. The Proposed Acquisition is conditioned on the satisfactory completion of Due Diligence by Buyer and through its representatives and agents, at Buyer's sole and absolute discretion.

2. Confidentiality Agreement. Buyer and Seller each acknowledge the existence of that certain Confidentiality/Non-Disclosure Agreement dated _____ by and between Seller and Buyer and continue to be bound by its terms and conditions.

3. Operations. Seller shall operate its business and maintain all its assets during the period from the date hereof until the closing date of the Proposed Acquisition in the same manner in which it has been operated and maintained in the past.

4. Third Party Dealings. Except as provided in the section entitled **Announcements** below, Seller shall not disclose to any third party, except its professional advisors, the terms and conditions of this Proposed Acquisition or that Seller is in communication with Buyer regarding a Proposed Acquisition. Through the Termination Date (defined below) Seller shall not solicit or entertain offers from, negotiate with or in any manner encourage, discuss, accept, or consider any proposal of any other person relating to the acquisition of the Seller's assets, business or shares of stock, in whole or in part, whether directly or indirectly, through purchase, merger, consolidation or otherwise. Through the Termination Date, Seller shall immediately notify Buyer regarding any inquiry to Seller or its representatives from any person regarding any offer or proposal or any related inquiry, negotiations or discussions for the sale (including, without limitation, by merger) or other disposition of any assets or capital stock of Seller.

5. Fees and Expenses. Each party shall be responsible for the payment of all fees, costs and expenses incurred by it in connection with the transaction contemplated hereby and shall not be liable to the other for the payment of such fees, costs and expenses, including without limitation, brokerage or finders' fees incurred by the other party.

6. Announcements. Unless required by law or by regulation of the Securities and Exchange Commission, prior to the execution of the Definitive Agreements, no party to this Letter shall disclose or issue any statement or communication to the public or any third party, except its professional advisors, regarding this Proposed Acquisition without the prior written consent of the parties hereto.

7. Termination. This Letter shall automatically terminate on the earlier of (i) _____, 20__, or (ii) the execution of the Definitive Agreements. Upon any termination of this Letter, the parties shall have no further obligations hereunder, except the obligations set forth in the Binding Provisions of this Letter and in the Confidentiality Agreement, each of which shall survive any termination of this Letter.

8. Controlling Law/Assignment. This Letter and the Definitive Agreements shall be construed in accordance with the laws of the State of Colorado. This Letter and the obligations hereunder may not be assigned by Seller to any person or entity.

9. Counterparts/Facsimile Signatures. This Letter may be executed in two or more counterparts, each of which shall be deemed to be an original, but all of which taken together shall constitute one and the same document. This Letter may also be executed by facsimile signature which will be accepted by the parties as an original signature. This Letter shall only be effective upon the signature of all parties.

With the exception of Binding Provisions, this Letter with the non-binding term sheet attached hereto as Exhibit A does not constitute a binding agreement between the parties. This Letter is written solely as a summary of terms upon which the parties would consider the Proposed Acquisition and is intended to serve merely as a guide to the preparation of the Definitive Agreements. It is expressly understood and agreed that (a) Exhibit A to this Letter is not considered to be a part of the Binding Provisions; (b) no liability or binding obligation is intended to be created between or among any of the parties to this Letter, except with respect to the Binding Provisions; and (c) other than with respect to the Binding Provisions, any legal rights and obligations between or among any of the parties to this Letter will come into existence only upon the parties' execution and delivery of the written Definitive Agreements, and then only in accordance with the terms and conditions of such Definitive Agreements.

If you are willing to proceed on the basis as outlined above, please sign and return one copy of this letter to Buyer no later than 5:00 p.m. Central Standard Time the _____ day of _____, 20___. This Letter will be null and void if not executed by all parties and delivered to Buyer before such time.

Yours very truly,

BUYER

ACCEPTED AND AGREED TO this _____day of

_____, 20__.

SELLER'S COMPANY,

a Colorado corporation

By: _____

Duly authorized signer, President

Attached to the Letter of Intent (as Exhibit A) is a non-binding term sheet like the one following. This Term Sheet is fairly comprehensive and is intended to be a checklist. Needless to say, each transaction is unique and many of these terms would not apply to all.

NON-BINDING TERM SHEET

1. Structure (Stock/Asset/Merger).
   - Stock Purchase
   - Asset Purchase
   - Merger
   - Tax Free Reorganization
   - Section 338(h) or (h)(10) Election
   - Divisional Purchase/Sale
2. Purchase Price/Purchase Price Calculation.
3. Purchase Price Adjustment.
4. Payment of Purchase Price.
   - Cash
   - Promissory note/security agreement
   - Stock
   - Options to acquire stock
   - Escrow/holdback
5. Escrow/Holdback.
6. Earn-Out.
7. Assumed Liabilities/Non-assumed Liabilities.
8. Non-Refundable Deposit/Break-up Fee.
9. Financial Condition of Closing (Revenues/Net Worth/EBIT).
10. Permitted Distributions.
11. Transition Consulting Agreement/Employment Agreement.
    - Principals
    - Key employees
12. Covenant Not to Compete.
13. Real Property Lease Agreement.
14. Real Property Purchase/Sale.
15. Finance Contingency (if any).
16. Other Contingencies (if any).
17. Anticipated Closing Date.

Book Order Form

Order **Deciding to Sell** Today

Please send _____ copy(s) of *Deciding to Sell Your Business The Key to Wealth and Freedom* @ $24.95 each (hardcover); $17.95 (paperback) plus $2.00 postage. Contact Minor & Brown for information about quantity discounts. (303) 320-1053 or *decidingtosell@minorbrown.com*.

Name: _____

Company Name: _____

Address: _____

City: _____ State: _____ Zip: _____

Phone: _____ Email: _____

TELEPHONE ORDERS:	Toll Free (877) 320-1053. Have your Visa or Master Card ready.
POSTAL ORDERS:	Minor & Brown PC 650 South Cherry Street, Suite 1100 Denver, CO 80246-1813.
ON-LINE ORDERS:	www.decidingtosell.com
PAYMENT:	❏ Check Enclosed
	❏ Visa ❏ MasterCard
	Credit Card number: _____
	Name on Card: _____
	Expiration Date: _____

For information about Minor & Brown PC or to contact Ned Minor, please call (303) 320-1053 or send an email to Ned at decidingtosell@minorbrown.com.

SERVICES & EDUCATIONAL MATERIAL FROM MINOR & BROWN, P.C.

LEGAL SERVICES

MERGERS & ACQUISITIONS

EXIT PLANNING

BUSINESS AND TAX PLANNING

ESTATE PLANNING

EDUCATIONAL MATERIALS

THE COUNSELOR
A one-page look at an issue of interest to the business owner.

THE EXIT PLANNER
A six-page newsletter for the owner who wants an in-depth look at a particular planning tool.

THE EXIT PLANNING REVIEW
An e-newsletter using case studies shows owners how various techniques apply to real-life situations.

THE COMPLETELY REVISED HOW TO RUN YOUR BUSINESS SO YOU CAN LEAVE IT IN STYLE

by John H. Brown. The definitive book on Exit Planning.

THE WORKBOOK FOR THE COMPLETELY REVISED HOW TO RUN YOUR BUSINESS SO YOU CAN LEAVE IT IN STYLE.

A hands-on approach to Exit Planning.

SEMINARS

Minor & Brown offers seminars both locally and nationally on topics of interest to the business owner.

For more information about these services and materials, please call (303)320-1053 or visit www.minorbrown.com.